HUBS OF EMPIRE

Hubs of Empire

THE SOUTHEASTERN LOWCOUNTRY AND BRITISH CARIBBEAN

Matthew Mulcahy

JOHNS HOPKINS UNIVERSITY PRESS
BALTIMORE

© 2014 Johns Hopkins University Press
All rights reserved. Published 2014
Printed in the United States of America on acid-free paper
9 8 7 6 5 4 3 2 1

Johns Hopkins University Press
2715 North Charles Street
Baltimore, Maryland 21218-4363
www.press.jhu.edu

ISBN-13: 978-1-4214-1469-0 (hardcover: alk. paper)
ISBN-13: 978-1-4214-1470-6 (pbk.: alk. paper)
ISBN-13: 978-1-4214-1471-3 (electronic)
ISBN-10: 1-4214-1469-4 (hardcover: alk. paper)
ISBN-10: 1-4214-1470-8 (pbk.: alk. paper)
ISBN-10: 1-4214-1471-6 (electronic)

Cataloging-in-Publication data is available from the Library of Congress.

A catalog record for this book is available from the British Library.

Special discounts are available for bulk purchases of this book. For more information, please contact Special Sales at 410-516-6936 or specialsales@press.jhu.edu.

Johns Hopkins University Press uses environmentally friendly book materials, including recycled text paper that is composed of at least 30 percent post-consumer waste, whenever possible.

Contents

Acknowledgments

THANKS FIRST TO ROBERT J. BRUGGER for the invitation several years ago to write this volume, for repeated inquiries about its progress, and for answering many questions along the way. Thanks as well to Juliana McCarthy, Melissa Solarz, Hilary Jacqmin, Catherine Goldstead, and Sara Cleary at Johns Hopkins University Press for their assistance with production. Michael Baker provided expert copyediting and offered numerous insightful suggestions. Robert Cronan of Lucidity Information Design drew the fine maps.

Whatever the merits or drawbacks of this book, it is much better than it would have been because of critical feedback from several friends and colleagues. Russell Menard, David Ryden, Philip Morgan, Natalie Zacek, Bradford Wood, Andrew O'Shaughnessy, Lawrence Peskin, and David Turnham read chapters, offered excellent suggestions that improved the manuscript in a variety of ways, and saved me from many errors. Those that remain, of course, are my own. I am especially grateful to two anonymous reviewers for the press whose comments helped me frame the project at an early stage and strengthen its arguments at the end. I presented a version of the preface at a symposium honoring Russell Menard at the University of Minnesota in May 2012 and a draft of chapter 2 to the Baltimore Early American History Writing Group in April 2011, and I benefited from the comments of participants at both. This book is a work of synthesis, and as such it draws on the published work of many scholars.

The essay on sources lists the major studies that I have consulted, but my intellectual debts go well beyond the works cited there, and I offer a general thanks to the large community of scholars who have produced a rich and growing literature on the people and places of the Greater Caribbean.

I have received a good deal of support in the research, writing, and the publication of this book. I made final changes to the manuscript during a sabbatical granted by Loyola University Maryland in fall 2013. I am especially grateful to the generosity of the Center for the Humanities at Loyola, which provided funds for the maps and images. My colleagues in the history department have created a lively intellectual environment in which to work. The staff of Loyola–Notre Dame library, especially Virginia Smack-Harper, Nick Triggs, and Peggy Field, assisted with my numerous interlibrary loan requests. I drafted a good chunk of the manuscript in Sawyer Library at Williams College during the summers of 2012 and 2013. Many thanks to the college librarian, David Pilachowski, for allowing me access to the library and its collections.

I remain very grateful for the support of my family, especially my mother, who shares my interest in history. Jennifer Turnham did not read (and reread) this time, and the book is weaker as a result, but it would not be finished at all without her. Rebecca and Sam have tolerated many excursions to historical sites, which, although loath to admit it, I think they (mostly) enjoyed. I hope they might enjoy this book in a few years, and I dedicate it to them.

HUBS OF EMPIRE

Rethinking Regions in Colonial British America

THE CONCEPT OF REGION PLAYS an important role in the teaching and writing of early American history. Historians often focus their research on topics within a specific region—New England, the Middle Colonies, the Chesapeake, for example— or on an individual colony within that region. College surveys and textbooks generally are organized by regions, with individual lectures or chapters comparing and contrasting developments in different parts of British America in the period before the American Revolution. A key reason for this emphasis on regions is that the process of colonizing America occurred at different times in different places and unfolded in different ways, reflecting the complex interactions among groups of Native Americans and European and African migrants in the varied physical environments of North America and the Caribbean. Out of these encounters developed diverse colonial societies distinguished by their demographic profiles, the products they exported, the way they organized land and labor, their political institutions and practices, and the way they spoke and dressed, among other characteristics. As Jack P. Greene and J. R. Pole suggested thirty years ago, recognizing and highlighting these "several distinct socioeconomic regions" provides a particularly effective means of exploring the history of colonial British America, and their argument forms the foundation for the series of which this book is a part.[1]

Although historians have long emphasized the importance of regions in early American history, what constitutes a region, and even how many regions existed, has been the subject of some debate. Many divide colonial British America into five major regions: New England, the Middle Colonies, the Chesapeake, the Lower South, and the West Indies. Others add a sixth region, the Backcountry, arguing that inland territories throughout mainland North America constituted a very different world than coastal communities. Still others argue for larger regional divisions. David Hackett Fischer's survey of British folkways in America, for example, posits four key regions: Greater Massachusetts, Greater Virginia, the Greater Delaware Valley, and the Backcountry. The geographer D. W. Meinig employs some of the same groupings, although he also argues that a Greater Carolina emerged in the southeast and he distinguishes several different Backcountry areas. Other scholars, however, suggest that these broad regional divisions can obscure as much as they reveal. Lorena Walsh, for example, argues that the Chesapeake actually encompassed three distinct regions, while Robert Gough maintains that the so-called Middle Colonies were really two separate regions.

Regions thus are not established or fixed entities. They are instead useful but artificial frameworks employed by historians, geographers, and other scholars to help make sense of the past and present. Regional definitions are dynamic and open to interpretation. Although physical geography—climate, terrain, land use patterns, and the like—plays a key role in defining regions, regions are as much cultural creations as they are physical ones. Shared history and experiences, common customs, practices, and mentalities, similar social and economic systems also can delineate regional boundaries.

With that in mind, this book makes an argument for considering the British plantation colonies in the Caribbean—particularly the major islands of Barbados, Jamaica, Antigua, St. Christopher, Nevis, and Montserrat—and the Carolina and Georgia Lowcountry—a coastal zone stretching from the Cape Fear River to the Altamaha River in Georgia and inland roughly fifty miles—as a distinct region, the British Greater Caribbean.

These colonies do not loom large in the historical imaginations of many Americans. The phrase "colonial America" is more likely to call forth images of Boston, Salem, or Williamsburg in the minds of most Americans rather than sugar plantations in Antigua or the governor's mansion in Spanish Town, Jamaica. One reason is that the island colonies did not join their mainland counterparts in the revolution against British rule in 1776. As a result, they often are ignored or marginalized in textbooks and courses dealing with the colonies that eventually formed the United States. Similarly, the Carolina-Georgia Lowcountry, with an economy focused on rice production and a majority population of enslaved Africans, has long been viewed as a place apart from the other mainland colonies. Its history and experiences often seemed too different, too distinct to fit into larger narratives concerning "the thirteen colonies" as anything other than exceptions.

This has begun to change in recent decades. The rise of Atlantic history, with its broad geographic scope, focus on the movement of people and commodities around the Atlantic basin, and greater attention to the centrality of slavery, has generated a good deal of scholarship on the colonies of the Greater Caribbean. At the same time, U.S. historians increasingly have recognized that the boundaries of colonial British America extended beyond the North American mainland, and several have highlighted links between the islands and the Lowcountry in particular. Nevertheless, few scholars consider these colonies as forming a coherent region akin to the more familiar groupings of New England, the Chesapeake, or the Middle Colonies. Generally historians lump the Lowcountry with adjacent Backcountry territories in North Carolina, South Carolina, and Georgia into one region—"the Lower South"—while the islands form a separate region—"the West Indies." There are good reasons, however, for thinking about the Lowcountry and the islands as parts of a broader region, as the Greater Caribbean.

One factor is shared history. All of the region's major colonies developed as social and economic extensions of Barbados. It was in Barbados that the deadly combination of sugar, slavery, and large landholdings first took hold within the British Empire during the 1640s, and it was migrants from Barbados searching for new opportunities who carried this plantation complex to Jamaica and the Leeward Islands during the 1650s and 1660s, and eventually to the South Carolina Lowcountry during the 1670s, where rice replaced sugar as the staple crop. South Carolina, in turn, served as the base for expansion south along the Georgia coast and, to a more limited extent, north into the Cape Fear region of North Carolina during the eighteenth century. The timing and process by which the plantation complex took root differed among the various colonies, but the end result was similar everywhere. As Jack Greene has argued, Barbados served as a "culture hearth" for the Greater Caribbean in much the same way that the social and economic models that emerged in Virginia eventually spread to neighboring Maryland and parts of North Carolina and those in Massachusetts influenced other parts of New England.[2]

In addition to shared history, the colonies of the Greater Caribbean exhibited a number of similar socioeconomic characteristics. The size and scale of plantation operations, including the average size of landholdings and slaveholdings, dwarfed those in the other major plantation zone in British America, the Chesapeake tobacco colonies of Maryland and Virginia. Sugar and rice plantations made colonists in the Greater Caribbean the richest in British America. The colonies became the center of Britain's Atlantic economy, "hub[s] of the British empire," to borrow the words of the great Trinidadian historian Eric Williams.[3] The great riches generated by sugar and rice exports enabled colonists to import vast quantities of British goods, to send their children to Britain for schooling, and for some, to retire to Britain, becoming absentee owners living off the profits of their distant plantations. Many Lowcountry planters became absentees of a different sort, living a good portion of the year in Charleston away from their swampy plantation lands. Ironically, although plantations dominated the landscape, the Greater Caribbean was home to several major urban centers, including, Kingston, Charleston, St. John's, Basseterre, Savannah, and Bridgetown. A larger percentage of colonists lived and worked in the region's cities and towns than in any other part of British America. Religion also served as a common bond, and a link to England as well, as the Anglican Church became the established church in all these colonies by the mid-eighteenth century.

Most importantly, enslaved Africans formed a majority, often an overwhelming majority, of the population in each of these colonies, distinguishing them from all others in British America. The size of the enslaved population, combined with the constant arrival of new slaves from Africa, meant that West African cultures—language, rituals, belief systems, material culture—remained stronger and more influential in the Greater Caribbean than in other parts of British America. No single West African culture dominated in any of the colonies. Rather, West Africans from diverse regions and cultures over time negotiated and borrowed from one another, and from Europeans, to produce a new, creole culture. African practices, in turn, influenced European colonists and culture. These ongoing "creative adaptations" among all groups produced colonial societies that new arrivals from both Britain and Africa found familiar in some ways and yet thoroughly alien in many others.[4]

Environmental factors also influenced social and economic developments within the region and further distinguished it from others in British America. No one mistook the Greater Caribbean for a new England, and the region's tropical and subtropical climate created distinct issues for colonists. European colonists marveled at the region's beauty, embraced its bounty of exotic plants and fruits, and profited from the production of tropical commodities such as sugar, rice, and indigo, but they also experienced its perils. Tropical diseases such as yellow fever and malaria took the lives of European colonists at rates that would have qualified as epidemics elsewhere, while diseases combined with brutal work conditions and inadequate food decimated the population of enslaved Africans. As a result, the Greater Caribbean became—and remained—the deadliest region in British America, an ongoing demographic disaster zone for blacks and whites alike. Moreover, the hurricanes that swept across the region and the earthquakes that shook the foundations of cities and plantations posed more frequent existential threats to these colonies than to any others in British America. The dangers of disasters and disease further encouraged many European colonists to flee the region, while the terrible mortality rates among enslaved Africans necessitated the continued importation of huge numbers of new slaves.

The threat from hurricanes, earthquakes, and disease rendered life in the region especially volatile and uncertain, even within the context of the early modern period. So too did rebellion and war. The size of the slave populations in the Greater Caribbean meant that colonists employed extraordinary violence and terror in an effort to maintain control. Their efforts never succeeded fully. Africans and African Americans resisted their enslavement in ways large and small, but most dramatically during numerous rebellions, including Tacky's War, the largest slave rebellion in British America during the colonial period. Colonists also found themselves surrounded by numerous hostile powers. Most of the British islands sat cheek by jowl with Spanish, French, Dutch, and Danish islands, as well as islands occupied by Carib Indians. The Lowcountry developed in the borderlands north of Spanish Florida and east of lands belonging to powerful native groups including the Creek and the Cherokee. The result was that the Greater Caribbean—and the sugar islands in particular—experienced frequent attacks and threats of attack throughout the seventeenth and eighteenth centuries. All colonies in British America faced enemies in one form or another at various times, but arguably no others faced such constant threats as did those in the Greater Caribbean. Hubs of trade, the colonies were also centers of conflict.

Important differences distinguished the sugar islands and the Lowcountry, to be sure. Almost a thousand miles separated the Carolina Lowcountry from the nearest island colony, Jamaica. The islands were, of course, islands, some of them volcanic, most of limited size and with limited resources. By contrast, the Lowcountry was, as its name implies, low and flat, formed part of the continental mainland, and was surrounded by abundant natural resources. The Lowcountry's subtropical climate approximated tropical conditions in the islands at times, but the Lowcountry also experienced occasional frosts, and the more limited growing season prohibited the cultivation of sugarcane. Rice required large-scale plantation operations and generated great wealth, but sugar plantations were more complex and sugar planters far wealthier than their Lowcountry counterparts. Production of the two crops also differed: slaves on sugar plantations generally labored under the brutal gang system, while the more flexible task system emerged on Lowcountry rice estates. Different labor regimes in turn influenced slave life and culture more broadly. Native Americans played a far greater role in the history of South Carolina—as trading partners, and as both military allies and foes—than they did in any of the islands during the seventeenth and eighteenth centuries.

These differences, however, should not eclipse the broad similarities that existed between the Lowcountry and the islands, particularly because the islands themselves exhibited significant variation. Barbados, small and relatively flat, was a far different place than rugged, mountainous Jamaica, and the two were separated by more than a thousand miles of ocean. Even the neighboring Leeward Islands differed significantly from one another in topography and climate. Sugar was the major crop in all of the islands, but Jamaica's size allowed for a more diverse economy and the island produced significant crops of cotton, indigo, and later coffee. Jamaica's economy in some ways more closely resembled that of the Lowcountry than the eighteenth-century sugar monocultures of Nevis or St. Kitts. The ratio of slaves to European colonists in the eighteenth century likewise varied significantly among the islands. Analyzing the Lowcountry and islands together, in other words, simply extends the boundaries of an already large and diverse Caribbean region that was nonetheless bound together by a shared history and common characteristics, among them a hazardous environment, high mortality rates, a tremendously wealthy and powerful planter class with strong ties to Britain, large slave majorities, and significant African cultural elements.

Such factors also distinguished the Lowcountry from its adjoining Backcountry territories. The colonial history of South Carolina and Georgia for the seventeenth and much of the eighteenth century is essentially the history of the Lowcountry. Significant expansion into the Backcountry began only in the middle decades of the eighteenth century, and although geographically contiguous, the two regions exhibited significant social and economic differences. The varied geography, small farms, overwhelmingly European population, and relative poverty of the Backcountry stood in stark contrast to the rich plantations and large African populations that defined the coastal Lowcountry. As one eighteenth-century traveler observed, the Lowcountry and Backcountry were "countries as different almost as Iceland

and Bengal."[5] The Backcountry was its own region, and its history is explored in a separate volume in this series.

Shared history, common socioeconomic and demographic characteristics, cultural similarities, and overlapping environmental conditions all provide a rationale for thinking about the Lowcountry and the islands as part of a single region. Nevertheless, it is worth asking, what is gained from such an approach? What difference does it make to group these colonies together? For students of U.S. history in particular, such a framework underscores the essential point that there were more than thirteen colonies in eighteenth-century British America, and that some of the most politically and economically important are those least studied in standard U.S. history classes. It also restores something of an eighteenth-century perspective to our understanding of Britain's American empire, placing these colonies at the center of analysis rather than at the periphery. Moreover, the idea of a Greater Caribbean helps render both the Lowcountry and the islands less anomalous within the larger context of colonial British America. The Lowcountry appears less an exceptional place on the mainland and more like the plantation colonies in British America as a whole, while the islands become more linked to the mainland plantation zone rather than distinct from it.

Finally, the idea of the Greater Caribbean highlights the diverse influences that shaped the development of colonial British America, and in the longer term, the development of the United States. Cultural influences did not simply flow across the Atlantic from Europe or Africa to the colonies. They also spread from existing colonies to new ones. Adopting the framework of a Greater Caribbean provides a clearer perspective for tracing the Caribbean origins of various ideas and practices that gradually took root in the southeast mainland. Seventeenth- and eighteenth-century commentators sometimes referred to the Carolina Lowcountry as "this part of the West Indies."[6] Exploring why they did so opens up new opportunities for thinking about the history of colonial British America.

ONE

Plundering and Planting the Greater Caribbean

THE GREATER CARIBBEAN WAS THE FIRST PART of the Americas to experience the shock waves of European colonization following the arrival of the Spanish in 1492. Diverse groups of Native Americans had lived in the region for more than a millennium prior to Columbus, their societies evolving over time in response to local conditions and encounters with other native groups. While the pre-Columbian Greater Caribbean was a dynamic place of movement and change, the Spanish conquest transformed the region and its peoples with lightning speed and on an unprecedented scale. As a result, Native Americans throughout the region had experience with Europeans, for better or worse—mostly for worse—long before the English arrived.

The first Englishmen who sailed to the region in the sixteenth century went with no other motives than raiding Spanish treasure fleets and enriching themselves. Gradually, English privateers and merchants recognized the benefits of permanent colonial settlements that could produce exotic staple crops like tobacco and sugar. Establishing those settlements took time, but by the middle of the seventeenth century England had claimed several islands and laid the foundations for the plantation system that would dominate the region for the next two centuries.

Unlike other parts of British America, the Greater Caribbean encompassed a vast territory with no contiguous boundaries or direct links between the colonies beyond well-traveled maritime routes that connected them to one another, and to the rest of the Atlantic world. Separated by distances ranging from 2 to almost 2,000 miles, the colonies exhibited tremendous diversity in their size and physical environments.

Permanent English settlements emerged first in Barbados and the Leeward Islands of St. Christopher (also called St. Kitts), Nevis, Antigua, and Montserrat, so named because of their position downwind from Barbados. The Leewards form part of the Lesser Antilles, a string of small islands stretching from the Virgin Islands in the north to Trinidad and Tobago in the south. The Lesser Antilles comprise two strings of islands, an inner arc

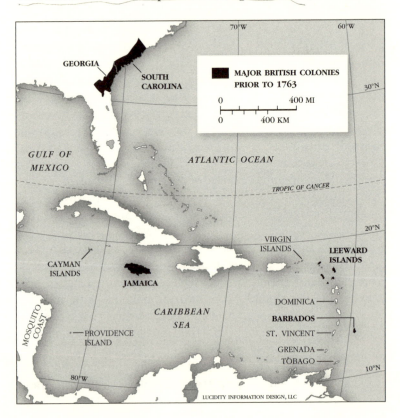

of volcanic islands that includes St. Christopher, Nevis, and Montserrat, and an outer arc generally formed from coral limestone on top of an older volcanic base, among which are Barbados and Antigua. The English islands in the inner arc are small—St. Christopher measures 76 square miles, Montserrat 40 square miles, and Nevis just 36 square miles—with tall mountains at their center. The white clouds surrounding Nevis's peak inspired Columbus to call it Nieves, or "snows." The mountains limited the amount of acreage available for plantation agriculture, but they also created abundant rainfall for planters. By contrast, Antigua, located just 60 miles away from Nevis and St. Christopher, is 108 square miles and relatively flat. It receives far less rainfall and lacks any rivers or streams to provide water, and as a result, suffered repeated droughts during the seventeenth and eighteenth centuries.

The other major English settlement in the Lesser Antilles emerged on Barbados, located some 300 miles south of the Leewards and 90 miles east of its nearest neighbor. Barbados is the largest English island in the Lesser Antilles at 166 square miles. Like Antigua, the island is relatively flat with a central plateau rising only 1,000 feet above the Atlantic. Barbados also lacks any significant rivers or streams, but it receives more rainfall than Antigua. Its location to the east of the other islands meant it often served as the first stop for ships arriving from England, although its isolated location also meant it was easy to miss. One early arrival compared finding the island from a ship to looking for a coin in the middle of an English field. Most importantly, it was on Barbados that the English began to plant sugarcane in the 1640s.

The English gained a foothold in the Greater Antilles in 1655, when they captured Jamaica from the Spanish. The Greater Antilles—Cuba, Hispaniola (now Haiti and the Dominican Republic), Puerto Rico, and Jamaica—are the largest islands in the Caribbean basin. Measuring some 4,440 square miles, Jamaica is more than ten times the size of Barbados and the four Leeward Islands combined. High, rugged mountains rising to over 7,000 feet in places—double the height of Nevis's peak—cut across parts of the island. This forbidding terrain provided a refuge for runaway slaves throughout the seventeenth and eighteenth centuries. Jamaica's size eventually made it the most valuable colony in British America, but it also meant it took decades to develop its agricultural potential fully. Moreover, Jamaica's location almost 1,000 miles west of the Leewards and roughly 1,200 miles north and west of Barbados rendered it somewhat isolated from the other English islands. The dominant trade winds in the Caribbean blow from east to west, making it easy to sail from Barbados to Jamaica. The return voyage sailing into the wind was far more difficult to navigate. As a result, it often took less time to sail from Jamaica to London than from Jamaica to Barbados.

Finally, migrants from the existing English settlements in the Caribbean, as well as from Europe, colonized the southeastern mainland coastal region beginning in 1670. Located approximately 1,000 miles north of Jamaica, the Lowcountry stretches some 350 miles from the Altamaha River in what is now Georgia to the Cape Fear River in southeastern North Carolina, extends about 50 miles inland, and includes dozens of coastal islands. Unlike the varied topography of the islands, the Lowcountry is flat, with the land rising no more than 70 feet above sea level. One contemporary wrote that the land was "soe plaine & levyll that it may be compared to a Bowling ally [*sic*]." Dozens of rivers and streams flow from the interior, including the Altamaha, the Savannah, the Cooper, the Ashley, and the Santee Rivers. So numerous were these coastal waterways that they appeared to "crumble the Continent into Islands," according to one early explorer.[1]

Jamaica, Barbados, the Leewards, and the Lowcountry became the major locations for English colonization during the seventeenth and eighteenth centuries, but England claimed or exploited other locations within the Caribbean basin as well. Providence Island off the coast of Nicaragua was the site of an early Puritan settlement before the Spanish expelled the English in 1641. Small groups of colonists raked salt, salvaged wrecks, and cut timber on the numerous islands of the Bahamas and Turks and Caicos, but these remained small and marginal settlements compared to the plantation colonies in the region. Indeed, the latter in particular formed part of what one scholar has termed the "Caribbean Commons," a frontier zone outside the formal jurisdiction of any one colony or colonial power but exploited by many. The Cayman Islands, likewise, attracted colonists from Jamaica and elsewhere to hunt green turtles for meat and hawksbill turtles for their shells, which were used in making combs, brushes, and mirrors. By the end of the seventeenth century, some forty or so ships sailed from Port Royal to the Caymans, returning with thousands of turtles each year. Several hundred logwood cutters with links to Jamaica established small outposts on the Yucatan peninsula during the second half of the seventeenth century, harvesting trees that provided valuable dyes needed in European textile production. After Spanish attacks in the early eighteenth century, the "Baymen," as they were termed, shifted operations to the Bay of Honduras (what is now Belize). Another small settlement emerged at the Black River on the Mosquito Coast, in what is now part of Honduras, by the middle of the eighteenth century. The roughly 150 whites, 170 mixed-race freedmen, and 800 enslaved Africans exported mahogany, sarsaparilla, and tortoise shells, much of it via Jamaica, but also through mainland ports such as New York.

Small groups of English colonists also developed plantations in the Danish West Indies (what are now the Virgin Islands), particularly St. Croix. Pushed out of the Leeward Islands during the shift to sugar in the second half of the seventeenth century, English planters remained on St. Croix when the Danes purchased the island from France in 1733, and they remained the dominant ethnic group, outnumbering Danish colonists 5 to 1 in 1741. Finally, many small islands, such as Barbuda and Anguilla, provided land for pasture and provisions, but these two and others served as appendages to the larger plantation colonies. In sum, Jamaica, Barbados, Antigua, Montserrat, Nevis, St. Christopher, and the Lowcountry became the sites of the most important English colonies in this Greater Caribbean, and they warrant the greatest attention from students and scholars of early British America.

The climate of the Greater Caribbean played a significant role in shaping the colonial societies that emerged there. The entire region is classified as tropical (the islands) or subtropical (the Lowcountry). Temperatures in the Caribbean basin remain relatively constant throughout the year, between 75 and 85 degrees—perfect for the growth of sugarcane—although these figures vary by location, and higher elevations are often noticeably cooler. Trade winds blowing east to west across the Atlantic temper the intense heat of the sun. In addition to providing cooling breezes, the trade winds accumulate tremendous amounts of moisture on their journey across the Atlantic, another essential ingredient for sugarcane cultivation. This moisture eventually falls as rain, although the amount of rainfall varies considerably among the islands, and even on different parts of individual islands. On Nevis, for example, the mountains force up the warm, moist air, which cools as it rises. The cooler air then condenses and falls as rain as it passes over the mountain peak. Locations to the windward and in higher elevations generally receive significantly more precipitation than those to the leeward side, which fall into what is called a rain shadow. Rainfall at higher elevations in Nevis is more than double that at lower elevations. Likewise, Port Antonio on Jamaica's north coast receives 125 inches of rain a year. Twenty miles inland, but higher up, the Blue Mountains receive over 200 inches. Kingston, by contrast, below the Blue Mountains on Jamaica's southern coast, receives less than 30 inches a year. Islands that lack significant mountains, such as Antigua, receive less rain, and water shortages are far more common. Although it can rain throughout the year, most islands have a rainy season between June and November, when precipitation is more frequent.

Temperatures in the Lowcountry vary more widely than in the Caribbean basin. Early colonists praised the Lowcountry climate as a perfect balance between the extreme heat of the tropics and the colder regions to the north. All expressed confidence that a variety of tropical crops, including sugar, oranges, lemons, and olives, would flourish, but experience soon proved otherwise. Lowcountry summers are hot and humid—between 70 and 90 degrees—and while the winters are mild—between 40 and 60 degrees—frosts do occur, and on rare occasions, snow. Early frosts killed off experiments with oranges and other crops, and sugar never took hold. Nevertheless the Lowcountry climate had much in common with the islands, and both differed dramatically from the temperate climate of northern Europe.

English colonists to the Greater Caribbean held mixed—indeed conflicting—ideas about the tropical and semi-tropical climates in which they settled. On the one hand, colonists believed that hot climates produced great wealth. Many in the early modern era associated gold, silver, and other precious metals with heat. The warmth of the sun, it was thought, drew such riches out of the earth. Moreover, exotic and valuable crops such as sugarcane, tobacco, indigo, cocoa, and ginger thrived in hot, moist conditions. So, too, did lemons, limes, pineapples, papayas, and a host of other exotic fruits. Colonists extolled the region's natural abundance and fertility. One visitor described the Liguanea section of Jamaica as "another Eden, whose trees are allways loaden with ripe and delitious fruites, the earth filled with choice hearbs and roots, and the ... aire filled with odourous perfumes." Accustomed to seasonal changes, colonists encountered "no Winter, or decay" in the islands but rather a "continual Spring." Similar images appeared in accounts of the Carolina Lowcountry, which more than one commentator noted occupied the same latitudinal position as the Garden of Eden.[2]

Alongside such images, however, existed others that emphasized the many dangers of hot climates, particularly for English colonists. Heat might nourish exotic plants, but it threatened English bodies more accustomed to the cooler climate of northern Europe. Early modern science held that individual bodies, and more specifically the "humors" inside the body—blood, black and yellow bile, and phlegm—were attuned to particular environments. Moving from temperate England to the tropical Greater Caribbean threatened to upset the delicate balance of these humors, with potentially fatal results. Colonists adopted the term *seasoning* to describe the period of acclimatization, during which newcomers were thought to be especially vulnerable. Even if they survived seasoning, the intense heat of the region took a physical and cultural toll. Several commentators observed that English colonists suffered a "great failing in the vigor, and sprightliness we have in colder Climates."[3] Tasks that required no great level of exertion in England left colonists exhausted. One eighteenth-century governor in Barbados complained that constant sun and heat weakened his eyesight, diminished his memory, and made reading and writing increasingly painful. Many feared a weakening of English virility and a gradual development of practices associated with what they viewed as the inferior Latin cultures of southern Europe. And it was not just the heat, as the saying goes, but also the humidity that rendered the atmosphere unwholesome. Excessive moisture in the air caused knives, swords, and other items to rust. Locks and keys did not function correctly because of the humidity, nor did watches and clocks. Letters to England advised new colonists not to bring leather clothing, because it would soon rot.

The heat and humidity allowed a range of tormenting insects to thrive. Gnats, ants, cockroaches, spiders, and mosquitoes caused constant itching and irritation for colonists. Early colonists slept in hammocks over smoky fires in an effort to ward off mosquitoes and other pests. Particularly annoying were chiggers. These small mites burrowed under the skin, causing a stinging sensation followed by terrible itching. Removal required digging them out with a sharp instrument, making the cure as painful as the problem. Beyond extreme discomfort, the failure to remove chiggers occasionally resulted in the loss of a toe, or in extreme cases, a foot.

Mosquitoes posed a far more serious threat to colonists' well-being, although no one knew it at the time. Mosquitoes serve as vectors for both yellow fever and malaria, two Old World diseases introduced to the region via the slave trade. A mild form of malaria existed in parts of northern Europe prior to colonization of the Americas, but colonists to the Greater Caribbean encountered a far deadlier form, *Plasmodium falciparum,* which quickly became a constant presence in the region. The yellow fever virus appeared more sporadically, but with far deadlier results. Colonists at the time had no understanding of the relationship between mosquitoes and disease, but they had ample evidence of the results, as yellow fever and malaria made the region a graveyard for Europeans. Enslaved Africans who came from regions where yellow fever and malaria existed likely had some immunity to the diseases, having survived exposure to them at an early age, but not all slaves had such immunity, and many perished alongside European colonists.

Finally, a range of natural disasters threatened the very foundations of colonial societies in the region. Drought took a heavy toll on crops in Antigua and other islands repeatedly during the seventeenth and eighteenth centuries. An infestation of caterpillars destroyed crops in several islands in 1662. More frequent were earthquakes, which shook all the colonies from time to time, although the danger was greatest in Jamaica and the Leeward Islands. Both experienced major earthquakes in the 1690s, the scale of which dwarfed the tremors that occasionally shook England or other parts of British America. The most spectacular was the 1692 earthquake that struck Jamaica, leveling houses and plantations throughout the island and plunging half the town of Port Royal to the bottom of the harbor. Thousands perished in one of the great disasters of the early modern Atlantic world. Not all earthquakes resulted in such destruction, but after 1692, even minor tremors raised the specter of another Port Royal.

More than anything else, however, colonists dreaded the onset of hurricane season. Hurricanes were an entirely new phenomenon for European colonists—the word itself comes from the Arawak *hurakan*—but they quickly became the most feared element of the region's climate. The storms routinely struck with an unimaginable fury, causing massive damage to houses, plantations, and crops. The level of destruction was so great, according to one seventeenth-century commentator, that a hurricane "puts us to begin the World anew."[4] Both sugar and rice planters routinely cautioned that, no matter how promising their crops appeared, nothing was certain until the hurricane season passed. Individual colonies sometimes went years, even decades, without a major storm, but it was a rare year that some colony in the region did not suffer from a hurricane, and colonists greeted the start of hurricane season with trepidation. The path of hurricanes meant that the islands suffered most frequently, but hurricanes regularly struck the Lowcountry as well. Indeed, several eighteenth-century commentators, including Edmund and William Burke and the naturalist Mark Catesby, believed that the Lowcountry represented the northern border of the hurricane zone. Although incorrect—hurricanes occasionally struck other parts of British America, including the mid-Atlantic and New England—such perceptions reinforced the ideas that the Lowcountry was part of the Caribbean world.

The heat, the humidity, the hurricanes, the strange and wondrous flora and fauna: all contributed to contemporary perceptions of the Greater Caribbean as an especially foreign, volatile, and uncertain world. Colonists who migrated to all parts of British America encountered new physical environments that presented both great challenges and great opportunities, but those who settled in the Greater Caribbean faced particularly novel and extreme conditions. As one colonist in Jamaica wrote to his sister in 1672, "We are but a month from you [England] by sea, if the wind be good, but indeed those who talk much of a new world of the Indies say more than they ofttimes know."[5]

NATIVE AMERICANS IN THE GREATER CARIBBEAN

Long before Europeans arrived, diverse groups of Native Americans lived in various parts of the Greater Caribbean. Much about the native societies in the region remains unknown, especially in the islands. Often a handful of pottery shards offer our only glimpse into the complex worlds of people living thousands of years ago. Not surprisingly, how to interpret this limited evidence has generated much debate among scholars.

There is general agreement that human occupation of the islands began about 6,000 years ago. The first wave of migrants likely came from two directions. Some of these Archaic peoples crossed over from the Yucatan peninsula to Cuba and the other islands of the Greater Antilles in the period 4000-3500 BCE. Roughly 2,000 years later, a second group of migrants moved north from South America and Trinidad. Beginning around 500 BCE, yet another wave of migrants moved north out of the Orinoco basin in South America. Rather than island-hopping, as has long been theorized, migrants may have traveled first to Puerto Rico and the Leeward Islands by canoe before moving to other islands in the Greater and Lesser Antilles. These Saladoid people, as they are termed, brought several plants with them from the mainland, including cassava (manioc), a hearty root crop that supplied a huge number of calories per acre cultivated. In addition, the Saladoid produced red clay pots decorated with white markings, a distinctive ceramic style that archaeologists use to identify Saladoid sites.

Gradually, between 500 CE and 1500 CE, Saladoid migration across parts of the Greater Antilles, cultural mixing with earlier Archaic peoples, increased agricultural activity, population growth, and ongoing environmental adaptations resulted in the development of new, more complex, and more hierarchical societies known as the Taino. The Taino emerged first on the eastern part of Hispaniola and Puerto Rico, but as the population grew— the result of increased agricultural production—they spread out, colonizing Jamaica in roughly 500 CE as well as the Bahamas, where they became known as the Lucayans. Taino culture also appeared in Cuba and in the northern Leeward Islands. The Taino generally lived in villages of 1,000–2,000 people, although some villages contained as many as 5,000 people, each under the control of a local chief (*cacique*). Individual villages were united into larger chiefdoms, led by the most powerful village chief. As was the case in many Native American groups, the Taino were matrilineal, meaning that they traced descent through the mother's lineage. Related families often lived together in a single thatch house. Inside, Taino men and women slept in woven cotton nets called hammocks, another Taino word, like *hurakan*, that quickly entered European vocabularies.

In many villages, circular or rectangular wooden houses surrounded a walled and paved central plaza. Among other roles, the plaza served as a court for an elaborate ball game in which two teams of thirty or so players squared off, each trying to move a rubber ball in the air to the other end of the court without using their hands or feet—knees, shoulders, hips, and other body parts had to suffice. Such games may have served as a form of staged competition between different chiefdoms as well as providing a form of entertainment.

More importantly, the plaza also functioned as the center of ritual and spiritual life. The Taino lived in an enchanted universe in which supernatural forces existed all around them. The Taino called these forces *zemis,* which was also the name of the carved wooden or stone figures that represented those forces. Some *zemis* were larger than humans and were placed around the central plaza. Others were smaller and kept by individuals in their homes. Shamans mediated between *zemis* and humans. Because *zemis* existed in all parts of nature—trees, rocks, the wind—the Taino, like other native groups, cultivated a relationship with the natural world characterized by respect rather than dominance.

The Taino relied heavily on cassava for food, but they also cultivated sweet potatoes, squash, beans, tobacco, and some maize, making use of a wooden digging stick called a *coa* to work the soil. Fish and green turtles provided additional protein. Women were responsible for cultivating the crops, while men helped clear the land, fished, and hunted. Large dugout canoes, some of which were capable of holding over a hundred people, allowed for communication and trade among villages on different islands.

The arrival of the Spanish in 1492 transformed and ultimately destroyed the Taino. Captivated by their gold jewelry, the Spanish quickly enslaved the Taino and put them to work digging for gold. Taino resistance only furthered the belief among Columbus and his followers that captured Taino "infidels" were prime candidates for slavery. Aided by dogs, horses, and guns, the Spanish conquered the Taino on the large island they named Hispaniola before moving on to nearby islands.

War and enslavement took a heavy toll on the Taino population in the Greater Antilles, but European diseases proved even deadlier. Native peoples throughout the Americas lived in a relatively disease-free environment prior to 1492. Because they had no contact with the rest of the world, they were never exposed to a range of diseases, including smallpox, chickenpox, measles, and influenza, and thus never developed any antibodies or immunities to them. Europeans unwittingly brought these diseases with them, unleashing what scholars term "virgin soil epidemics." Such epidemics often resulted in the death of up to 90 percent of an exposed population within fifty years or so of contact, although the loss was most dramatic in the initial years. Estimates for the population on Hispaniola prior to 1492 vary, but it is likely that between 1 and 2 million people lived on the island. That population was reduced by half by the mid-1490s and continued to fall dramatically. By 1508, only 60,000 Taino remained on Hispaniola. A few years later, in 1518, the number was 11,000. By midcentury, the Taino had become virtually extinct in the Greater Antilles.

A different group of natives, the Kalinago, occupied the islands south of Montserrat. The Kalinago spoke Cariban, an Arawakan dialect, and thus became known to Europeans as the Caribs. The origin of the Caribs, whose name was soon given to the sea and the larger region, remains the subject of debate. One theory posits that the Caribs arrived in the Lesser Antilles just a generation or two before Columbus and conquered the natives on those islands. A second, and increasingly dominant, theory suggests that the Caribs, like the Taino, emerged from the descendants of the Saladoid migration, but environmental conditions in the Windward Islands and ongoing contact with the

South American mainland gave rise to a distinct cultural formation. Resolving the issue with any certainty is difficult, given the limited evidence, although it is clear that Taino and Kalinago culture differed in significant ways. Columbus reported that the Taino described the natives to their south as an aggressive, warring, and possibly cannibalistic people. Subsequent colonists reified the distinction, counterpoising the peaceful Taino and the warlike Caribs, but such distinctions likely reveal more about Spanish perceptions than native realities.

The Caribs occupied a number of the Windward Islands, but some—notably Barbados—were unoccupied at the time English colonization began in the seventeenth century. One scholar estimated a total Carib population of between 7,000 and 15,000, spread across various islands. Like the Taino, the Caribs were skilled hunters and fishermen, but they also cultivated cassava and other crops, often mixing them with fish and peppers to make a spicy stew. The Caribs lacked the political hierarchy that marked Taino life. Small villages ruled by a headman served as the primary political unit, but they had no strong chiefs. Instead, Caribs elected temporary chiefs to lead war or raiding parties. Raids on neighboring groups aimed to take captives rather than territory. The Caribs generally adopted female captives and children into the villages, but they tortured and killed male captives. A number of European writers stated that the Caribs practiced cannibalism with their captives, but whether such allegations are true is, again, the subject of debate. Significantly, no Europeans actually witnessed acts of cannibalism.

Spain's focus on the larger islands of the Greater Antilles, and then on the mainland in Mexico and Peru, meant that Caribs in the Lesser Antilles did not experience the full onslaught of European colonization until the early seventeenth century. French and English ships plying the waters of the Caribbean frequently stopped at Carib islands, exchanging axes, pots, and cloth for provisions and hammocks, but they made no effort to establish permanent settlements. Both groups benefited from these arrangements, but when the English, and then the French, began to view the islands as more than places to water and trade, the Caribs resisted. Conflict continued sporadically throughout the seventeenth and eighteenth centuries, even as Carib numbers and territory shrank.

The English encountered a different native world when they began reconnoitering the Lowcountry coast in the 1660s. Humans had lived in the southeast for thousands of years. By 600 CE, native peoples throughout the region had begun to cultivate the classic crops of native agriculture—corn, beans, and squash—which in turn supported the growth of more complex and hierarchical societies. The most significant of these were the Mississippian people, also known as the Mound Builders because of the large ceremonial earthworks and plazas they constructed. Mississippian chiefdoms dominated large parts of the southeast from about 1000 CE until the arrival of Europeans. Although the extent to which Mississippian culture influenced natives in the Lowcountry is unclear, some scholars suggest that the Guale in Lowcountry Georgia and the diverse groups that eventually became known as the Cusabo in the Carolina Lowcountry shared basic social structures and belief systems and had links with the Mississippian groups farther inland.

As in the islands, the arrival of the Spanish transformed native life in the Lowcountry, even though the Spaniards' physical presence was less pronounced. The first Spaniards arrived in the Lowcountry in the 1520s and unsuccessfully attempted to establish a permanent settlement near the Pee Dee River. The French arrived next, establishing an outpost at Port Royal in 1562 and another one at Fort Caroline, near Jacksonville, Florida, in 1564. Neither lasted long: colonists abandoned the first within a year, while a Spanish expedition drove out the second in 1565. Concerned about such intrusions into territory they claimed and anxious to protect shipping lanes, the Spanish constructed a string of forts along the southeastern coast, including one at Port Royal (which they called Santa Elena). The largest and most important was St. Augustine, built in 1565, making it the oldest continually inhabited settlement in North America. Alongside fortifications, the Spanish established missions to Christianize natives. The Spanish had less direct influence on groups farther north in the Carolina Lowcountry, but by the time the English arrived in the 1660s, all the Indian peoples in the coastal zone had some familiarity with Europeans and European culture. When William Hilton dropped anchor near Port Royal on a reconnaissance mission in 1663, he reported that the natives spoke some Spanish and were quite familiar with guns. They were "as little startled at the fireing of a Piece of Ordnance, as he that hath been used to them many years."[6]

The Edisto people whom Hilton encountered were one of over a dozen small, independent groups of Native Americans living in the region between the Santee and Savannah Rivers by the middle of the seventeenth century. Other groups included the Escamacu, Etiwan, Kiawah, Stono, Kussoe, and the Sewee. A 1707 treaty listed several of these groups as Cusabo, and scholars sometimes use that term as shorthand to refer to Lowcountry Indians, but there is no evidence to suggest that native peoples used or recognized this identification. Instead, they appear to have maintained distinct identities even in the face of declining numbers.

Relatively little is known about these natives, especially in comparison to the larger and better-documented groups in the interior, such as the Cherokee or Creek. Even their language is something of a mystery, although it appears at least two different languages were spoken in the region. North of the Ashley River, the Sewee spoke a Siouan dialect, while groups south of the Ashley may have spoken a language distinct from either Siouan or Muskogean and which some scholars call Cusaboan.

Regardless, enough evidence exists to suggest that Lowcountry groups had much in common with other groups living in the coastal areas of North America. As was the case elsewhere, Lowcountry natives engaged in seasonal migration to take full advantage of the diverse resources available in the region. Each spring they migrated to coastal locations and formed into small villages of twenty or so houses. These were round, wooden structures tied together with bark rope, with thatched roofs made of palmetto leaves. Some groups also built larger structures that served as town or "state" houses in which the entire group could meet. These too were circular buildings, perhaps sixty-five feet or more in diameter, with a raised seat for the "Cassique," or leader, and rings of benches. Next to the houses, they cleared fields and planted a wide variety of crops, including corn, beans, squash, and watermelons. In many parts of North America, Indian women had primary responsibility for the fields and crops, and this likely was true among the Lowcountry groups as well.

Many English observers found native agricultural practices lacking. Unlike English farms, there were no fences around fields. Corn, beans, and squash were intermixed rather than grown in separate grounds. This gave the fields an unkempt appearance, and colonists criticized the natives for their "lasinesse." But these same observers also noted that Indian fields produced bumper crops. However much it offended English sensibilities, the practice of mixing crops together contributed to the growth of each; beans replaced some of the nutrients taken out of the soil by other crops; cornstalks functioned as beanpoles; and the cover provided by squash and beans inhibited the growth of weeds. Indeed, Indian fields produced enough food to feed colonists who settled in 1670 and who likely would have starved without such aid. Indians often used fire to clear areas for fields, which in the short run provided nutrients to the soil and in the long run created open spaces in the forests. Colonists only partly appreciated that the savannas they praised as similar to parks in England resulted from deliberate burning by natives.

While they waited for the crops to grow, natives fished and gathered wild plants, as well as oysters and clams. Dugout canoes, some large enough to hold ten people, facilitated ocean fishing as well as travel and communication on Lowcountry rivers. After the crops had been harvested in the late summer and early fall, villages broke apart into smaller kin groups and moved into the interior, traveling between ten and fifty miles. During the fall and winter months, they gathered acorns and walnuts and hunted deer, turkeys, and other game. In the spring, natives returned to their coastal locations and began the cycle again.

The various Lowcountry groups were politically independent, but because of their small numbers, individuals often married into neighboring groups. One result was a relative degree of harmony among the various groups. Early colonists reported that they did not fight each other but rather had common enemies in the interior who threatened them, particularly the Westo. As was the case elsewhere in eastern North America, Lowcountry Indians were matrilineal, meaning that they traced descent through the mother's family. Men generally served as leaders, but many women also played key leadership roles. One document ceding land to the colonists in 1675 was signed by twenty-eight natives, at least eleven of whom were women.

Descriptions of religious practices among Lowcountry natives are limited. Most accounts suggest that they worshipped one great god, who had created the universe, and some note special reverence for the sun and moon, but few details exist about general beliefs or practices. It is clear that several groups believed in an afterlife, where rewards awaited the good and punishments, the evil. They paid special attention to the dead. Several accounts of Etiwan burial practices note that after a body had decomposed, the bones were cleaned, placed into a chest, and stored in a special structure built on posts. Doing so allowed natives to carry the dead with them when they moved.

For the Etiwan and others, the number of burials increased significantly during the seventeenth century. Although population figures are problematic, one estimate suggests that roughly 1,750 lived in the region in the 1560s, but that number had declined to around 664 by 1682, and continued to fall in the ensuing decades. Disease played the biggest role in this decline, particularly in the first years after English settlement, a fact celebrated by one early eighteenth-century colonist who wrote that "the Hand of God was eminently seen in thining the Indians, to make room for the English" by sending "unusual Sicknesses amongst them."[7]

Several other groups surrounded the Etiwan, Escamacu, and other Cusabo Indians in the Carolina Lowcountry. To the north lived several groups known as the Cape Fear Indians, whose culture resembled that of their neighbors in Carolina. In the Georgia Lowcountry to the south lived the Guale, Muskogean-speaking peoples whose territory stretched from the Ogeechee River to the Savannah River and included several major sea islands. Economic activities resembled those to the north, but unlike the decentralized groups in the Carolina Lowcountry, the Guale were organized into larger chiefdoms. Individuals living in villages paid tribute in crops or labor to one of five regional chiefs. Relations with groups to the north varied; the Guale were at war with the Escamacu in the 1560s, but there is also evidence of some trade links in the seventeenth century. By that point, however, Guale power had weakened considerably under the onslaught of Spanish military and missionary endeavors. The combination of warfare, forced labor, and disease reduced the population considerably from 3,000 or so in the early sixteenth century to less than 1,300 in 1600 to roughly 250 by 1675, at which point many began to migrate to new locations closer to Spanish settlements in Florida.

Finally, perhaps one hundred miles south and west of Charleston lived the Westos. The Westos were an Iroquoian group who had been pushed out of western New York in the 1650s by the more powerful Five Nation Iroquois. They settled briefly in Virginia, where they began exchanging Indian slaves for guns. Raiding for slaves carried them south into the Carolinas, and by the 1660s they had settled in a fortified town on the Savannah River. From there they raided Lowcountry groups for slaves, whom they traded to Virginia colonists. The Westos quickly earned a reputation as fearsome warriors, and Westo raids ended the lives of thousands of Indians in the southeast and terrified those who escaped. One early English settler reported that the Kiawah and other Lowcountry groups were "affraid of ye very foot step of a Westoe." When the English arrived in 1670, the Kiawah and others welcomed them as potential allies against the Westo.[8]

Deeper in the interior lay territory belonging to the Catawba, Creek, and Cherokee. These groups, and others even farther inland, established trade connections with colonists and alternately allied with and fought against English newcomers to the region, but their worlds lay far beyond the borders of the Lowcountry. Nevertheless, the presence of so many Indians, both along the coast and in the interior, distinguished the Lowcountry from other parts of the Greater Caribbean. Periodic trade and conflict with the Caribs occurred in the sugar islands, but native peoples played a far greater role in the political, economic, military, and cultural life of the Lowcountry during the seventeenth and eighteenth centuries.

EARLY ENGLISH INCURSIONS: PRIVATEERING AND THE TOBACCO TRADE

Until the end of the seventeenth century, only the Spanish had established permanent colonies in the Greater Caribbean. The 1494 Treaty of Tordesillas granted Spain dominion over all of the Americas, except for Brazil, which fell under Portuguese control. By the middle of the sixteenth century, the Caribbean served as the gateway to Spain's mighty American empire and a highway for the great fleets of treasure ships carrying gold, silver, pearls, and emeralds, as well as exotic commodities such as sugar, tobacco, ginger, and chocolate, to markets in Seville and Madrid. The vastness of Spain's American territory, however, rendered it impossible to defend, and its great riches soon attracted other nations seeking to prey on its vulnerable points. French corsairs began to raid Spanish ships and ports in the 1520s, and they continued to do so for the next three decades as part of larger, sporadic conflicts between the two nations. In 1559, the two sides agreed to a treaty, but the peace did not extend to the Indies. Instead, there was "no peace beyond the line," meaning that actions in areas south of the Tropic of Cancer and west of the mid-Atlantic would not affect European affairs. Spain continued to claim exclusive rights to American territories and the right to capture all foreigners found there, while the French continued to insist on their rights to sail to the region.

The English entered these turbulent waters relatively late. At least one English vessel visited the Greater Antilles in 1527, but almost another forty years passed before English ships became a regular presence in the area. Three decades of political and religious instability following Henry VIII's conversion to Protestantism in the 1530s, England's relative poverty compared to Spain and France, and the movement to conquer and colonize Ireland, begun in the 1550s, all contributed to the delay. Elizabeth I's accession to the throne in 1558, however, secured England's Protestant allegiance and ushered in a period of remarkable transformations in English life, including a growing interest in overseas ventures beyond Ireland. State support for such ventures remained limited. Instead, individual merchants and members of the gentry organized and financed voyages across the Atlantic. The quest for wealth animated these West-Country Men, as they became known, but so too did the desire to challenge Spain's growing power in Europe and its dominance in America. Fiercely anti-Catholic, they took aim at Spanish ships and ports in the Caribbean, seeking to interrupt the flow of wealth into Spanish, and, by extension, papal coffers, while simultaneously advancing England's (and their own) fortunes and the Protestant cause. So interwoven were these various motives that by the 1570s, according to one historian, "Protestantism, patriotism, and plunder became virtually synonymous."[9]

Among the first to venture out was John Hawkins. Hawkins was the son of a Plymouth merchant who had experience trading in Spain and West Africa. Following in his father's footsteps, Hawkins sailed to the west coast of Africa in 1562, where he "got into his possession, partly by the sworde, and partly by other meanes" three hundred slaves.[10] He then sailed to Hispaniola, where he sold the slaves to Spanish planters (illegally, as Spain prohibited foreigners to trade with its colonies) in return for sugar, ginger, pearls, and hides. Hawkins sent the goods to an English trader in Spain, hoping they would be recognized as legitimate cargo. Instead, Spanish officials seized the goods. Undeterred, Hawkins organized subsequent voyages in 1564, 1566, and 1567. The last ended in disaster when Hawkins ran into Spanish warships at San Juan de Ulúa, the fort guarding the harbor at Vera Cruz, Mexico, in 1568. Hawkins survived, but he lost several ships, three hundred men, and most of his trade goods.

Interest in the contraband slave trade waned even before news of the San Juan de Ulúa debacle reached England. The risks of the trade were too great and the profits too small. Plenty of other Englishmen, however, ventured to the region in search of plunder. Between 1570 and 1577, at least thirteen English expeditions sailed to the Indies, hoping to capture Spanish treasure. Perhaps the most famous of these "Sea Dogs" was Hawkins's cousin, Francis Drake. Drake made moderately successful raids on Panama in 1570 and 1571, but he struck it rich on his third voyage in 1572–73. Teaming up with a group of runaway slaves in Panama, the *cimarrones,* as well as with French Huguenot (Protestant) privateers, Drake and his men captured £40,000 in gold, silver, and pearls.

Plundering expeditions gained a degree of official sanction when open hostilities broke out between England and Spain in 1585. English pirates became privateers, licensed or semi-licensed raiders seeking to damage the enemy and enrich themselves. Drake commanded one of the first and largest ventures. Officially sent out to present a show of force to the Spanish in European waters, Drake's main goal was Caribbean treasure. He sailed from England in September 1585 with a fleet of twenty-two ships, including two of the Queen's vessels, and 2,300 men. After making a brief appearance on the Spanish coast, he sailed to the Cape Verde Islands and then to Hispaniola. He attacked and destroyed Santo Domingo and seized 25,000 ducats, a significant sum, but far less than he had hoped. He then moved on to Cartagena (Colombia), one of the central shipping points for American gold and silver. Drake easily captured and ransacked the city in early 1586. With his men increasingly succumbing to disease, Drake abandoned plans to attack Panama and sailed north. In May, he burned St. Augustine to the ground and sailed to the recently established English settlement at Roanoke, North Carolina, where he evacuated the struggling colonists and returned to England.

Drake's voyage yielded less booty than anticipated, but he exposed the weakness of Spain's Caribbean defenses, which other privateers soon sought to exploit. Between 1550 and 1624, roughly 900 English ships manned by some 25,000 sailors traversed Caribbean waters, many returning home with significant prizes. During the peak years of privateering in the 1590s, the value of prize goods entering England fluctuated between £100,000 and £200,000 per year, of which American goods accounted for 70 percent of the total value. Privateers hoped for, and occasionally seized, prizes carrying gold, silver, or pearls, but most of their loot came in the form of valuable products like sugar, hides, indigo, and logwood. A Spanish observer in London in 1591 complained that the privateers' haul was such that the price of sugar was lower in London than in Lisbon. Not all privateering ventures were successful, but most captured enough goods to make the enterprise profitable, and some struck it rich.

A few Elizabethans sought a more direct source of gold and silver than raiding Spanish ships and settlements. Rather than sailing from one place to another in search of what he dismissed as "Ordinarie prizes," Sir Walter Ralegh set off in February 1595 with four ships and 300 men in a quest for El Dorado, the fabled city of gold located deep in the interior of South America, whose ruler reportedly covered his body in gold dust. Here was the prospect of riches even greater than those flowing out of Mexico and Peru. Ralegh landed at Trinidad in March 1596 and quickly destroyed the major Spanish settlement at San Josef, executing most of the Spaniards he captured. He then set off up the Orinoco River basin in mid-May. He formed alliances with local Indians along the way with promises to help fight the Spanish but eventually turned back after encountering massive waterfalls and increasing powerful river currents fueled by summer rains. Ralegh returned to London anxious to publicize his exploits and promote English colonization ventures to the region. He published *The Discoverie of the Large, Rich, and Beautiful Empire of Guiana* in 1596, but with no actual gold to support his case, his efforts generated little interest.

Ralegh's quest for El Dorado failed, but English privateers continued to cruise the region in search of Spanish loot throughout the 1590s and early 1600s. Many of these men gradually discovered they could make significant profits by trading illegally with Spanish colonists in Trinidad and other places on the poorly defended northern coast of South America. Spain's decision to strengthen fortifications at important port cities and to organize new fleets of galleons to guard those cities following Drake's raid in 1585–86 left other, more marginal parts of the empire less defended and less well supplied. English privateers stepped in to fill the void, exchanging European goods with these neglected Spanish colonies in return for a variety of commodities, particularly for a new product increasingly in demand in England—tobacco.

Native Americans had long used tobacco in a variety of rituals and ceremonies, but Europeans were slow to adopt the plant. At some point in the sixteenth century, local colonists began to smoke and sniff tobacco, as did visiting sailors. Sailors, in turn, likely introduced tobacco seeds and habits of consumption to Spain and the rest of Europe by the 1570s. Francis Drake's men traded for tobacco with Caribs on Dominica when they cruised through the region in 1585–86, suggesting that they were already acquainted with the plant. Although wary of tobacco's association with "heathen" rituals, elite Europeans eventually embraced tobacco as a medicinal wonder, a means of relieving headaches, toothaches, respiratory problems, and upset stomachs, among other ailments. One English writer in the 1590s suggested that tobacco could even help with food shortages, because it relieved hunger and thirst for days at a time. Not everyone was enamored with the new plant: King James I issued *A Counterblaste to*

Tobacco in 1604, claiming that its use promoted "sinnefull and shamefull lust" and that it was "a custome loathsome to the eye, hatefull to the Nose, harmefull to the brain, [and] daungerous to the Lungs."[11] His warnings, however, did little to curb growing demand. England already was importing close to 100,000 pounds of tobacco each year by 1611, well before Virginia and Bermuda had begun to export the crop. Most of it came from Trinidad and the Orinoco basin.

That contraband trade in turn generated interest in establishing permanent plantations that could produce tobacco for the English market. Charles Leigh and Robert Harcourt led separate efforts to develop a tobacco colony in Guiana in 1604 and 1609, respectively, but neither lasted more than a few years. Others turned their attention farther south in the 1610s and 1620s, seeking to produce tobacco in the Amazon basin. The Amazon Company managed to get 150–200 men to the region between 1619 and 1623 before the colony collapsed.

Despite their failure, these early efforts at colonization, along with privateering and the contraband trade, played a key role in the eventual development of successful colonies in the Greater Caribbean and elsewhere in British America. The English gained valuable experience and knowledge about the physical and political geography of the Americas from these early ventures. As the historian N. A. M. Rodger observed, "In 1558 there was probably not one Englishman capable unaided of navigating a ship to the West Indies, and in 1568, only one."[12] By the early seventeenth century, however, thousands of Englishmen had sailed in the Greater Caribbean and many captains had made multiple voyages, including Christopher Newport, who had sailed to the region thirteen times before he led the Virginia Company ships through Caribbean waters on their way to Jamestown in 1607.

Likewise, the sea war with Spain promoted the growth of English shipbuilding and associated trades. The size of the English merchant fleet, as well as the size of individual vessels, increased dramatically during the sixteenth century. Moreover, the profits from illegal trade and plunder provided necessary capital to finance many of the early colonization efforts.

Finally, although early settlements in the Orinoco and Amazon basins failed, interest in establishing more permanent settlements remained strong and pushed others to search out new options for colonization. James I's desire to maintain peaceful relations with Spain following the 1604 Treaty of London while also claiming the right of Englishmen to settle unoccupied parts of the New World—that is, unoccupied by the Spanish—meant that those interested in developing permanent colonies had to look on the margins of Spain's empire. Such marginal places included Virginia, which was far enough away from the heart of Spanish power that it attracted only minimal protests from Madrid; New England, even farther away and where the Pilgrims of 1620 turned after determining that a settlement in Guiana was too great a diplomatic risk; and, finally, the smaller islands of the Lesser Antilles that remained undesirable to the Spanish, and thus unoccupied by them. It was on those islands that the English established their first permanent colonies in the Greater Caribbean.

COLONIZATION OF THE LEEWARD ISLANDS AND BARBADOS

Efforts to colonize the Lesser Antilles began in 1605, when a group associated with Charles Leigh's Guiana colony landed on St. Lucia. Caribs on the island eagerly traded with colonists, but they had little interest in permanent neighbors and quickly destroyed the fledgling settlement. Only a few survivors escaped to tell the tale. Carib resistance likewise doomed an effort to settle Grenada in 1609. The next major effort, led by Thomas Warner over a decade later, focused on the Leeward Islands at the northern end of the Lesser Antilles. Warner was the son of a middling farmer from Suffolk and a neighbor of the Puritan leader John Winthrop. He had sailed to the Caribbean as part of a venture to the Amazon basin in 1620. That effort, like so many others, failed, but on his return voyage to England Warner followed a tip from a friend and sailed to the Leeward Islands. At St. Christopher he found "a very convenient place for ye planting of tobaccoes, which ever was a rich commodetie."[13] Warner quickly "became acquainted" with the leaders of several Carib groups, although whether any agreement was reached regarding an English settlement is unclear. Regardless, Warner returned to England, secured financial backing from London merchants, outfitted a small group of colonists, including his wife and son, and sailed to the Caribbean.

Warner and his group arrived on St. Christopher in January 1624. They immediately set about clearing land, building houses, and planting tobacco. In all these activities, they almost certainly followed native practices, burning parts of the woods to clear ground and constructing simple, round dwellings with roofs made from palmetto leaves. The colonists encountered a major setback when a hurricane swept across the island in September and destroyed their tobacco crop. Undeterred, the colonists quickly rebuilt and replanted, and by 1625 Warner returned to England with a crop of tobacco to exchange for more supplies.

Little documentary material for the early settlement of St. Christopher exists, and we can only guess at the nature of relations between the English and Caribs in the initial period following colonization. By 1626, however, relations had turned decidedly violent. A small group of French settlers had arrived on St. Kitts the year before to establish a settlement and, despite a general disdain for one another, the two groups of Europeans quickly made common cause against the Caribs. English accounts suggest that the Caribs had begun preparations to attack the Europeans and to destroy their settlements. Whether such rumors were true or not, the English and French joined forces and launched a preemptive raid on the Caribs. They attacked at night and massacred more than a hundred Indians while they slept in hammocks. The Caribs counterattacked the following year, but the colonists defeated them and gained control of the island. Faced with the possibility of attacks from Caribs on neighboring islands and from the Spanish, the English and French colonists agreed to divide St. Christopher between them in 1627. The French occupied the two ends of the island, while the English occupied the interior.

Another hurricane in 1626 again wiped out their tobacco crop along with their provisions, leaving hungry and miserable colonists struggling to feed themselves. Three years later, the Spanish invaded and destroyed crops, fields, and buildings. Many colonists fled, but others found sanctuary in the mountains or on nearby islands, and once the Spanish fleet departed, they returned and began rebuilding. New arrivals from England soon augmented their numbers. The population was likely 3,000 or so before the Spanish attack, including at least 60 enslaved Africans. It took several years to recover from that attack, but St. Kitts's population grew steadily in the following years.

As St. Kitts's population expanded, so too did tobacco production, and with limited land on the island, some colonists sought new opportunities on surrounding islands. Anthony Hilton led the movement to nearby Nevis in 1628. Hilton had come to St. Kitts a few years earlier to seek his fortune. The Caribs had destroyed his first effort to develop a plantation on the island's windward side, but he quickly rebuilt on the leeward side and soon produced a good crop of tobacco. He returned to England, recruited a small group of colonists, and sailed for Nevis in 1628. They were soon joined by 150 colonists, who migrated from St. Kitts. The colonists had only started constructing houses before the Spanish invaded in 1629, but as happened on St. Kitts, displaced planters returned quickly and began rebuilding soon after the Spanish left.

A few years later, in 1632, migrants from St. Kitts fanned out to nearby Montserrat and Antigua. Thomas Warner's son Edward led the migration to Antigua and served as the island's first governor. The Caribs attacked the infant settlement repeatedly, killing or capturing dozens of colonists, and Antigua's situation remained precarious for years, but by the 1650s the island had a population of roughly 1,200 men. Many of the more recent arrivals had migrated from Barbados as land became scarce on that island following the transition to sugar. Montserrat became a haven for Irish Catholics who arrived in the Caribbean, some as political prisoners, others as indentured servants. Thomas Warner doubted the loyalty of these men, with good reason, as Irish servants on Nevis greeted invading Spanish forces in 1629 with cries of "Liberty, joyfull Liberty." Warner feared the Irish would align themselves with the French on St. Kitts and thus encouraged them to settle on nearby Montserrat. Additional Irish Catholic settlers arrived from Virginia and from Ireland itself, recruited by the island's governor, an Irishman named Anthony Briskett.

Even before colonists from St. Kitts began to spread out to other islands, another group of English adventurers established

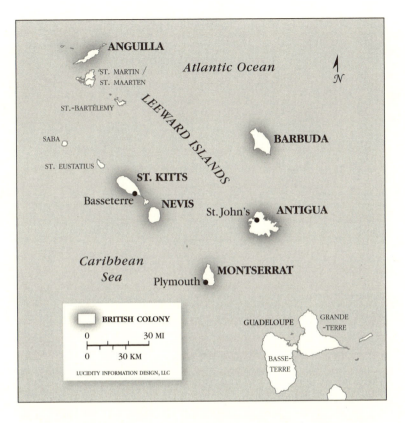

A colony far to the south on the unoccupied island of Barbados. As with St. Christopher, interest in Barbados developed from trading expeditions to South America. Captain John Powell visited the island in 1625 while returning from Brazil on behalf of Sir William Courteen, a wealthy London merchant with trading interests in Spain, Portugal, West Africa, and the Americas. Unlike St. Christopher, Barbados was uninhabited, although there was evidence that Caribs had lived there or hunted there in an earlier period. Powell's report on the island encouraged Courteen to finance an expedition led by Powell and his brother Henry. The first colonists arrived in Barbados in 1627, among them Henry Winthrop, whose father John would soon lead another group of English colonists to Massachusetts. The group also included eight or ten enslaved Africans who had been captured en route. After dropping off the colonists, Henry Powell sailed to

Guiana, where he obtained a variety of plants, including tobacco, corn, cassava, and sugarcane for use on Barbados. He also enslaved thirty-two Arawak Indians to instruct the colonists in the cultivation of these crops.

Courteen was not the only one interested in the island, and while his men were the first to arrive, he had not secured the necessary legal title to the island. Before he had done so, Charles I granted a favorite courtier, the Earl of Carlisle, proprietary title to Barbados *and* the Leeward Islands. As proprietor, Carlisle had the power to appoint governors and ruling councils and to collect rents and taxes from the colonists. With letters patent in hand, Carlisle appointed Thomas Warner governor of St. Kitts and Charles Wolverston governor of Barbados. Wolverston sailed to Barbados in April 1628 with seventy colonists to assert Carlisle's patent. Before that group left, Courteen had enlisted the aid of the Philip Herbert, Earl of Montgomery, and later Pembroke, and together they managed to secure a separate patent from Charles naming him proprietor. (Charles was notoriously inattentive to such matters—one Barbadian governor claimed he signed whatever paperwork was put in front of him without reading it.) As a result, Barbados had two competing proprietors and two separate settlements during the late 1620s: Courteen's men at Holetown and Carlisle's men at what became Bridgetown. Violence ensued as the two sides dueled for control of the island, taking turns raiding each other's settlements and capturing the opponents' governor.

Carlisle eventually secured his claim to Barbados and the Leeward Islands in 1629, but he had little interest in the colonies beyond their ability to provide money to pay his debts. The governors he appointed ruled as petty tyrants. One ordered his predecessor executed for leading a group of hungry colonists who had demanded access to ships loaded with provisions during a food shortage. Another routinely jailed those who challenged his actions, threatening to make one dissident "shorter by the heade." One prominent planter spent an hour in the stocks without his hat under blazing midday sun for asking about another, "If all whoremasters were taken off the Bench, what would the Governor do for a Councell [?]"[14] Needless to say, such conditions did not inspire the colonists to great deeds. When Sir Henry Colt arrived in Barbados in 1631, he found the colonists

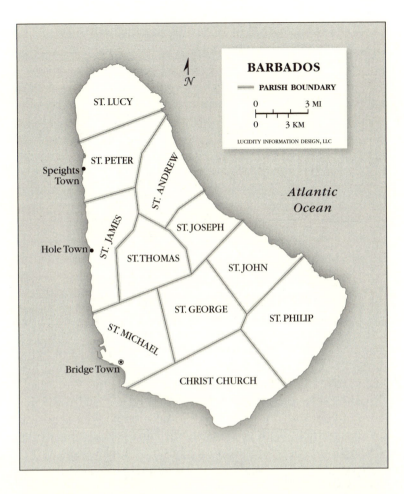

BARBADOS

PARISH BOUNDARY

0   3 MI

0   3 KM

LUCIDITY INFORMATION DESIGN, LLC

ST. LUCY

ST. PETER

Speights
Town

ST. ANDREW

ST. JAMES

ST. JOSEPH

Hole Town

ST. THOMAS

ST. JOHN

Atlantic
Ocean

ST. GEORGE

ST. MICHAEL

ST. PHILIP

Bridge Town

CHRIST CHURCH

engaged in heavy drinking and constant quarreling, but little labor. He claimed that servants on the plantations he visited did no work over the course of ten days.

Colt may have exaggerated, but Barbados remained a rough-and-tumble place for many years. Similar conditions prevailed in the Leeward Islands. In 1642, colonists in St. Christopher revolted against proprietary taxes and Warner's arbitrary rule as governor. Reports indicated that 1,500 armed men confronted Warner and forced concessions from him, including the creation of a representative assembly. Tensions, however, remained high, and Warner feared another revolt would result in the "Cutting of throates" and the "Island ruyned forever."[15]

In between political quarrels amongst themselves and with the proprietor or his representatives, colonists gradually went about the business of building farms and plantations, a process discussed in chapter 2. With the outbreak of the Civil War in England during the 1640s, however, colonists, particularly in Barbados, seized the opportunity to take greater control over local affairs. They asserted their neutrality, stopped paying taxes to the proprietor, and essentially became a self-governing state. An informal peace emerged between factions on Barbados during the mid-1640s. According to one account, anyone who uttered the words "Cavalier" or "Roundhead," the names given to competing sides in the Civil War, had to buy a meal for all who heard him. Distracted by events in England, neither the king nor the proprietor nor Parliament had the means to assert much control from 3,000 miles across the Atlantic.

As the Civil War intensified in the late 1640s, however, numerous Royalist refugees fled to Barbados, enflaming passions on both sides and destroying the island's neutrality. Royalists eventually managed to seize control of the government in the name of the king. Parliament, in turn, organized a fleet of ships under Sir George Ayscue to retake the island. Ayscue and his men arrived in late 1651, and within a few months, Barbadian Royalists surrendered. The terms of surrender included the return of confiscated property and no taxation without approval by the assembly. With peace established and parliamentary rule declared, colonists returned to the business of planting. Ayscue then sailed to the Leeward Islands and secured a similar settlement with colonists there.

Renewed competition for the proprietary rights to Barbados and the Leewards followed the Restoration of Charles II to the throne in 1660. One group based their claim on the Carlisle patent, another on the Pembroke/Courteen patent, while yet another group of merchants and planters in Barbados sought to escape proprietary rule altogether. Ultimately Charles asserted his power by annulling the proprietary patent and placing the colonies under control of the Crown. In exchange for royal recognition of their title to lands, colonists in Barbados and the Leewards agreed in 1663 to pay the Crown a tax of 4.5 percent on all goods exported.

By the time of the Restoration settlement, colonists in Barbados had abandoned tobacco and turned to planting sugar, amassing huge fortunes and providing a model of plantation development soon embraced by colonists in the Leeward Islands, Jamaica, and the Carolina Lowcountry. Although prospects of plundering the Spanish initially lured the English into the tropical Caribbean waters in the sixteenth century and tobacco provided the impetus for the development of colonies in the early seventeenth century, it was sugarcane that would transform the islands from mildly prosperous settlements into tremendously wealthy plantations, the crown jewels of Britain's American empire.

TWO

The Sweet Negotiation of Sugar

THE ENGLISH MEN—and it was almost exclusively men at first—who ventured to the Caribbean in the early seventeenth century came in search of riches. As the historian Richard Dunn remarked, these early adventurers "did not attempt calypso-style Holy Experiments, nor did they build palm-fringed Cities on a Hill."[1] Neither religious persecution nor the desire to establish new, model societies motivated the majority of colonists. That is not to say that religion played no role in the development of English colonies in the Caribbean, but there is little doubt that the search for individual wealth occupied a particularly prominent place in the minds of these men. As one early visitor stated, colonists "came here in order to become wealthy."[2]

Colonists in Barbados and the Leeward Islands pinned their initial hopes for riches on tobacco. They gradually cleared land, built up farms, grew provision crops along with tobacco for export, and used the profits to purchase more and more indentured servants. Tobacco provided solid, if unspectacular profits for several years, but prices dropped in the 1630s and colonists began to search for other crops that could generate revenue. Beginning in the 1640s, a few planters in Barbados learned the secrets of making sugar from the Dutch in Brazil, and within a few decades the island had become an economic juggernaut.

The development of sugar plantations had momentous consequences for Barbados and other colonies in the region. Sugar generated fantastic wealth for a few planters, altered the social structure and demography of the island, and accelerated the growth of African slavery. Sugar production also hastened deforestation, exhausted the soil, undermined the production of provision crops, necessitated importation of large numbers of animals, and aided the spread of deadly disease. Sugar, in short, transformed the economy, society, and ecology of Barbados with remarkable speed. Barbados, in turn, provided a model for the Leeward Islands. The shift to sugar took longer in the Leewards, but by the end of the seventeenth century the basic patterns associated with sugar production on Barbados had repeated themselves, providing an early example of the extension of the Barbados culture hearth.

TOBACCO AND COTTON SOCIETIES

Tobacco had obvious appeal to early colonists. The leaf had a ready market in Europe, and it required little more than seeds, a few simple tools, and basic labor to produce. Hoping to emulate Virginia's recent success, colonists in the islands set about clearing the dense forest cover on the islands by chopping or burning trees and planting seeds amidst the charred remains. Their slash-and-burn methods did not impress visitors—Sir Henry Colt complained that the landscape of Barbados resembled the ruins of a fire-ravaged village, a "desolate and disorderly shew" of small clearings and half-burned trees set against dense forest.[3] Nevertheless, colonists in Barbados, St. Christopher, and elsewhere cleared enough land to produce several crops of tobacco in the first few years, and a fortunate few made handsome profits. James Drax earned enough from his initial tobacco crops in the late 1620s to purchase fifty indentured servants, which in turn allowed him to expand operations.

But while Drax and others managed to earn good profits, many colonists struggled. Part of the problem was that new tobacco production in the West Indies alongside increased output in Bermuda and Virginia flooded the market in the 1620s and early 1630s and pushed down prices. No data exists for West Indian tobacco, but Chesapeake prices fell from 11.60 (pence sterling per pound) in 1625 to 9.10 in 1627—the year Barbados was colonized—to 5.30 in 1630 to 2.90 in 1632. In addition to falling prices, colonists in Barbados produced a lower-quality tobacco. John Winthrop complained that the tobacco that his son Henry sent from Barbados was so "ill conditioned, fowle, full of stalkes and evill coloured" that no one wanted to purchase it.[4] Barbados tobacco was so bad that even many colonists smoked imported Virginia tobacco. Colonists in St. Christopher produced better-quality tobacco, perhaps the result of the island's rich volcanic soil, but falling prices limited their prospects for great riches as well.

Colonists continued to plant tobacco, but in the face of declining profits, a number of planters turned to other crops, including ginger, indigo, and, most importantly, cotton. Cotton required a larger capital investment, but it also generated larger profits and, unlike tobacco, Barbadian cotton had a good reputation in European markets. "The trade of Cotton fills them all with hope," wrote Colt in 1631, and something of a cotton boom took place on Barbados during the 1630s as planters expanded operations.[5]

Regardless of what crop they planted, the key to success for early colonists was having enough laborers to clear the land and work the fields. One contemporary observed in the 1630s that "a plantation in this place is worth nothing unless there be some good store of hands upon it."[6] Planters utilized a number of different forms of labor to meet their needs, but the most important in the early decades of settlement was indentured servitude. Although indentured servitude had some precedents in the English practice of hiring agricultural laborers for one year, the Virginia Company appears to have originated the idea of shipping servants to the colonies to work for longer periods of time, and colonists in Barbados quickly adopted the practice.

Indentured servants sold their labor in exchange for payment of their passage to the New World. Some servants signed contracts stipulating the length of service before they left. Others were sold on arrival according to the "custom of the country." The number of years varied by age and other factors, but most servants served for four or five years. During that time, their labor was the property of their owners and could be sold or traded away at any point. When they completed their contracts, servants received "freedom dues," generally £10–20 worth of commodities to start them on their new lives.

Servants came from a variety of backgrounds. Some were convicts transported to the colonies in lieu of prison time. Others were political prisoners, captured in Oliver Cromwell's wars against Scotland and Ireland in the middle of the seventeenth century. Later, men involved in Monmouth's Rebellion in the 1680s were shipped to Barbados to get rid of them. Indeed, for a period of time, Barbados became a verb, as officials sought "to barbadoes" various disorderly elements of society. The majority of servants, however, were voluntary migrants. Most were young, single men who had few economic prospects at home. One list of passengers sailing to the island from London in 1635 reveals that 94 percent of the 983 passengers were male, and 70 percent were between the ages of fifteen and twenty-four. Most of these passengers, perhaps as many as three-quarters, were indentured servants. Very few families and younger children traveled to the Caribbean in the seventeenth century. Instead, Barbados and the Leeward Islands attracted those hoping to find new economic opportunities or served as a dumping ground for the rebellious or the unwanted. As one visitor remarked, Barbados was "the dung-hill whereon England doth cast forth its rubbish. Rogues and whores and such like people are those which are generally brought here. A rogue in England will hardly make a cheater here: a Bawd brought over puts on a demure comportment, a whore if handsome makes a wife for some rich planter."[7]

Life as a servant was difficult. Richard Ligon, who arrived on Barbados in 1647, wrote that whether a master was "merciful or cruel" shaped the experience of individual servants, but most faced a bleak and brutal existence. Servants were called out by a bell at six in the morning and worked until eleven. They went back to the fields at one in the afternoon and remained there in the grueling afternoon sun until six in the evening, when they returned to small huts made of sticks and plantain leaves. Their food was dull and monotonous, consisting mostly of potatoes and boiled cornmeal. Ligon wrote that they received "bone" (fresh) meat only when an ox died. "If they complain," Ligon wrote, "they are beaten by the Overseer; if they resist, their time is doubled." Ligon was appalled by the violence employed to discipline servants. "I have seen an Overseer beat a Servant with a cane about the head, till the blood has followed, for a fault that is not worth the speaking of . . . Truly, I have seen such cruelty there done to Servants, as I did not think one Christian could have done to another." The fact that many servants were Irish

Catholics only heightened tensions. Planters viewed them as a "riotous and unruly lot" ready to overthrow the English at the first opportunity. The Irish servants viewed the masters with similar disdain. One received twenty-one lashes for declaring he would eat more meat if there was as much English blood on the tray. Shortly before Ligon arrived on Barbados, eighteen servants were executed for plotting rebellion. Ligon wrote in the late 1640s—during the transition to sugar—but similar treatment, and accompanying servant unrest, characterized earlier years as well.[8]

Despite miserable working conditions, migrants poured into Barbados, lured by the hope of economic prosperity. Although the documentary base for calculating the number of migrants is limited, a very rough estimate suggests that more than half of the estimated 40,000 European migrants to British America during the 1630s went to the Caribbean. Most came as indentured servants and most ended up in Barbados. The number of migrants rose to over 68,000 in the 1640s, with perhaps 80 percent of them going to the Caribbean. The constant influx of servants and others resulted in rapid population growth during the 1630s and 1640s, so that by 1655, the island had a population of roughly 23,000 Europeans and approximately 20,000 enslaved Africans.

Former indentured servants hoped to acquire land and establish themselves as freemen, but few managed to do so. Those who did generally were early arrivals who acquired land during the 1630s, when it was still relatively inexpensive and available. They also frequently formed partnerships with others, which enabled them to pool resources and limit risk. Given the small size of Barbados, however, most former servants never achieved their goal of owning land and continued their quest for wealth and security elsewhere.

Indentured servants provided the majority of labor for Barbados during the 1630s and early 1640s, but planters also utilized slave labor. Some slaves were Native Americans from other islands or the mainland. The thirty-two Arawaks who came from Guiana with Henry Powell in 1627 were enslaved either before or shortly after their arrival on Barbados, and Ligon encountered Indian slaves in the late 1640s, some of whom were likely Pequots captured during their war with New England colonists a decade earlier. Colonists purchased Native American slaves throughout the seventeenth century, including captives from King Philip's War in New England and from South Carolina, but their numbers were never large.

Early colonists also exploited Africans as slaves. Several enslaved Africans arrived with the first English colonists in 1627, captured en route and retained by Powell, and Africans appear in at least one inventory of property from the 1630s. Slaves, however, were expensive, and few planters growing cotton or tobacco could afford them during the first decade or so of settlement.

By 1640 Barbados had emerged as a relatively prosperous colonial society of small planters, numerous indentured servants, and a few enslaved Africans and Native Americans, producing cotton, indigo, ginger, and tobacco, along with provision crops. Much of the interior remained uncultivated, but colonists had cleared coastal areas and established farms and settlements. No one was getting terrifically wealthy, but prospects remained good enough to draw in thousands of servants and other migrants hoping to improve their lot. The colony's population had grown to about the same size as Virginia and Massachusetts. Similar conditions characterized St. Christopher and the other Leeward Islands, although the relative success of cotton production in Barbados gave colonists there better access to credit from London merchants, which allowed them to expand operations more quickly.

The general economic prosperity of the 1630s, however, gave way to more challenging conditions in the early 1640s. Cotton and tobacco prices plummeted, and many planters faced uncertain futures. Tobacco planters on Barbados, with their notoriously inferior product, were particularly hard-hit. Both cotton and tobacco prices rebounded by the mid-1640s, but in the meantime, colonists in Barbados searched for a new crop that could produce large profits. They found one in sugar.

THE KING OF SWEETS

Native to southeast Asia and the Pacific Islands, sugarcane spread gradually to Persia by the seventh century CE. From there, as the saying goes, sugar followed the Koran. The cane, and more importantly the irrigation and milling technology needed to grow and process sugar, were carried by Muslim armies to the Levant, then across North Africa, as well as along the eastern Mediterranean from Cyprus to Sicily, and eventually into parts of Spain and Portugal by the tenth century, if not earlier. The taste for sugar, particularly among northern Europeans, increased as a result of the Crusades at the end of the eleventh century. Crusaders began to produce sugar in territories they occupied, and they brought samples with them when they returned to Europe. By the early fifteenth century, a significant sugar trade had developed between northern Europe and the sugar-producing regions of the Mediterranean.

Europeans craved sugar for a variety of purposes. First viewing it as a medicine, Europeans gradually began to use it as a spice to enliven the flavor of meats and vegetables. They also used it as a preservative, and beginning in the late seventeenth century, as a sweetener for coffee and tea. By the 1680s, English elites started mimicking the French custom of eating meals with multiple courses, including a final sweet course. In addition, sugar could be combined with other substances such as almonds to form a paste that could be sculpted in various ways. Guests at a royal wedding in Brussels in 1565 were treated to a display of various fruits from around the world that were displayed in bowls, plates, and cups on a table with napkins and candelabras—all made out of sugar. Only the wealthy could afford to use sugar for such decorative displays, and it remained a luxury through much of the early modern period. Nevertheless, consumption spread gradually across different levels of society. Per capita consumption of sugar in England rose from about 2 pounds per person in the 1660s to 4 pounds per person by the 1690s and continued to expand in the eighteenth century. By the time of the American Revolution, every man, woman, and child in England on average consumed 23 pounds of sugar a year, enough to allow regular use of sugar in food and drinks. British colonists on the North American mainland imported less than half as much sugar, about 14 pounds per person in 1770, but made up for it with a much higher consumption of sugar's by-products, rum and molasses.

The Portuguese and the Spanish carried sugarcane beyond the Mediterranean basin and into the Atlantic, first to the Atlantic Islands—the Azores, Madeira, the Canary Islands, Cape Verde, and São Tomé during the fifteenth century—and then to the New World. Columbus brought sugarcane to the New

World on his second voyage in 1493. A small sugar industry developed on Santo Domingo in the sixteenth century, but gold and silver captured the imagination of Spanish authorities and colonists far more than sugar. As a result, it was the Portuguese in Brazil who emerged as the major sugar producers in the New World. By the 1540s, a number of mills operated in Pernambuco and Bahia in northeast Brazil, and by the end of the sixteenth century, Brazil had emerged as Europe's main supplier of sugar. The wealth generated by Brazilian plantations proved a tempting target for other European powers, and in 1630 the Dutch captured Pernambuco and held it until 1654. It was from the Dutch in Brazil that the English in Barbados would learn the secrets of sugar.

Sugarcane was a complicated crop to grow and process. The growing season was long—between twelve and sixteen months—and the canes required a great deal of water and heat once they had been planted, so climate limited where canes could grow. With average year-round temperatures of 79 degrees and high seasonal rainfall, Barbados and many of the other Caribbean islands provided ideal environments for sugar production. At first, colonists planted cane pieces in long trenches about two feet apart from one another, but by the beginning of the eighteenth century they switched to the cane-hole system, which involved planting canes in two- or three-foot squares, about five or six inches deep, separated by a small bank of land. Canes were planted in the rainy season between September and December and were cut roughly fourteen months later in the dry spring season, after they had reached a height of about eight feet. The stumps of the cut canes would sprout again the following year. This was known as the ratoon crop. Ratoons did not yield as much cane juice, and after a year or two, planters allowed a field to lie fallow for a period before new canes were planted.

After the canes were cut, they were brought to mills to be crushed. Servants and slaves fed the cane pieces through a vertical three-roller mill that extracted the juice. Because canes begin to lose their sucrose content within twenty-four hours of being cut, it was important to get the canes to the mills quickly, and during the harvest season mills operated constantly. The mills were powered at first by animals, but colonists later adopted windmills, the remains of which still dot the landscapes of various islands.

After the canes were crushed, the cane juice flowed from the mill into a large kettle in the boiling house and then was transferred into a series of ever smaller and hotter kettles. Boiling eliminated impurities and gradually reduced the liquid to a syrupy substance. At a certain point lime was added to temper the substance and aid crystallization, and then at just the right moment, the sugar was "struck" and transferred to another cistern to cool. Knowing how much lime to add and when to transfer the sugar required a good deal of skill and expertise, and the boiler was an important position on all sugar plantations. One planter wrote that regardless of the size and quality of the cane crop, if there was "neglect in the boyling house the proffit will be little."[9] Boiling was also a difficult and dangerous position. Boilers worked in an oven-like atmosphere of intense heat over pots filled with scalding liquid. "If a Boyler get any part into the scalding Sugar," one planter observed, "it sticks like Glew, or Birdlime, and 'tis hard to save either Limb or Life."[10] Condi-

Sugarcane harvest. This image is from the early nineteenth century. Enslaved Africans would have had less clothing during the seventeenth and much of the eighteenth centuries. From William Clark, *Ten Views in the Island of Antigua* (London, 1823). Courtesy of the John Carter Brown Library at Brown University.

A seventeenth-century sugar mill. From Charles de Rochefort, *Histoire naturelle et morale des iles Antilles de l'Amerique* (Rotterdam, 1665). Courtesy of the James Ford Bell Library, University of Minnesota.

tions inside the boiling house were so hot that slaves sometimes had to splash water on the roof shingles to keep them from catching fire.

After the sugar had cooled for about twelve hours, it was transferred to the curing house and into clay pots with holes in the bottom. Over the course of a month, molasses slowly drained out of the sugar and was collected in buckets below each pot. The end product was a loaf of brown sugar known as muscovado. Planters in Barbados initially made only muscovado sugars, but in response to falling prices in the latter part of the seventeenth century they began to whiten the final product by applying wet clay to the curing pots. Water from the clay slowly dripped through the sugar, washing away more molasses and turning the sugar a whiter color. Clayed sugar took longer to produce but brought higher prices. Planters also increasingly made use of the collected molasses. Some sold it as it was, but others distilled it into rum for export and for consumption. The relatively complex infrastructure needed to mill, boil, and cure sugar, as well as to distill rum, gave sugar plantations something of an industrial character and distinguished them from traditional agricultural enterprises in England.

Henry Powell introduced sugarcane to Barbados in 1627, but it was not until the early 1640s that colonists learned how to process and make sugar. Exact details are murky, but it appears that several planters, including James Drax and James Holdip, learned the basics of mill design and sugar processing from Dutch planters in Brazil. Ligon wrote that "the great work of Sugar-making, was but newly practised by the inhabitants" when he arrived in 1647, and he observed that after having acquired canes from Pernambuco, planters continued to make trips to Brazil to "improve their knowledge." Slaves also may have played a major role in the transfer of information. It is perhaps not a coincidence that the leading sugar planter on Barbados, James Drax, owned several slaves who had been "bred up amongst the Portuguese," which likely meant they were from Brazil.[11] Why the Dutch were so willing to share their knowledge is not clear, but it seems likely that they appreciated the growing demand for sugar in Europe and thought that they could profit as middlemen. For many years historians argued that the Dutch also provided the financing that allowed colonists to establish sugar plantations, but more recently, Russell Menard has argued that English merchants were the key investors, often buying land directly in Barbados or partnering with local planters to produce sugar. Menard found that one London merchant family alone, the Noells, invested close to £10,000 sterling in Barbados in 1646–47, buying up five plantations totaling 600 acres.

Financed with capital from England, several Barbados planters began to produce sugar for export by 1643. Sugar did not immediately displace cotton, tobacco, and indigo on Barbados plantations. Local planters often built on their experiences with these other crops to purchase more servants and slaves on credit and then shifted into sugar. When the *Marie Bonadventure* arrived in Barbados from the west coast of Africa in July 1644, for example, planters quickly purchased the 251 slaves on board. Most were purchased on credit, and 54 percent of the credit transactions promised future payment in cotton, tobacco, or indigo. Only 17 percent promised payment in sugar. That would soon change. Barbados continued to export cotton and some tobacco for several more decades, but they quickly became marginal products. "The wealth of this island," stated one visitor in 1654, "consists of sugar."[12]

Sugar dominated Barbados's economy in the decades following the 1640s. By the middle of the 1660s, 91 percent of all exports from Barbados were sugar or its by-products, rum and molasses. That figure grew to 96 percent by the end of the seventeenth century, by which point, according to one historian, "Barbados was probably exporting more, proportionate to its size and population, than any other colony or state of its time, or indeed, in the history of the world up to that point."[13]

The transition to sugar ushered in a number of dramatic changes in Barbados. The price of land skyrocketed from £1.80 per acre (Barbados currency) in 1641 to £5.50 per acre in 1650. Ligon noted that one newly arrived gentleman in 1647 paid £7,000 sterling for half ownership in a 500-acre plantation whose total value before the introduction of sugar was £400. With land so valuable, colonists quickly set about clearing the woods that still covered much of the interior. While more than one-half of the island remained forested in 1647, within two decades, colonists had deforested the island and roughly 80 percent of the available land was planted in sugar. By 1676, the governor reported to officials in London that "there is not a foot of land in Barbadoes that is not employed even to the very seaside."[14] The almost complete deforestation of the island left Barbados dependent on outside supplies of wood required for building and for making sugar. Colonists imported wood and coal from England and the mainland colonies to meet the demand. They also began to innovate by making use of the crushed canes, called *bagasse,* for fuel. The ashes that resulted became fertilizer.

Colonists also became dependent on outside supplies of food. Planters who had cleared land had little interest in planting foodstuffs on it. They wanted all good land planted in sugar. As early as 1647, one colonist reported to John Winthrop that "men are so intent upon planting sugar that they had rather buy foode at very deare rates than produce it by labour, soe infinite is the profitt of sugar workes after once accomplished."[15] Winthrop and other New Englanders were quick to respond, and a lucrative trade in provisions soon linked New England to Barbados.

The deforestation of the island and the shift to sugar had other environmental consequences as well. Without trees, bird populations decreased significantly, so much so that some new arrivals to Barbados commented on the lack of birdsong. Trees also help maintain nutrients in the soil, particularly in tropical environments. By burning trees colonists provided added nutrients to the soil for a short period, but in the long run, the loss of trees undermined the soil's fertility and promoted erosion. As early as 1661, officials complained that some land in Barbados "is much poorer, and makes much less sugar than heretofore," and the issue worsened in the following decades.[16] Planting canes in trenches complicated the issue of erosion, because the trenches provided a ready channel for runoff during periods of heavy rain or storms. The runoff was so great during a four-day storm in 1668 that charging waters carried off over a thousand coffins from Christ Church's burial grounds. Many colonists constructed walls around parts of their estates to help limit runoff. The development of cane-holing in the eighteenth century represented another effort to deal with the issue of erosion. In order to maintain the fertility of the soil, innovative planters used increasing quantities of animal dung. By the 1690s, one planter wrote, an acre of land required thirty cartloads of dung. Some small producers on more marginal lands became dung farmers to meet the needs of sugar plantations.

In addition to being a source of dung, imported horses, oxen, and cattle provided the power for sugar mills. Turning the mills was grueling work, however, and animals died quickly. Because canes needed to be crushed immediately after being cut, having a steady supply of animals was essential, and many frustrated planters turned to windmills by the end of the seventeenth century. Planters also used animals to transport the sugar from the fields to the mills and from plantations to the warehouses and docks in Bridgetown. Colonists experimented with camels in the 1640s and 1650s—the animals make a striking sight on Ligon's map of the island—but small donkeys called assinegoes imported from the Azores quickly replaced them. One of their great advantages, according to Ligon, was that after carrying canes to the mill they returned to the fields themselves without a guide.

Finally, the development of sugar plantations created conditions especially well suited for *Aedes aegypti* mosquitoes, the primary carrier of the yellow fever virus. Both the mosquito and the virus arrived from Africa via the slave trade by the 1640s, and both soon flourished in Barbados. *A. aegypti* breed in water, and sugar plantations, with lots of cisterns and clay pots collecting water, created ideal breeding grounds. At the same time, deforestation reduced the population of birds that preyed on mosquitoes. Moreover, mosquitoes could feed on cane juice, which allowed them to live longer, creating more opportunities to bite humans and transfer the yellow fever virus. The arrival of African monkeys in Barbados also may have helped keep the virus alive. The first outbreak of yellow fever occurred in 1647, almost immediately after the beginnings of large-scale sugar production, and epidemics would strike repeatedly in the following centuries. The disease killed thousands in Barbados and elsewhere and, as we shall see, influenced military operations and geopolitical relations throughout the region during the seventeenth and eighteenth centuries.

Sugar thus reshaped the physical environment in Barbados with remarkable speed. Although colonists had begun clearing land and building farms in the tobacco and cotton eras, the shift to sugar production dramatically accelerated these developments, creating an entirely new landscape within just a few decades.

THE RISE OF SLAVERY

The work of clearing the island and planting sugarcane required a massive amount of labor, and the social transformations accompanying the shift to sugar were as dramatic as the environmental changes. Barbados's population surged during the 1640s and 1650s. By the middle decades of the seventeenth century, the island had a higher population density than anywhere in the British Atlantic world except London. Most new migrants were indentured servants, who continued to pour into the Caribbean during the 1650s. Although data is limited, the average number of indentured servants working on a plantation rose from between one and two in the years 1640–41, to three in 1646–49, to five in 1650–57. English indentured servants, however, could not meet demand, and as a result planters increasingly turned to enslaved Africans.

The use of West African slaves on sugar plantations first developed in the Atlantic Islands during the fifteenth century.

The Spanish and Portuguese initially enslaved the native Guanche on the Canary Islands to work the fields alongside wage laborers, but as the Guanche fell victim to disease and brutality, the Iberians also began to trade for slaves from West Africa. Slavery had a long history in sub-Saharan Africa, and various groups and states employed captives from wars as domestic servants and agricultural laborers. African leaders traded captives to the Portuguese in exchange for metal goods and cloth. By 1482 the Portuguese had established a fortification, El Mina, on the coast of present-day Ghana to facilitate the trade, and the use of enslaved Africans for sugar production increased, especially on the island of São Tomé, located in the Gulf of Guinea just off the West African coast.

The Portuguese transferred what historians call the plantation complex—large landholdings, production of a single staple crop for export, and the widespread use of enslaved labor—to the Americas when they colonized Brazil in the early 1500s. As in the Atlantic Islands, the Portuguese at first exploited local Native Americans for labor, but as disease killed many natives, they turned to Africans. One plantation, or *engenho,* in Bahia illustrates the trend. Africans formed only 7 percent of the labor force in 1572, increased to 37 percent in 1591, and by 1638 the entire labor force was African or Afro-Brazilian. African slavery was thus firmly established when Barbadians began to learn about sugar from the Dutch in Brazil.

The English had only limited experience with slavery or Africa before the 1640s. Although John Hawkins and a few other privateers attempted to profit from the sale of slaves to the Spanish and Portuguese, few other English captains followed their lead. Instead, the Dutch and Portuguese dominated the trade in slaves during the sixteenth century. Only a small number of Africans lived in England at the beginning of the seventeenth century. They were concentrated in a few key port cities, and their precise status is unclear, although most were in some form of servitude.

It is clear that the English held negative views of Africans. Skin color played some role in shaping these attitudes, as the English associated black with evil, but culture and religion were even more important. The English viewed Africans as savages and infidels, outside the social contract that existed among

Christians, and thus as candidates for enslavement. They also were aware that the Spanish and the Portuguese held Africans in permanent bondage in their colonies. For whatever reason or combination of reasons, English colonists adopted slavery as a form of labor during the initial years of colonization. Several enslaved Africans arrived with the first colonists to Barbados in 1627. The previous year, Maurice Thompson, a major London merchant and early planter on St. Kitts, imported sixty slaves to labor in his tobacco fields. Although scholars have long debated the status of the "20 and odd Negroes" who were sold at Jamestown in 1619, most now agree that colonists viewed them as slaves for life, and it is clear that colonists in Barbados and the Leeward Islands adopted similar attitudes toward Africans. By 1636, Barbados officials declared formally that all Africans and Indians would serve for life, the earliest articulation of that policy in any of the English colonies.

While the English exhibited no hesitation about enslaving other human beings, they had neither the need for large numbers of slaves nor the resources to purchase them until the middle decades of the seventeenth century. Some planters who had great success with cotton began to purchase slaves in the 1630s, but the shift to sugar generated a massive demand for laborers that the servant trade could not meet. The number of indentured servants on plantations increased during the 1650s, but the number of slaves increased even more dramatically. An estimated 25,877 slaves were sold in Barbados during the 1640s, 16,212 in the 1650s, 32,496 in the 1660s, and over 40,000 in the 1680s. As one colonist explained in 1645, "The more [slaves] they buie the better able they are to buye; for in a yeare and a halfe they will earne (with gods blessing) as much as they cost." Slaves had become "the life of this place."[17]

The transition to slave labor in Barbados was aided by a steady increase in the supply of enslaved Africans and a decline in price over the later decades of the seventeenth century. The initial demand for labor generated by the shift for sugar drove up the price for slaves during the 1640s and 1650s, but prices began to fall in the 1660s, testimony to increased efficiency in the ghastly business of transporting human beings from Africa to the New World. At the same time, the cost for servants— measured by the length of their terms—increased, so that by the 1660s, the cost of an adult male slave (£20) who worked for life was only somewhat higher than the cost of an adult male servant (£12) who labored for four years. The number of slaves in Barbados equaled the number of whites in 1660, roughly 20,000 each, and from that point on, the white population declined while the slave population increased significantly. By the early eighteenth century, enslaved Africans numbered 50,000 and constituted almost 75 percent of the island's population. Although the specific figures would vary, by the early eighteenth century large African slave majorities would distinguish all the colonies of the Greater Caribbean.

Colonists in Barbados responded to the growing number of enslaved Africans by drafting a comprehensive slave act in 1661. Early colonists had created a number of laws dealing with indentured servants, but the slave act represented a new and harsher system of control, one for which no English precedents existed. The preamble manifested the prevailing attitudes toward Africans, labeling them "an heathenish, brutish and uncertaine, dangerous kinde of people," before moving on to specific regulations.[18] By law, masters had complete control over the lives of slaves. They could punish slaves as they saw fit; there was no consequence for killing slaves while punishing them, and only a fine for outright murder. Slaves who physically assaulted any "Christian" faced a series of draconian penalties, ranging from branding to having their noses slit, and ultimately, to death. Planters did not extend the English tradition of trial by jury to slaves. Instead, a committee composed of two justices of the peace and three freeholders passed judgment. Rebels and suspected rebels were tried by a court-martial.

The 1661 Barbados law served as the model, directly or indirectly, for slave laws in other colonies throughout the region. Colonists in Jamaica copied it extensively in 1664 but added new language, including clauses concerning runaways and slave provision grounds, when they revised the law twenty years later. The 1684 Jamaican law, in turn, provided the model for colonists in South Carolina, who adopted it almost word for word when they passed a slave law in 1691. Colonists in Antigua drew on the Barbados and Jamaica laws when they drafted their slave act in 1697.

In addition to the rapid expansion of slave labor, sugar transformed patterns of landholding on the island. During the tobacco and cotton era, landholding was relatively dispersed, with many planters owning small farms of 20 or 30 acres. Sugar operations, however, required a much larger capital investment, and colonists gradually discovered that the ideal plantation size was between 100 and 200 acres of cane land. As sugar took hold, emerging elites bought out smaller neighbors and consolidated their landholdings in larger plantations, each with its own mill. Various natural disasters at times aided the process. Damage from a major hurricane in 1675, for example, appears to have forced a number of small planters off Barbados, allowing more established planters to take over their properties.

Thousands of colonists emigrated from Barbados in the decades following the rise of sugar, and the island served as something of a nursery for the development of plantation societies in Jamaica and elsewhere. Governor Sir Jonathan Atkins reported that by 1680, "people no longer come to Barbados, many having departed to Carolina, Jamaica, and the Leeward Islands in hope of settling the land which they cannot obtain here."[19] Small farmers did not disappear entirely on Barbados, but they increasingly occupied only marginal lands along the northern and southern coasts of the island.

A detailed census assembled by Atkins in 1680 provides striking evidence of the economic might of the leading planters in Barbados. A small group of 175 planters who each owned 60 or more slaves (a huge number by seventeenth-century standards) dominated the island's economy. Although less than 7 percent of all property owners, they owned 53.4 percent of the total acreage on the island, 53.9 percent of servants, and 54.3 percent of all slaves. They also dominated the island politically. Twenty of the island's 22 elected assemblymen owned 60 or more slaves, as did 10 of the 12 members of the governor's council, 19 of the 23 judges, and 48 of the 64 justices of the peace. Barbados had become a plantocracy, a government of the planters, by the planters, and for the planters.

By 1680, what Ligon called the "sweet Negotiation of sugar" generated wealth for elite planters in Barbados on a scale unknown in other parts of colonial America. James Drax told Ligon that he would not return to England before he was in a position to purchase an estate that generated £10,000 a year. One colonist assured a relative in England that an investment of

£1,000 would soon generate £2,000 a year in income. No reliable figures exist for the average wealth of the Barbadian sugar magnates in this early period, but two leading economic historians suggest a conservative estimate of £4,000 sterling—four times higher than wealthy tobacco planters in the Chesapeake at the time. By all measures, sugar had transformed Barbados into the richest colony in English America.

LEEWARD ISLAND TRANSITIONS

The sugar plantation complex that developed in Barbados gradually spread to the Leeward Islands during the course of the seventeenth century, but the process took some time to complete. Most colonists in the Leewards remained focused on tobacco, indigo, and provisions. Those on the small island of Nevis were the first to shift to sugar, beginning in the 1650s. As in Barbados, planters relied at first on indentured servants, but they also began to purchase more enslaved Africans, and ships from Africa began to sail directly to Nevis as early as the 1650s. A 1678 census highlights the transition, as sugar made Nevis the wealthiest of the four Leeward Islands. Governor William Stapleton estimated the value of Nevis plantations at £384,000, compared to £196,500 for the other three islands combined. Nevis also had the most slaves, 3,849 compared to 2,172 in Antigua, 1,436 in St. Christopher, and 992 in Montserrat. Only about 25 percent of the available acreage in St. Christopher was planted in sugar and indigo. Tobacco, provision crops, and pasture ground occupied the rest. Large parts of Antigua and Montserrat remained undeveloped, and most colonists worked small holdings of fifty acres or less. Tobacco remained the primary crop in Antigua until the 1680s. The Leewards remained something of a frontier zone in the early Caribbean, and since land remained available on some islands, a number of former servants and others moved there from Barbados hoping to improve their economic prospects.

Several factors help explain the slower transition to sugar in the Leeward Islands. Geography was one. Nevis, St. Christopher, and Montserrat are rugged and mountainous islands, and clearing land was difficult. Antigua is relatively flat but far more arid, making sugar a riskier enterprise. In addition, colonists lacked access to creditors, who would help finance the development of sugar. Many were small farmers engaged in subsistence agriculture who lacked the connections and collateral to attract credit from England. Moreover, both tobacco and cotton prices recovered somewhat by the end of the 1640s, decreasing the incentive to shift to a new crop that required such a large capital investment.

Finally, and perhaps most significantly, the Leeward Islands suffered repeated destruction from military conflicts and natural disasters during the seventeenth century. Unlike isolated Barbados, the Leewards were close to French and Dutch islands, and in the case of St. Christopher, the English and French shared the island. Violence between the two broke out repeatedly. Carib Indians on Dominica also presented a threat, particularly to Antigua. Conflicts with these various enemies repeatedly resulted in significant destruction to plantations. One of the most damaging conflicts occurred in 1666–67, when French troops and rebellious Irish servants ravaged St. Christopher, Montserrat, and Antigua (Nevis generally escaped the worst of it). The combined forces burned homes, crops, and settlements across the islands and made off with thousands of confiscated slaves. So great was the impact that a St. Kitts planter named Christopher Jeaffreson claimed ten years later that the island still had not recovered fully. "The wars here are more destructive then [*sic*] in any other partes of the world," Jeaffreson declared, "for twenty yeares' peace will hardly resettle the devastation of one yeares' war."[20] The islands suffered damage again during the Nine Years War (1688–97) and Queen Anne's War (1702–13). The Treaty of Utrecht in 1713 finally resolved the vexing issue of joint control of St. Christopher, as France ceded its claim to the island to the English, but the threat of outside invasion remained.

Natural disasters also took a heavy toll. The Leewards suffered numerous hurricanes during the seventeenth century, including major storms in 1638, 1667, 1669, and two in 1681. These storms claimed numerous lives and caused significant damage to property, tearing up fields, destroying mills, and leveling houses. In addition to damaging sugar crops, and with them planter profits, hurricanes destroyed provision crops and often resulted in what Jeaffreson called a "sickly and scarce time." Food shortages weighed especially heavily on enslaved Africans, who found themselves pushed to rebuild plantations while enduring famine-like conditions. Although hurricanes struck Barbados as well, they did so with less frequency, meaning fewer major disruptions for planters.

The combination of war and disasters complicated the shift to sugar in the Leewards, but colonists gradually expanded production during the later decades of the seventeenth century. One of the first to make the transition on Antigua was another of John Winthrop's sons. Samuel Winthrop arrived in the Leeward Islands in 1649. Serving at first as a merchant and business agent for other colonists, he built up his savings, purchased hundreds of acres of land, bought enslaved laborers, and shifted to sugar cultivation. By the 1660s, Winthrop's slaves were producing 20,000 pounds of sugar per year for export. Other colonists soon followed his example. Jeaffreson reported in 1677 that on St. Christopher, "it is now esteemed here a great folly for a man to expose his tyme or goods to the hazard of indigo or tobacco, sugar being now the only thriveing and valuable commodity."[21]

As sugar took hold in the Leeward Islands, the plantation complex established in Barbados repeated itself. The islands became increasingly deforested, smaller farmers were displaced, an elite group of powerful planters consolidated land into larger estates, all available land was shifted into sugar cultivation, and the number of enslaved Africans increased dramatically. The Leewards even experienced their own period of outward expansion as rich planters engrossed the best lands and displaced small planters sought new opportunities in the smaller, nearby islands of Barbuda, Anguilla, Tortola, Virgin Gorda, and St. Croix. A few eventually established sugar plantations, but most colonists on these islands grew minor crops, including cotton, or provided provisions to sugar estates on the four major islands. Ironically, the destruction caused by conflicts with the French between 1689 and 1713 appears to have aided the consolidation of land in the Leewards, as poorer farmers were ruined and their lands bought by emerging sugar elites. By the early eighteenth century the transition was complete. Muscovado sugar dominated exports from the islands. Statistics are not available for St. Christopher, but sugar accounted for 99 percent of exports from Nevis and Montserrat and 82 percent from the slightly more diversified Antigua. The combined white population on the islands dropped from 10,408 in 1678 to 7,311 thirty years later. The slave population rose dramatically from 8,449 to 23,500 during the same period, with the largest expansion occurring in Antigua, where the slave population grew sixfold, from 2,172 to 12,960. Everywhere enslaved Africans heavily outnumbered European colonists, and colonists in the Leewards developed comprehensive slave laws modeled on the 1661 Barbados act.

One parish in Antigua provides a microcosm of the social changes accompanying the rise of sugar. There were 53 taxpayers in St. Mary parish in 1688. Sixteen were slaveholders, but only 6 owned 20 or more slaves. By 1706, the number of taxpayers fell to 36, 30 of whom owned slaves. Sixteen planters owned 20 or more slaves, while 4 owned more than 100. Similar patterns emerged elsewhere. On Montserrat, the 30 largest plantations composed over 78 percent of the island's agricultural land and held 60 percent of the island's slaves in 1729. Each plantation held, on average, 115 slaves.

These trends continued to accelerate over the course of the eighteenth century as the ratio of slaves to whites and the percentage of sugar among total exports increased even further. The slave population in St. Kitts rose from little more than 3,000 in 1708 to over 19,000 by 1745, while the white population essentially stagnated, increasing from 1,670 to only 2,377. On Antigua, the slave population more than doubled, from 12,943 to 27,892, during the same period, while the white population dropped by one-third between 1724 and 1745. The growth was less dramatic but still significant on the smaller islands of Montserrat and Nevis. Overall, sugar production among the islands soared from 7,044 tons in 1700 to 17,584 tons in 1748. As the sugar economy expanded, elite planters continued to consolidate their landholdings. The number of sugar estates on St. Kitts plunged from 360 in 1724 to just 110 by 1783. On nearby Nevis, consolidation reduced the number of individual estates from roughly 100 in 1700 to 61 by the 1770s.

The Leeward Islands represented the first—and an extreme—replication of what the historian Jack P. Greene has called the "Barbados culture hearth." As Greene notes, the social and economic infrastructure associated with the production of sugar that emerged on Barbados during the 1640s and 1650s proved "remarkably capable of re-creation and, with appropriate modifications, transferable to other areas in the Anglo-American world."[22] Barbados and the Leeward Islands developed in tandem during the early decades of colonization, and it is not surprising that once colonists in Barbados had mastered the art of making sugar, solved the problem of finding enough laborers, and developed large-scale sugar plantations, planters in the Leeward Islands would eventually follow their lead. The process took longer in the Leewards, but economic developments there eventually mirrored changes in Barbados. Meanwhile, just as colonists in the Leewards began the transition to sugar, others were beginning to replicate the Barbados culture hearth in two newer colonies—Jamaica and the Carolina Lowcountry.

THREE

Jamaica

W ITHIN JUST A FEW YEARS of the sugar boom, the increasingly crowded conditions in Barbados prompted many colonists to seek opportunities elsewhere. One of the earliest ventures was to nearby Surinam on the South American coast, where by 1651, 150 Barbadians had established a small settlement. A decade later, the population had swelled to 4,000. Early colonists tended livestock to supply the Barbados market, but some also began to grow sugar in Surinam's rich soil, much to the chagrin of established planters on Barbados, who feared increased competition would eat into profits. The English attempt to develop Surinam, however, was cut short by the outbreak of the Second Anglo-Dutch War in 1665. The Dutch conquered the colony in 1667 and secured their possession as part of the Treaty of Breda. Some displaced colonists migrated to the still-developing Leeward Islands, where they began "hewing a new fortune out of the wild woods," as one put it.[1] Others, however, set out for a new colony in Britain's expanding American empire, Jamaica.

The English captured Jamaica from the Spanish in 1655. Located 1,000 miles to the north and west, the island differed from Barbados in almost every way. It was far larger, measuring 4,411 square miles, compared to Barbados's 166 square miles. Unlike relatively flat Barbados, Jamaica was mountainous, with the tallest peaks in the Blue Mountains rising to over 7,400 feet. Whereas Barbados sat apart from the rest of the islands of the Lesser

Antilles, Jamaica was surrounded by the larger Spanish islands of Cuba, Puerto Rico, and Hispaniola.

Several thousand Barbadians joined the expeditionary force that captured Jamaica from the Spanish, and hundreds more migrated in the 1660s, hoping to emulate the success of the Barbados plantation complex. Jamaica's size and location, however, meant that its path of social and economic development differed in some ways from Barbados. Privateering and illegal trade with the Spanish generated more wealth than planting in the early decades, while a shortage of labor and war with groups of runaway slaves known as Maroons slowed the expansion of plantation agriculture. The transition to sugar thus occurred more gradually in Jamaica than in Barbados. Moreover, the island's size and the varied terrain ensured that its economy remained more diversified. Nevertheless, the Barbados sugar complex provided the model for colonists, and by the middle of the eighteenth century Jamaica had emerged as Britain's leading sugar producer and the crown jewel among its American possessions. It became the wealthiest and most important colony in British America, and its most violent and exploitative.

JAMAICA AND THE WESTERN DESIGN

The English conquest of Jamaica had its origins in an earlier, failed effort at colonization in the western Caribbean. In 1630, just as colonists led by John Winthrop landed in Massachusetts Bay, a group of prominent English Puritan leaders, including many involved with efforts to settle Massachusetts, established a colony on a small island 110 miles off the coast of Nicaragua they named Providence (now part of Colombia). Located in the heart of the Spanish Empire, these Puritans envisioned Providence Island both as a plantation colony and as a staging ground for attacks on Spanish ships and possessions on the mainland that would weaken Spain and advance the Protestant cause.

Problems, however, plagued Providence Island from the start. Tensions existed between military and religious leaders regarding the colony's mission. The company's insistence that colonists work the land as tenants rather than as freeholders frustrated many. The tobacco that many hoped would provide a steady income proved as poor quality as that produced in Barbados. After repulsing a Spanish attack in 1635, the colony organized several privateering ventures, which yielded some profits, but never enough. Promoters sought to recruit more settlers from New England, and one ship carrying some forty settlers left Massachusetts in early 1641, but by the time they arrived, the Spanish had captured the island.

The Providence Island colony failed, but the vision of establishing a foothold in the center of Spanish dominions remained strong and found renewed support when Oliver Cromwell assumed power as lord protector of England in 1653. Cromwell's bold "Western Design" ultimately envisioned the conquest of all of Spanish America, but the first step was capturing individual colonies. Unlike earlier colonization efforts, including Providence Island, the Western Design had the full backing of the state. Cromwell's government, however, had limited resources, and he turned to London merchants for financial support. Among the most important of these backers were several men with experience in Barbados, including Martin Noell, Maurice Thompson, and James and William Drax.

English officials initially set their sights on capturing the large island of Hispaniola. An expedition of 3,500 men under the command of Admiral William Penn (father of the founder of Pennsylvania) and General Robert Venables sailed from England in December 1654. They arrived in Barbados six weeks later and spent ten weeks gathering provisions, supplies, and new recruits. Most of the recruits were indentured servants or former servants hoping to escape the brutality of the sugar regime or to find the fortune that had eluded them, although planters complained that many were simply escaping their debts. Ultimately, 3,500 men from Barbados and another 1,200 from the Leeward Islands joined the expedition, for a total force of over 8,000.

The invasion of Hispaniola in April 1655 was a disaster. The fleet landed in the wrong location, and the troops had to march over land for several days with limited supplies. By the time the expedition reached the capital, Santo Domingo, the men were weakened by hunger and disease. The Spanish repulsed the attack and the English withdrew, having lost over 1,000 troops in just a few weeks. Hoping to salvage something from their losses, the commanders turned their attention to nearby, and lightly defended, Jamaica. Spanish Jamaica had a small population of no more than 2,500 people including slaves. A few sugar mills

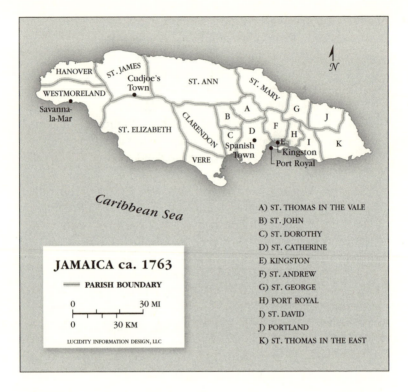

JAMAICA ca. 1763

— PARISH BOUNDARY

0   30 MI

0   30 KM

LUCIDITY INFORMATION DESIGN, LLC

A) ST. THOMAS IN THE VALE
B) ST. JOHN
C) ST. DOROTHY
D) ST. CATHERINE
E) KINGSTON
F) ST. ANDREW
G) ST. GEORGE
H) PORT ROYAL
I) ST. DAVID
J) PORTLAND
K) ST. THOMAS IN THE EAST

operated in the countryside surrounding the major town, St. Jago de le Vega, a few miles inland from Jamaica's southern coast, but the island functioned mainly as a source of provisions and livestock for other nearby colonies. Faced with a large invasion force, the Spanish governor quickly surrendered—the terms were the same as those forced on the colonists from Providence Island in 1641—but not before buying enough time to allow many colonists and their slaves to flee into the island's rugged interior. From there, they would continue to harass the English for the next five years.

While the English, in theory, had captured Jamaica, they struggled to establish a functioning colony. The invasion occurred at the start of the rainy season, and disease—likely malaria—took an immediate toll. Within three weeks, 3,000 men were sick, and many soon died. By November, only 3,700 troops of the initial invasion force of over 8,000 remained alive. One commander wrote that the bodies of dead soldiers were "lying unburied in the highways, and among bushes . . . [Those] that were alive, walked like ghosts or dead men, who, as I went through the town, lay groaning and cried out, bread for the Lord's sake."[2] As was the case during the early years in Virginia, too many of the "colonists" were soldiers who came to plunder rather than plant. As a result, the new settlement at what the English named Spanish Town struggled to feed itself for several years. Colonists also had to fend off guerrilla attacks from the Spanish and their slaves sheltered in the interior. As word of conditions in Jamaica spread, potential new colonists hesitated to emigrate. Cromwell hoped that "godly" colonists from New England would migrate to Jamaica, but few did. Colonists in Barbados likewise stayed away, scared off by reports of disease and death. A group of 1,400 settlers from Nevis arrived in 1656, but two-thirds of them died within a few months. The situation in these early years was so dire that if the Spanish had mounted an invasion to retake the island they almost certainly would have succeeded. Fortunately for the English, they did not. By 1660, the English managed to defeat the remaining Spanish guerrillas and gained control of the island, although Spain did not formally recognize the English conquest until the Treaty of Madrid in 1670. Even then, groups of runaway slaves remained free in the mountainous interior.

PLANTING, PLUNDER, AND TRADE

Officials encouraged the soldiers who conquered Jamaica to develop farms and plantations, and they laid plans to recruit "poor maids" from English towns (and prisons) to provide wives for the colonists. Nevertheless, the island remained more of a military camp than an agricultural settlement in its first years. That began to change with the appointment of Sir Thomas Modyford as governor in 1664. Modyford had been a prosperous sugar planter in Barbados, and he brought his extensive knowledge and experience as a planter with him to Jamaica. He also brought 1,000 colonists, many of them small planters who owned slaves and faced limited prospects for growth on crowded Barbados. They were soon joined by experienced planters and over 1,000 slaves who fled from Surinam following the Dutch conquest in 1667. Modyford encouraged settlement by handing out generous land grants of 30 acres to each new colonist and an additional

30 acres for every family member, including indentured servants and slaves. He claimed over 20,000 acres for himself and other family members. He also managed to exempt Jamaica from the 4.5 percent duty on exports paid by planters on Barbados and the Leewards. Jamaica's total population increased significantly during Modyford's time, rising from 4,205 in 1662 to 15,198 in 1670. The population of enslaved Africans increased most dramatically, rising from 552 in 1662 to over 9,504 in 1673. Nevertheless, Jamaica's population remained small relative to the size of the island, and while over a million acres of land had been patented by 1683, the limited number of servants and slaves meant that much of it remained uncultivated.

Early colonists engaged in a variety of economic pursuits. Some followed the lead of their Spanish predecessors and focused their energies on cattle ranching and provision crops. One young colonist named Cary Helyar, who arrived in Jamaica in 1664, wrote to his brother in England that there were many ways to build a fortune in Jamaica, "but a small stock of cattle is no bad beginning."[3] Others took advantage of the cacao trees left behind by the Spanish. Europeans craved chocolate, and a number of colonists, including Governor Modyford, believed that cacao was the island's most promising commodity because, although the trees took time to grow, they required little effort and generated large profits. Cacao generated great excitement in the 1660s, but high hopes for the crop proved short-lived, as blight struck in 1670, destroying the trees. Still other colonists developed small plantations dedicated to established staple crops: tobacco, cotton, ginger, and indigo. These crops required relatively little capital investment and brought good returns for colonists who lacked the resources to establish sugar plantations. Together they accounted for more than half of all commodity exports from Jamaica until the 1680s.

Then there was sugar. Early colonists to Jamaica were well aware of the tremendous profits generated by sugar on Barbados, and many sought to emulate that success in the new island. Indeed, "If Barbadoes have risen to be so rich by sugar alone, where land is dear and cattle, provisions, and wood scarce," one official report from 1670 asked, "what may Jamaica arrive to, where all these are in plenty?"[4] Sugar production, of course, required a large investment of capital, including many laborers.

One seventeenth-century commentator estimated that developing a plantation of 100 acres required an initial outlay of £5,625, including £1,250 for 50 slaves and over £4,000 to pay for land, construct a mill, and purchase the necessary copper kettles and other equipment. Annual operating expenses were several hundred pounds more. (The cost of establishing a good-sized Virginia tobacco plantation in 1690, by contrast, was roughly £550, and farmers could grow tobacco on a smaller scale with fewer costs.) Those colonists who arrived in Jamaica with adequate capital or connections set up sugar estates immediately. Among them was Thomas Modyford, who had made a fortune in Barbados with sugar and soon replicated his success in Jamaica. By the time he died in 1679, he lorded over an estate valued at £11,327 that included three plantations worked by over 440 slaves.

Only a few big planters from Barbados or elsewhere, however, moved to Jamaica in the early decades following its capture from Spain. Most migrants were smaller men on the make, and many had come directly from England. They lacked the capital to invest in sugar and thus sought to build fortunes by other means. Some embraced what Cary Helyar called the "Barbados custom" of building a plantation. Just as colonists on Barbados built the sugar complex from profits gained from tobacco and cotton, Helyar outlined a similar process of development for Jamaica. A small farmer should start with provision crops, he argued, along with a small amount of acreage devoted to export crops like tobacco and cotton that required relatively little capital investment. The profits from those crops were then used to purchase "a Negroe or two more, and they will beget others, so that in 7 years time, it will produce a hopefull business." An expanding labor force and growing profits, in turn, gradually provided the capital needed to shift into sugar. This "Barbados custom" of developing a plantation was "no new thing," Helyar wrote to a correspondent. "This Sir is what my eyes see every day."[5] And indeed it was. The number of sugar estates on Jamaica grew substantially during the 1670s, from 57 in 1671 to 246 in 1684. Some of this growth reflected investment by new planters migrating to the island, but in at least 40 cases planters followed the Barbados custom: listed as growing indigo, cacao, and provisions in 1671, they had switched to sugar by 1684. By that point, sugar products accounted for 54 percent of total commodity exports from Jamaica, a figure that would grow to 76 percent within a decade, although the island still produced less sugar than tiny Barbados.

A major impediment to the development of plantations in Jamaica was a lack of labor. As in Barbados, colonists in Jamaica utilized indentured servants and enslaved Africans to work the fields. The number of both servants and slaves increased dramatically during the 1660s and 1670s, and by 1673 the island already had over 9,500 slaves, more than the Leeward Islands. But supply never kept up with demand. Part of the problem was Jamaica's location. The island was over a thousand miles from the more established market in Barbados and thus received fewer ships from England and Africa.

The other major impediment to agricultural expansion was competition from privateers. Privateering formed an essential part of Jamaica's economy from the beginning. As one official noted, many of the earliest English colonists to Jamaica were "looser sorts" who came to plunder rather than to plant. The Western Design had envisioned an island base for attacks on Spanish ships and port cities, and Jamaica, "in the heart of the Spanish Dominions," was situated perfectly to "gaule them on every side."[6] Governor Edward D'Oyley furthered that goal in 1657 by inviting English buccaneers—so named for their practice of grilling meat on a wooden rack called a *boucan,* what we now call a barbecue—who had been operating from the small island of Tortuga to shift their operations to Jamaica. D'Oyley hoped that the buccaneers would defend the island from Spanish attacks as well as plunder Spanish ships and ports. On that score, the buccaneers did not disappoint. Between 1655 and 1671 Jamaican privateers pillaged eighteen cities, four towns, and thirty-five villages in Spanish America. One of the most spectacular early heists was led by Christopher Myngs. While raiding the Venezuelan coast in 1659, Myngs and his men landed at the small town of Coro, where they stumbled upon twenty-two chests filled with silver coins. Why the treasure was there is something of a mystery, as Coro was not a regular stop for the fleets on their return voyage to Spain, but that mattered little to Myngs and his men, who reportedly returned to Port Royal, the home port for the buccaneers, with over £40,000. Privateering raids rarely resulted in yields as large as Myngs's Coro booty, but the privateers did provide an important boost to the island's economy. One observer wrote in 1669 that Jamaica's trade "now consists principally in plate, money, jewels, and other things brought in by the privateers, who sell them cheap to the merchant, and then are sent to New England and the Madeiras and returned chiefly in wine, brandy, and victuals."[7]

Privateering, however, hindered the growth of Jamaica's plantation economy to some extent. It offered an appealing alternative to agricultural work, and many young men chose to seek their fortunes at sea rather than on land. Raiding entailed a number of risks, and notwithstanding a few spectacular successes, the rewards could be quite small. Compared to the hard work and harsh discipline that governed the lives of indentured servants on plantations, however, privateering appeared as an attractive option. Governor Lord Vaughan reported in 1676 that "the only enemy to planting is privateering," and because "these Indies are so vast and rich and this kind of rapine so sweet . . . it is one of the hardest things in the world to draw those from it which have used it so long."[8]

Sir Thomas Modyford had orders to rein in the privateers when he was appointed governor in 1664, but he found it more profitable to align himself with the buccaneers. He authorized missions against the Dutch and Spanish in the 1660s and happily accepted his percentage of goods captured at sea. And it was during Modyford's tenure that perhaps the most famous seventeenth-century buccaneer operated. Henry Morgan led a series of plundering expeditions against the Spanish in the 1660s. In 1668, Morgan left a trail of terror and destruction in Cuba and Panama, netting himself and his men 250,000 pieces of eight (about £75,000) and a variety of goods and commodities. A few years later he sacked Panama City, one of the major stops in the route that brought silver from Peru to Spain. Morgan and 1,400 men landed on the coast in January 1671, fought their way upriver, captured the city, and sailed into Port Royal with an estimated £30,000 in loot. They also returned to the news that England and Spain had signed a peace treaty the previous year. Morgan's raid became an embarrassment, and English officials promptly ordered Morgan and Modyford arrested and returned to England. Modyford spent time in the Tower of London, but his and Morgan's disgrace proved short-lived. Spain's unwillingness to open American ports for trade frustrated English officials, and Morgan soon found himself knighted for his actions against the Spanish and sent back to Jamaica as the lieutenant governor, while Modyford later served as the island's chief justice.

While privateers raided Spanish ships and towns, other colonists profited from illegal trade with Spanish settlements in the region. Spain prohibited its colonies from trading with those of any other nation, but its inability to supply colonists with essential goods created an opening for enterprising foreign merchants with a tolerance for risk. English merchants in Port Royal were well placed to fill the gap. They sent out cargoes of European manufactured goods and North American provisions and brought back dyewood, hides, and most of all, bullion. Governor Lord Inchiquin reported in 1691 that Jamaica sent home over £100,000 in Spanish coins, worth more than the island's sugar exports, valued at £88,000. Indeed, while other English colonies used various commodities such as sugar or tobacco as currency, colonists in Jamaica used Spanish coins. By the end of the 1660s, one official estimated that only about 25 percent of the goods carried on ships returning to England from Jamaica were produced in the colony. The majority were products obtained from the Spanish.

Merchants in Jamaica also supplied the Spanish with enslaved Africans. The 1494 Treaty of Tordesillas between Spain and Portugal prevented Spanish access to the west coast of Africa, so Spain relied on other nations to supply its American colonies with slaves. Spain tried to control this trade by granting an exclusive contract, the *asiento,* to Genoese merchants, but the Genoese subcontracted out to others, including in 1663, the English. By the 1680s, Spain even stationed an *asiento* agent in Port Royal to facilitate the trade. The English government, for its part, sought to control participation in the slave trade by creating a monopoly company, first the Company of Royal Adventurers, replaced in 1672 by the Royal African Company. Jamaica provided an ideal transshipment location, and a small group of merchants in Port Royal soon dominated the flow of enslaved Africans to Spanish colonial markets. The merchants bought slaves from the Royal African Company—and from private slave traders who violated the company's monopoly—and then resold them to the Spanish, often at a hefty profit. Port Royal merchants pocketed an additional 35 percent for transporting the enslaved Africans from Jamaica to Spanish ports, where they collected payment, an arrangement the Spanish accepted to avoid the risk of losing shipments of gold and silver to pirates. As one planter commented, the trade was "a much easier way of making money than making sugar."[9] Smaller planters in Jamaica complained that the *asiento* limited their ability to purchase slaves, thereby hindering their own economic prospects, but when the governor was aligned with the merchants, their complaints fell on deaf ears. Although few sources document the specific size of the early *asiento* trade, the historian David Eltis estimates that perhaps as many as 50,000 of the 160,000 enslaved Africans imported into Jamaica between 1662 and 1713 were resold to the Spanish.

Finally, colonists in Jamaica profited from the logwood trade out of the Yucatan and the Bay of Honduras (what is now Belize). Logwood yielded dyes used in textile manufacturing, and it generated good returns, between £25 and £30 a ton in the second half of the seventeenth century. As England cracked down on privateering missions in the 1670s, many of the men turned to woodcutting. Indeed, Thomas Modyford informed London officials that he thought the logwood trade would keep "these soldierly men . . . within peaceable bounds," but at the ready if war again broke out with Spain.[10] Logwood, however, became a source of conflict with Spain. The colonists declared that they cut wood only in uninhabited territories, but the Spanish claimed all territories on the mainland as their own and attempted to force out the English cutters. Spanish territorial assertions, however, went well beyond their means to enforce those boundaries, and a brisk trade in logwood through Jamaica continued for the remainder of the seventeenth and into the eighteenth centuries.

The hub of these various trading activities, as well as the privateer's home base, was the bustling town of Port Royal. Jamaica's political capital remained inland at Spanish town, but Port Royal became the colony's commercial center during the seventeenth century, and arguably the most important port city in all of English America. The town developed on a small cay of little more than twenty acres at the end of a strip of sand and gravel jutting out into Kingston harbor. As the population expanded, colonists sought to enlarge the town by sinking ship hulls and posts to create landfill. By the 1680s, they had succeeded in doubling the town's size to fifty-three acres. Some 6,500 people, including 2,500 enslaved Africans, crowded into Port Royal's houses, taverns, and warehouses, giving it a population density as great as central London prior to World War II.

Trade formed the lifeblood of the town. Over 40 percent of probate inventories (lists of all items in an estate at the time of the owner's death) for the years between 1686 and 1692 belong to merchants. In Boston, by contrast, shipping registers suggest only about 10 percent of men were merchants. John Taylor, who visited Jamaica in the 1680s, reported that "the merchants and gentrey live here to the hights of splendor, in full ease and plenty, being sumptuously arrayed and attended on and served by their Negroa slaves."[11] Even humble tradesmen made good livings, commanding wages three times higher than their counterparts at home in England. Because land was so scarce, colonists built tall, multistory structures that resembled those in London, Bristol, and other English cities, and Taylor claimed that the rents were as high as in the metropolis. Residents feasted on imported meats and wine as well as local delicacies, including manatee, which Taylor called the best meat in the world. The only thing wanting, Taylor noted, was good European bread. For recreation, they drank, attended cockfights and bear-baiting exhibitions, went target shooting, played billiards, and drank some more.

Numerous artisans and craftsmen set up shop in Port Royal, including, not surprisingly, several goldsmiths and jewelers. A large number of taverns and brothels lined the town's streets, and observers decried the level of debauchery involving wine and women funded by privateer loot. More surprising perhaps, Port Royal was also home to an Anglican church, Quaker and Presbyterian meetinghouses, a Catholic chapel, and a synagogue that served the town's small but economically important Jewish population. Few commentators emphasized the town's religious culture, however. Far more often they characterized the town's residents as a particularly ungodly people, a motley crew of pirates, prostitutes, and profaners. As one minister wrote, "Sin [was] very high and religion very low" among the colonists in seventeenth-century Port Royal.[12]

A good deal of the loot from privateering and illegal trade ended up in Port Royal's licit and illicit economy, but over time some of the profits also funded agricultural expansion. Leading merchants and privateers sought legitimacy and security by owning land, and they often used their profits to purchase plantations and slaves. As early as 1669, Governor Modyford reported that many "privateers have turned merchants . . . ; some of the best monied are turned planters."[13] Among them was the great buccaneer himself, Sir Henry Morgan. When Morgan died in 1688, he was the owner of a large plantation worked by 122 slaves and valued at £5,263. Peter Beckford left an even greater estate. Beckford initially made his money as a merchant and by the 1680s had become involved in the *asiento* trade. As his profits grew, he invested steadily in plantations and slaves. By the time of his death in 1710, he reportedly owned a stake in some twenty plantations and over 1,200 slaves. One study of Port Royal merchants found that more than half of the 508 merchants who operated out of Port Royal between 1664 and 1700 invested money in agricultural properties.

The expansion of sugar plantations, however, increasingly heightened tensions between planters and privateers during the 1670s. In addition to luring away laborers, privateering raids threatened to generate reprisals against the island and against ships carrying planters' crops, both of which were bad for business. Moreover, privateers were not always careful to distinguish under whose flag a ship sailed, and they sometimes attacked English vessels trading to Jamaica. Gradually, two distinct parties emerged in Jamaica, one representing the interests of the larger planters and major merchants who traded with the Spanish, the other representing the privateers and smaller planters. The 1670s and 1680s witnessed a series of conflicts as different governors aligned with one faction or the other. But as the number of plantations increased, along with revenues from sugar and other products, pressure mounted against the buccaneers, who gradually shifted their operations to more welcoming situations in St. Domingue (now Haiti) and the Bahamas. The planters secured their position when the pro-buccaneering governor appointed by James II died after a massive drinking binge in September 1688, and James himself was forced from the English throne during the Glorious Revolution.

A final, symbolic denunciation of the buccaneers came in 1692, when a great earthquake struck Jamaica. The tremor caused damage throughout the island, but Port Royal suffered particular devastation. Within minutes over half of Port Royal sank to the bottom of the harbor and over two thousand colonists died. Ministers in Jamaica and elsewhere lost little time in proclaiming that the colonists in Port Royal had received a just punishment for their sins, although at least a few commentators also suggested that Port Royal's unstable foundation of sand, gravel, and landfill had contributed to the level of damage. Regardless, local officials laid plans for a new trading town across the harbor. Efforts to develop Kingston stalled almost immediately, as disease claimed the lives of thousands of colonists. Survivors relocated back to Port Royal, which was rebuilt during the 1690s and again served as Jamaica's main port.

Port Royal suffered another calamity in 1703, when a fire destroyed the town. Local officials passed a law to prohibit resettlement at "that fatall spott," but residents protested vehemently, claiming that Kingston was too sickly and Port Royal was a better location for trade. Queen Anne voided the law in 1704. Port Royal was rebuilt again and remained a significant center of trade until a major hurricane in 1712 destroyed the city yet again. The hurricane served as a tipping point for most merchants and other colonists, who, in the wake of this third major disaster, finally moved their operations to Kingston. By the middle of the eighteenth century, Port Royal served mainly as a naval base, the town a small shadow of its former glory. Kingston now dominated trade in and out of Jamaica, and as Jamaica's economy expanded, so too did Kingston. Its population increased from 4,461 in 1730 to 26,748 in 1788, of whom some 16,659 were enslaved Africans. By the middle of the eighteenth century, it ranked as the fourth largest city in British America.

The destruction of Port Royal in 1692 and the loss of thousands of lives in the earthquake and from disease marked the beginning of a difficult period for colonists in Jamaica. The French invaded the island two years later, burning dozens of estates and capturing 1,600 slaves before the colonists managed to expel them. The threat of invasion and disruptions to shipping lingered during the remainder of King William's War (1688–98) and during Queen Anne's War (1702–13), hindering agricultural development. Nevertheless, planters gradually expanded their operations in the early eighteenth century, and as

Broadside announcing the Port Royal earthquake, published in London, 1692. Courtesy of The British Library Board, 719.m.17.(15).

sugar took hold, the transitions that occurred in Barbados repeated themselves on an even larger scale by the early decades of the eighteenth century. Planters gained possession of the best lands and consolidated them into sugar estates whose size far exceeded those in Barbados and the Leewards. Relatively little new land was patented in the 1690s and early 1700s; instead, planters expanded operations on existing, uncultivated lands. To do so, colonists imported increasing numbers of enslaved

Africans. An estimated 35,000 enslaved Africans arrived in Jamaica during the 1690s. That figure grew to nearly 54,000 during the first decade of the eighteenth century and to over 75,000 during the 1720s.

Even as sugar increasingly dominated Jamaica's economy, several factors beyond warfare and disaster slowed the development of plantation agriculture during the opening decades of the eighteenth century. First, increased production as well as greater competition from newer and more productive French islands lowered sugar prices in European markets. Second, a shortage of labor remained an issue, limiting the ability to bring new lands into production. Although more and more enslaved Africans arrived in Jamaica during the 1710s and 1720s, many were resold to the Spanish. England had won the coveted *asiento* to supply Spain with slaves at the end of Queen Anne's War in 1713, but while the *asiento* generated wealth for select Kingston traders who supplied the South Sea Company with slaves, as had been the case with the earlier trade, it resulted in increased competition and higher prices for planters.

Finally, ongoing war with the Maroons prevented planters from moving on to new lands in the north and west of the island. As noted above, conflict with Maroons had plagued the English in Jamaica from the beginning. The original Maroons formed from the Spanish slaves who ran away during the English invasion. They established a series of settlements in the mountains of eastern Jamaica and became known as the Windward Maroons, their numbers periodically augmented by runaway slaves from plantations. A second group of Maroons emerged during the 1670s and 1680s, decades marked by a series of rebellions led by recently arrived Africans. Hundreds of slaves rose up against the English in 1673, 1678, 1685, and 1690, and many who were not captured or killed fled to the mountains in the central and western part of the island. This group became known as the Leeward Maroons.

Differences between the groups faded over time as both gained new members from runaway slaves and established settlements in Jamaica's densely wooded and mountainous interior, which rendered English efforts to find and defeat them almost impossible. By the 1720s the population of Maroons had grown from several hundred to several thousand. Colonial officials made sporadic attempts to defeat the Maroons, but their efforts brought no results. Even when they managed to destroy a settlement, they rarely captured the inhabitants. The Maroons simply moved on and resumed their attacks on English plantations. During the 1730s, however, local officials launched a new, aggressive campaign against the Maroons with the aid of hundreds of British troops. They had some success against the Windward Maroons, forcing many to flee to the Leeward group, but by 1738 the war against the Leeward Maroons, led by a man named Cudjoe, had reached an impasse. The English had spent thousands of pounds and lost hundreds of men, but victory remained elusive. Although Cudjoe and his followers remained unbeaten, the war had taken its toll on their numbers and destroyed many of their provision grounds. In March 1739 the two sides agreed to a treaty that granted Cudjoe and his troops land and autonomy in return for halting their attacks on plantations and returning runaways to their owners. A few months later the Windward Maroons agreed to a similar treaty.

"A CONSTANT MINE"

The end of the Maroon Wars marked the beginning of a period of explosive economic growth in Jamaica. Coinciding with a steadily increasing demand for sugar in Britain, planters expanded rapidly, particularly in the north and west of the island, during the middle decades of the eighteenth century. The number of sugar estates increased from 419 to 648 between 1739 and 1768. The largest increase occurred in the western county of Cornwall, where the number of sugar estates rose from 143 to 265. Sugar production, in turn, rose significantly. The amount of sugar imported into England from Jamaica exceeded 400,000 cwt. (hundredweight) for the first time in 1750, and with two exceptions (1751 and 1752), it never fell below that figure for the reminder of the pre-Revolutionary era. Although production of sugar in the Leeward Islands also increased dramatically during the middle of the eighteenth century, by the end of the 1750s, Jamaica's output far surpassed that of the Leewards. Jamaica alone supplied nearly half of the total sugar imported into Britain. As was the case elsewhere, the best land came under the control of a small group of planters. By the middle of the eighteenth century, 467 planters, each owning at least 1,000 acres, controlled over 78 percent of the patented land, although not all of it was in production.

Although Jamaica represented another extension of the Barbados model of large-scale sugar production, the island's size and its varied topography enabled its economy to remain more diversified. Colonists harvested huge numbers of mahogany trees, which had emerged as the wood of choice for fine furniture in Britain. By the middle of the eighteenth century, Jamaica supplied Britain with over 90 percent of its mahogany imports. Trade, legal and illegal, remained important, especially after Spain awarded England the *asiento* contract in 1713. Merchants sold slaves and other goods to the Spanish in return for plantation goods and bullion. The historian Trevor Burnard has estimated that during the 1730s and 1740s, the value of trade with Spanish America rose to as high as £1,000,000 a year. Moreover, Jamaica's size meant that more land was available for provisions, cattle, and timber and for the production of other export crops. Livestock pens expanded rapidly on the island during the eighteenth century, and the number of cattle on the island almost doubled between 1740 and 1768. Colonists continued to produce small but significant quantities of ginger and cotton, and beginning in the middle of the eighteenth century, coffee emerged as an export crop. Aided by a preferential tariff in England, coffee exports from Jamaica rose from 50,367 pounds in the mid-1740s to 102,526 pounds in the early 1750s to over 252,000 pounds in 1764. Although today's Blue Mountain coffee is a premium brand that commands high prices, Jamaican coffee in the eighteenth century was generally a low-grade variety that could not compete with that grown in the East Indies or Arabia. The primary market for Jamaican coffee was in Germany and areas of North America with large German populations. Germans of all social ranks consumed coffee, and strong demand provided an outlet for Jamaica's cheaper, lower-quality beans. Together, woodcutting, livestock, minor staple production, and skilled occupations in urban areas such as Kingston meant that, by 1768, 4 out of every 10 slaves in Jamaica did not labor on sugar plantations.

A detailed census from St. Andrew parish in 1753 highlights the diversity of land use in eighteenth-century Jamaica. The parish adjoined Kingston on the island's south coast and was one of the first areas to shift to sugar production. The 1753 census, however, revealed that only 6 percent of the parish's land was planted in sugar. Most land, 53 percent, remained wooded, while 14 percent was planted in provisions and 24 percent was pasture. Planters grew ginger, cotton, and coffee on the remaining 2 percent of the land.

Nevertheless, despite a more diversified set of agricultural activities, sugar dominated St. Andrew and the rest of Jamaica. Eighty-five percent of export revenue from St. Andrew came from sugar or its by-products, molasses and rum, and sugar planters had the largest landholdings and the most slaves. What was true in St. Andrew was true throughout the island. Indeed, even the lands dedicated to timber and pasture ultimately supported the sugar economy. Timber lands provided a ready supply of fuel for the boiling houses, while the cattle provided manure and, more importantly, the power to turn the sugar mills. Although Jamaica's economy exhibited a degree of diversity not found on the other islands, it was ultimately sugar that made Jamaica, in the words of one eighteenth-century visitor, "a constant Mine, whence Britain draws prodigious Riches."[14] The profits from sugar production made white Jamaicans the richest men and women in British America. One historian has estimated the per capita wealth of whites in Jamaica on the eve of the American Revolution at an astonishing £2,201, compared to just £60.2 for whites in the thirteen mainland colonies. As happened in Barbados in the seventeenth century, much of this wealth was concentrated in the hands of a small elite. The top 10 percent of Jamaican property holders controlled two-thirds of the island's wealth by the middle of the eighteenth century.

Ultimately, of course, the riches associated with sugar came from the labor of African slaves. Jamaica's enslaved population increased steadily in the early eighteenth century, but as sugar production expanded, particularly after 1740, huge numbers of Africans arrived on the island. Jamaican planters and merchants imported an estimated 69,977 slaves during the 1740s and over 84,000 in the 1750s. Although contraband trade to the Spanish colonies continued, most of these new arrivals labored on Jamaican sugar plantations, where disease, malnutrition, and brutal treatment at the hands of an increasingly outnumbered white minority resulted in a demographic catastrophe. Although the island's enslaved population roughly doubled between 1740 and the outbreak of the American Revolution, rising from approximately 100,000 in 1740 to 192,787 in 1774, the increase of 92,000 in that thirty-four-year period required the importation of over 272,000 Africans. The loss of human life on Jamaica's sugar estates was horrific, but planters accepted such conditions with little thought or concern. According to one, the generally prosperous conditions during the 1750s and 1760s meant that slaves paid for themselves in three years. Jamaican planters had little incentive to keep slaves alive for any length of time. Instead, they literally worked them to death and then purchased new laborers.

Jamaica's white population also increased during the eighteenth century, but at a very slow rate and only as a result of ongoing immigration from Britain. Although exact figures are lacking, it appears that at least 30,000 whites migrated to Jamaica in the first half of the eighteenth century, but the white population increased by only a few thousand, rising from 7,365 in 1693 to 8,230 in 1730 to roughly 10,000 at midcentury. Two key reasons for this were the skewed sex ratio among immigrants—with most migrants being young men in search of fortunes—and disease. For those that survived, Jamaica held the promise of great material advancement, but many migrants never lived to see their hopes fulfilled. These factors, along with the ongoing importation of large numbers of enslaved Africans, meant that slaves greatly outnumbered whites. By the middle of the eighteenth century the ratio of slaves to whites was 11 to 1, far higher than in Barbados, and rose to 15 to 1 by the early 1770s.

Heavily outnumbered by their slaves and facing the prospect of an early grave, whites in Jamaica adopted an ethos that emphasized immediate material gain. Colonists cared little about the future, as they sought profits in the present regardless of the social costs. Although deadly and dehumanizing conditions characterized sugar plantations throughout the Americas, including Barbados and the Leeward Islands, Jamaica represented an especially stark manifestation of the brutality and exploitation at the heart of slavery. One eighteenth-century visitor to the island wrote, "No Country excels them in a barbarous Treatment of Slaves, or in the cruel Methods they put them to Death."[15] As we shall see, slaves in Jamaica resisted such conditions more frequently and more violently than elsewhere in the region.

Jamaica thus represented a distinct variation of the sugar plantation complex that first emerged in Barbados. A number of factors, including Jamaica's size and geographic location, meant that the shift to sugar took longer in Jamaica than in Barbados and that Jamaica's economy remained more diverse. But those factors also allowed the sugar plantation complex to emerge on an even grander scale. Everything about Jamaica was big in the context of the seventeenth- and eighteenth-century British Greater Caribbean: the size of landholdings, the number of enslaved Africans, the ratio of slaves to whites, the amount of sugar produced, the wealth generated by plantation crops, the violence employed against slaves, and the frequency and intensity of slave resistance. Captured as an afterthought from the Spanish in 1655, by the middle of the eighteenth century it had become Britain's richest and most important possession in its American empire.

FOUR

"Carolina in ye West Indies"

JUST A FEW YEARS AFTER the conquest of Jamaica, Barbados again served as a "nursery" for a new colony, this time on the southeastern coast of North America. The same factors that pushed colonists to Surinam and to Jamaica in the 1650s—namely, the scarcity of land and the need for a supply of timber, provisions, and other essential supplies no longer available on the island—led many Barbadians to migrate to the Lowcountry in the 1670s. Many of these early migrants brought slaves and capital with them. Not all new colonists arrived from Barbados and the other islands, but Barbadians played an outsized role in the social, political, and economic development of the Lowcountry during the early decades of settlement.

The Lowcountry landscape these migrants encountered differed from that of the sugar islands in obvious ways. The Lowcountry was part of a continental landmass, not an island, although the region included dozens of islands just off the coast. While the islands represented distinct political units (with the exception of the Leewards, which originally were governed by Barbados and later as a federated colony), the Lowcountry cut across what eventually became three distinct colonies. Diverse Native American groups lived in the Lowcountry and the surrounding areas. Finally, the Lowcountry's semi-tropical climate did not allow for the cultivation of sugarcane.

Colonists, however, soon discovered their own valuable staple crop, rice. Rice never dominated the Lowcountry as thoroughly as sugar dominated the islands. Even more than in Jamaica, diversity characterized the Lowcountry economy, as colonists exported deerskins, livestock, naval stores, provisions, and indigo as well as rice. Moreover, the process of producing sugar and rice differed greatly, as did markets for the two crops. Nevertheless, rice cultivation fostered the development of a plantation society in the Lowcountry that resembled that of the islands far more than it did the plantation society in the Chesapeake to its north. In its origins and in several key features, including large landholdings, tremendous wealth, and a population in which enslaved Africans greatly outnumbered European colonists, South Carolina represented another extension of the Barbados culture hearth. Contemporaries had good reason to reference "Carolina in ye West Indies."[1]

The rice plantation complex emerged first along the Ashley and Cooper Rivers in South Carolina, but during the middle decades of the eighteenth century it spread north into the lower Cape Fear region of North Carolina, and even more fully south into the new colony of Georgia. By the 1760s, what might be termed the "greater Lowcountry" stretched from the Cape Fear River to the St. Mary's River along the Florida border, although the South Carolina Lowcountry remained the region's vital center and Charleston its undisputed hub. Overall, the Lowcountry exhibited many of the key characteristics that defined all of the colonies of the Greater Caribbean, but it also underscores the diversity of places comprising the vast region.

THE COLONY OF A COLONY

In 1663, Charles II granted the land south of Virginia and north of Spanish Florida (he later expanded the borders in 1665) to a group of eight proprietors: Sir John Colleton, Sir William and Lord John Berkeley, Anthony Ashley Cooper, the Earl of Clarendon, the Earl of Craven, the Duke of Albemarle, and Sir George Carteret. Many of these men had direct experience with the Caribbean colonies. Colleton was a Royalist who had fled to Barbados during the Civil War and made a fortune in sugar. Ashley had owned part of a plantation in Barbados in the 1640s and had invested in the slave trade. Clarendon owned plantations in Jamaica and had correspondents in Barbados, as did Albemarle.

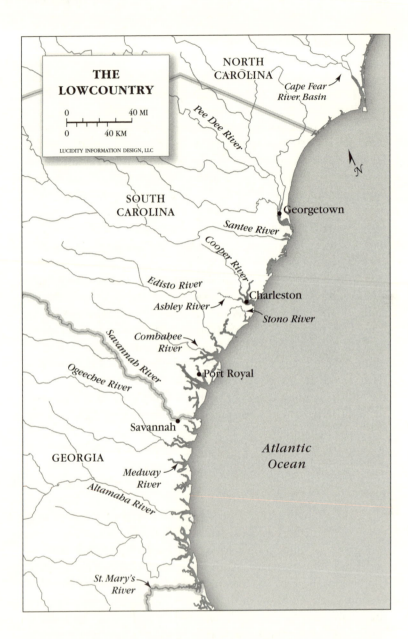

The proprietors' grant for "Carolina" encompassed a vast territory that eventually split into three colonies—North Carolina, South Carolina, and Georgia. Several of the proprietors also received a grant for the fledgling settlements in the Bahamas, which they ruled until 1718. From the beginning, however, the proprietors focused most of their attention on the Ashley River settlement that became South Carolina. The proprietors assumed that the new colony would find many eager recruits in Barbados and the other islands as well as from England itself. Glowing accounts suggested that the Lowcountry's climate lacked the intense heat of the tropics but that conditions were favorable for the production of sugarcane, oranges, silk, and other exotic crops. Carolina offered seemingly unlimited land for plantation development, and to facilitate migration, the proprietors promised generous land grants. Early colonists received 150 acres, as well as additional land for each family member, servant, and slave who accompanied them. Colonists who migrated later received smaller, but still significant, land grants. The prospect of large land grants appealed especially to servants and former servants from the islands who hoped to better their economic prospects as well as to younger sons of established planter elites in Barbados who were unlikely to inherit any property on the island.

Several different groups organized efforts to settle Carolina in the mid-1660s, including two efforts led by prominent Barbadians, but lack of supplies, internal conflicts, and poor relations with Indians undermined each attempt. These early failures prompted increased involvement by the proprietors, particularly Anthony Ashley Cooper, later the first Earl of Shaftesbury, in 1669. Shaftesbury became the leading force pushing to develop a colony in the southern part of the Carolina proprietary. Carolina became Shaftesbury's "Darling," and the rivers on each side of Charleston were named for him. Shaftesbury persuaded his fellow proprietors to invest £500 to outfit an expedition of settlers and supplies from London. He and his physician, the philosopher John Locke, drafted *The Fundamental Constitutions of Carolina,* a document that outlined a form of government and social organization for the new colony. *The Fundamental Constitutions* envisioned the creation of an aristocratic society in the New World, complete with titled nobility and "leet-men," agricultural laborers tied to the land in a state of neoserfdom. Aristocrats were to control two-fifths of all the land, while the rest was reserved for freemen. In an effort to lure potential migrants, the document promised religious toleration and a representative assembly. And, to mitigate any possible concern among potential migrants from the sugar islands, the document stated clearly that "every freeman of Carolina shall have absolute power and authority over Negro slaves." The *Fundamental Constitutions* was never ratified by the colonists, but elements of it took effect and it played an important part in ongoing disputes between the colonists and proprietors throughout the seventeenth and early eighteenth centuries.

Several hundred colonists sailed from London in 1669 with a copy of the *Fundamental Constitutions* in hand. The three ships—the *Port Royal,* the *Albemarle,* and the *Carolina*—followed the common route of the time, sailing first to Barbados, where they picked up supplies and additional colonists and replaced the damaged *Albemarle* with the ship *Three Brothers.* After leaving Barbados, a storm scattered the fleet, sending ships to Bermuda, the Bahamas, and Virginia. Roughly a hundred colonists eventually arrived on the Carolina coast in March 1670. Initial plans called for a settlement in the southern end of the territory near Port Royal, but the Kiawah Indians, hoping the colonists could serve as allies against the Westos, convinced the colonists to move north to a site near modern Charleston, along what the colonists soon named the Ashley River (the town was moved again to its current location in 1680). Within a few months, ships returned to Barbados seeking more colonists, at least a hundred of whom arrived in February 1671.

Migrants from Barbados and the other islands formed a significant percentage of the early colonists in the Lowcountry. For many years historians argued that a majority of colonists in the first two decades came from Barbados—one estimate suggested 54 percent—but more recently some scholars have argued that 30 percent or so is a more accurate figure. Regardless of the specific number, colonists from Barbados functioned as something of a "charter group" in Carolina, a group whose early arrival and initial leadership, actions, and decisions shaped subsequent developments.[2] Several of Carolina's early governors came from Barbados and other sugar islands, including Sir John Yeamans, James Colleton, and Sir Nathaniel Johnson, who previously had served as governor of the Leeward Islands before moving to Carolina. Many migrants from the islands were servants or former servants, but others came from prominent families. At least 18 of the 175 big planting families in Barbados—those with more than 60 slaves—acquired land in South Carolina, as did 33 "middling" families—those with between 20 and 59 slaves. Many of these migrants brought servants and slaves with them. Indeed, at least one-quarter and perhaps as many as one-third of the first colonists in South Carolina were enslaved Africans. Many, if not most, of these early Africans likely were Igbos or others from the Bight of Biafra, as that region supplied about half of all slaves reaching Barbados in the five years prior to the colonization of the Lowcountry.

Not all island planters actually migrated to the Lowcountry. Some, like John Lucas of Antigua, grandfather of Eliza Lucas Pinckney, became absentee landowners, remaining in the islands while servants and overseers developed their lands. Regardless, planters, servants, and slaves from the islands played a key role during the early decades of settlement. Letters from the colony in the first few years suggest that colonists from England looked to the Barbadians for advice on a wide variety of matters related to planting and farm building. Migration, moreover, continued in the early decades of the eighteenth century as families from Barbados and the other islands sought out land and opportunity in the Lowcountry, although they maintained their interest in the islands. The Middletons, Bulls, and Colletons were among the prominent families who owned estates in both Barbados and the Lowcountry throughout much of the eighteenth century. When South Carolina officials mapped out parish boundaries in the early eighteenth century, six of the ten parishes shared names with those in Barbados.

The proprietors initially welcomed the arrival of so many migrants from the islands, particularly wealthy planters and other "considerable" men who commanded the necessary labor, resources, and knowledge to develop plantations. Their opinion soon changed. A "Barbados Party" emerged in the Lowcountry that challenged proprietary efforts to structure the colony to their ends. As early as 1671 one colonist reported to Sir Peter Colleton that "the Barbadians endeavour to rule all."[3] Because many of the Barbados planters congregated along Goose Creek, a branch of the Cooper River, they became known as the "Goose Creek Men." Not all the Goose Creek Men were from Barbados—a number of key leaders, including Maurice Mathews, hailed from

England—but these men shared a desire to pursue their own wealth and advancement at the expense of the proprietors' larger vision for the colony.

In part to offset the influence of the Barbadians, the proprietors recruited colonists from other quarters, including New England, New York, and the Chesapeake region. They also encouraged other groups of European migrants during the 1680s, notably Scottish dissenters and French Huguenots. The former established a settlement called Stuart Town near Port Royal in 1684, but it was destroyed by the Spanish two years later. The Huguenots arrived in the wake of Louis XIV's revocation in 1685 of the Edict of Nantes, which had granted French Protestants limited rights and toleration. A few hundred Huguenots migrated to Carolina in the 1680s, and the group formed about 15 percent of the colony's population by 1700. The recruitment of Huguenots and dissenters reflected a number of factors. Shaftesbury and the other proprietors were strongly anti-Catholic, and they sought to aid their suffering fellow Protestants. In addition, the Huguenots had experience cultivating silk and wine, two crops the proprietors hoped Carolina would produce. But the proprietors also hoped that the new migrants could counter the political power of the Goose Creek Men. The Huguenots, however, focused on securing their own political rights, thereby adding to an increasingly factious political climate.

Wherever they arrived from, colonists quickly set out to transform the landscape into what they viewed as productive land, ignoring proprietary plans for development. The proprietors had hoped that colonists would settle in towns, both because towns represented order and civility and because scattered settlements often encroached on Indian lands, prompting raids in retaliation. Colonists, however, immediately set out to claim the best available land they could find. Rather than congregating in Charleston, they spread out along major rivers. The proprietors also hoped that colonists would concentrate their energies on developing a viable staple crop for export to England, but within a year or two, plans for producing sugarcane, oranges, and other tropical crops succumbed to the realities of Carolina's climate and to colonists' desire for immediate profits.

Instead of developing crops for the English market, colonists, led by the Barbadians, focused much of their energy on producing goods for the islands. As colonists cleared land, they shipped lumber to heavily deforested Barbados for use in construction and in making barrels and staves to hold sugar and molasses. Following native agricultural practices, they burned fields and planted a mixture of corn, peas, and beans to provide food for themselves and items for export to Barbados and the other islands. The combination of widespread burning and harvesting of trees for export had an immediate and significant impact on the environment. Charleston and its surroundings experienced a timber shortage as early as 1682—just twelve years after the colony was established.

Lowcountry colonists also turned to ranching, which offered good returns for little investment. Colonists marked their cattle and hogs with a distinct brand and then turned them loose to graze in the open savannas of the Lowcountry, fencing them only at night to protect against wolves and other predators. Free-range grazing had some English precedents, but colonists also may have learned such techniques from the Spanish in the Caribbean or from enslaved Africans, many of whom came from regions that tended cattle using similar practices. Regardless, colonists embraced ranching as a quick means of generating profits. The animals were slaughtered, salted, and sent to the sugar islands.

The focus on trade to the islands frustrated the proprietors. Shaftesbury fumed that colonists, led by the Barbadians, wanted "our own plantation soe ordered that in Reputation, people, and Improvement itt might arrive att no other pitch then [*sic*] to be Subservient in Provisions and Timber to the Interest of Barbados." Shaftesbury wanted "Planters . . . not Graziers" in Carolina, colonists who would produce exports to England as a way of paying their debts to the proprietors.[4] But supplying the islands with provisions and timber made good sense to the colonists, because the trade provided immediate returns and allowed them to begin to build farms and plantations. One colonist, echoing Cary Helyar, wrote that it required only a little credit from local merchants to obtain a few pigs and cattle and that with "Care and Industry" an individual would soon "be able to enlarge his Stock of Cattle, and purchase more Land, and also, by Degrees, purchase Slaves to work with him in his Plantation."[5] Early colonists built fortunes by raising livestock, planting orchards, cutting timber, and growing provisions and other commodities, the profits of which financed the acquisition of slaves and the expansion into plantation agriculture. There is no record that anyone in the Lowcountry called it the "Barbados custom" of building a plantation, but the process was the same.

In addition to supplying the islands, colonists also profited by supplying pirates and privateers. As officials in Jamaica increased efforts to suppress piracy during the 1670s, some buccaneers shifted their operations northward. They found a ready welcome in Charleston, where they refitted their ships, exchanged loot for provisions, and spent freely in the town's taverns and brothels. Indeed, Charleston emerged as something of a miniature Port Royal during the 1670s and 1680s, and its craftsmen included a surprising number of silversmiths for a colony with relatively little trade. The pirates brought so much specie into the region that Governor Thomas Lynch in Jamaica observed in 1684 that Lowcountry colonists were "now full of pirates' money."[6] It is impossible to quantify the extent or impact of pirate loot, but the lord proprietor's demand of quitrent payment in "Spanish money" suggests that it played a key role in the region's early economy.

Finally, and of greater importance than trade with pirates, colonists quickly developed a lucrative trade with Native Americans. Even before colonists had landed in the Lowcountry, various Cusabo groups expressed a desire for trade. One of the colonists who arrived in 1670 recalled that as the English approached the coast near Port Royal, they were met by a group of natives eager to exchange deerskins for guns, knives, clothing, and other European manufactured goods. Colonists soon established regular links with native groups in the region, including groups far into the Backcountry. The proprietors attempted to monopolize the trade with Indians for themselves, but colonists ignored these directives in their search for profits.

Deerskins served as one major item of trade. Buckskin, the name for deerskins after the hair had been removed, provided good leather for gloves, hats, shoes, and other items and was in high demand in England during the late seventeenth and early eighteenth centuries. Buckskin proved especially popular for breeches, so much so that one historian has written that buckskin breeches "served as the eighteenth-century equivalent of modern denim jeans."[7] The number of whitetail deer roaming the Lowcountry astonished colonists when they arrived in 1670, and they quickly initiated a trade with natives. Carolina exported an average of 53,000 deerskins a year between 1699 and 1715, and deerskins became the colony's most valuable export for a period. Exports dropped in half during and immediately after the Yamasee War, but the trade resumed in the 1720s and deerskins remained a major export item throughout the eighteenth century.

In addition to deerskins, colonists also traded for Indian slaves. Native groups in the southeast had long raided their enemies for captives. Captured warriors were often killed to avenge the loss of one of the group's own warriors, but women and children captives frequently were adopted to help maintain a group's population. English traders transformed the practice by offering European goods, especially guns, in exchange for captives. Traders offered the goods up front on credit, collecting payment when raiding parties returned with either captives or deerskins. The trade was a dangerous business, however, and it reshaped native communities. Native practices involved capturing relatively few individuals, but the slave trade required a steady stream of captives. In order to maintain access to guns and other European goods, native groups soon found themselves traveling great distances to secure captives. Failure to capture enough slaves pushed Indians into deeper debt, while aggressive and unscrupulous traders often violated established protocols, seizing friends and foes alike.

The Cusabo Indians had welcomed the English when they arrived in 1670 because they viewed the colonists as potential allies against the Westos. But Carolina traders soon formed an alliance with the Westo and forced the Cusabo to agree to several land cessions in the mid-1670s and 1680s. The Westos served as the primary source of slaves for several years, but they soon found themselves victims of the trade when colonists developed an alliance with two other groups in the 1680s, the Savannah and the Yamasee. From the 1680s through 1715, the Yamasee in particular raided groups throughout the southeast to supply Carolina traders with slaves. Yamasee raids nearly eliminated Spanish Florida's native population by the early eighteenth century.

In the 1710s, the Yamasee fought alongside the English against the Tuscarora in North Carolina in order to capture slaves.

Between 1670 and 1715, at least 24,000 and perhaps as many as 51,000 Indians were captured in slave raids in the southeast. Colonists retained some of these slaves, especially as plantations started to develop in the early 1700s. The number of Indian slaves in Carolina increased from about 200 in 1700 to 1,500 by 1710 and formed almost one-quarter of the colony's total slave population. Most, however, were traded to other colonies, where an unfamiliar landscape limited the ability to run away (or so it was thought). Some were sent to the islands in exchange for African slaves, while others were sold to New York, Pennsylvania, Virginia, and New England. The size of the Indian slave trade was so great that for the period before 1715, Carolina *exported* more slaves than it imported.

The trade in Indian slaves came to a sudden end in the mid-1710s. The Yamasee had fallen into debt to Carolina traders for an amount equivalent to 100,000 deerskins. Years of raiding and overhunting left them with fewer deer and potential captives to repay that debt. When Carolina traders began to take Yamasee children as payment, the Yamasee and their allies, including the Creek and the Catawba, fought back. Historians have suggested a number of underlying causes for the Yamasee War. Some have highlighted abuse by traders, including kidnapping captives who had been adopted into native groups, while others point to larger English violations of diplomatic and trading protocol. Some argue that expanding rice production and cattle ranching threatened Yamasee lands. Still others suggest that major disease epidemics in the late 1690s and early 1700s decimated Indian populations, both reducing the number of potential captives and creating a desire among the Yamasee to keep more captives to maintain their own population. Ultimately, perhaps no single explanation can capture the motivations of the numerous Indian groups who fought in the war.

Fearing that they would soon fall victim to English slave raids, the Yamasee attacked Carolina settlements on April 15, 1715. They began by killing English traders living in their towns and then, along with their Creek and Catawba allies, launched attacks against scattered farms and plantations. They destroyed fields and buildings and killed hundreds of colonists as panicked survivors fled into Charleston. The Yamasee War may have been the closest Native Americans ever came to completely defeating the English during the colonial period, but colonists survived the initial wave of assaults, recovered, and then organized counterattacks. The colonists' success was aided by native dependency on European guns and gunpowder, which undermined the ability of the Yamasee to continue to wage war. In addition, the colonists received assistance from the Tuscarora, who sought to avenge their earlier defeat, and, more importantly, from the powerful Cherokee, who feared the growing power of their traditional enemies, the Creek. The Yamasee offensive collapsed by 1716, and the Yamasee abandoned their lands, effectively ending the conflict.

The Yamasee War had several major consequences for the Lowcountry. Most immediately, the trade in native slaves came to an end. As with privateering in Jamaica, the profits from the slave trade helped finance the expansion of plantation agriculture in the Lowcountry, but slave raiding created too much instability. Raids and counterraids increasingly threatened plantations and profits. Planters preferred to establish alliances with native groups to help patrol the increasingly large number of enslaved Africans who worked those plantations and prevent the formation of Maroon communities. Colonists, in other words, abandoned Indian slavery to secure African slavery. Officials also took steps to regulate trade more carefully to maintain the profitable trade in deerskins.

In addition, the war heightened colonists' long-standing complaints about the proprietors' inability to provide adequate defense for the colony against Native Americans, the Spanish, and the French, whose new settlement in Louisiana created additional threats for the Lowcountry, as well as pirates, who had become increasingly unwelcome in the colony as rice production expanded. Rather than providing an economic boost, pirates, including the infamous Captain Edward Teach (aka Blackbeard) now raided ships that transported rice and other commodities to European markets and blockaded Charleston harbor. Colonists' concerns about defense climaxed in 1719, when rumors of a Spanish invasion circulated. Colonists overthrew the proprietary governor, established a temporary government, and, believing that the Crown would provide greater security, petitioned the king to take control of the colony. The king accepted the offer and appointed a provisional governor in 1720. It took several more years to reach an agreement for buying out the proprietors, but by 1729 Carolina officially became a royal colony.

Third, the war generated calls for the creation of a new colony between Charleston and Spanish Florida to help protect Carolina from attack. That desire was realized with the colonization of Georgia in 1733. Finally, the war contributed to the continued marginalization of Cusabo groups in the Lowcountry. A number of groups fought with the English against the Yamasee, but the war, combined with outbreaks of smallpox and other diseases, reduced their population significantly. Some survivors migrated west and were absorbed into larger groups. Others remained in the Lowcountry as "settlement" Indians and carved out an existence within the colonial economy as hunters, traders, tanners, and slave catchers. Indians never disappeared entirely from the Lowcountry, and they retained their culture as best they could. Nevertheless, the 250 or so settlement Indians living in the region by the 1750s occupied only a marginal place in the larger social landscape.

THE RICE REVOLUTION

Although colonists had cleared land, built houses and farms, and established a profitable trade with native groups, the Lowcountry remained something of a struggling outpost in the Greater Caribbean by 1700. The population remained small, fewer than 6,000 colonists, as high mortality rates and a migrant pool dominated by men limited the possibility of natural growth. The trade in provisions, lumber, and slaves to the islands, as well as the deerskin trade to England, anchored the Lowcountry economy and provided a certain degree of prosperity, but no great wealth. Overall, the Lowcountry remained a "colony of a colony."[8]

The Lowcountry's economic profile began to change in the first decade of the eighteenth century. First, aided by a parliamentary bounty in 1705, colonists began to exploit the region's abundant pine trees to produce tar, pitch, and turpentine—what were known as naval stores—essential items for caulking ships and waterproofing rope. By 1712, colonists exported almost 7,000 barrels of pitch and tar. Production rose to almost

45,000 barrels in 1724. English shipbuilders, however, complained about the quality of Carolina naval stores compared to those from the Baltic states, and officials cut the bounty in 1724. They reinstated it in 1729, although with different rates, and while Lowcountry exports resumed, by that time the primary center of production had shifted to the pine barrens of North Carolina.

More importantly, colonists identified a staple crop that would transform the Lowcountry: rice. One source suggests that colonists shipped some rice to Barbados as early as 1674, but it was not until the 1690s that colonists began to produce rice on a significant scale, and it would take two more decades for rice to emerge as the Lowcountry's signature crop. Together, rice and naval stores ushered in an export boom in the early eighteenth century that accelerated economic growth, environmental change, demographic shifts, and social transformation.

Colonists initially grew rice inland on dry soils, relying on rain to water the crop, but they soon recognized the need for a steadier supply of water. Early in the eighteenth century, they began to shift their operations to marshy swamplands that covered large segments of the Lowcountry. Slave workers drained the swamplands and constructed an elaborate series of embankments, canals, and reservoirs to store water. This water allowed planters to flood the fields a few times during the planting season to aid the growth of rice plants, but increased use of water also meant more weeds, which created more work for slaves. By the middle decades of the eighteenth century, some innovative planters took advantage of the tidal flow of the Lowcountry's rivers as a source of irrigation. Rising tides pushed freshwater upstream on top of the heavy saltwater below. Planters then installed a system of floodgates to control the entry of freshwater onto the fields. Tidal planting allowed for more frequent and regular flooding of the fields, which reduced the amount of hoeing required by slaves and increased the amount of rice produced. The construction of the infrastructure needed to control the supply and movement of water, however, involved moving a massive amount of earth, particularly on tidal plantations. On one plantation, fields were surrounded by sloping embankments that were five feet high, three feet across at the top, and over twelve feet across at their base. Contemporaries compared the amount of work involved in laying out an eighteenth-century rice plantation to building the Great Pyramids. Eighteenth-century observers suggested that setting up a rice plantation required an investment of somewhere between £1,000 and £2,000. This was a smaller capital investment than sugarcane required, but the labor and infrastructure requirements for rice far exceeded those of tobacco or other mainland crops.

Slaves planted rice in the spring and spent the summer months at the grueling work of hoeing the fields to keep them free of weeds. Rice was harvested in late August and early September. After the plants had been cut and dried, slaves began processing the grain. They first threshed the rice to separate the grains from

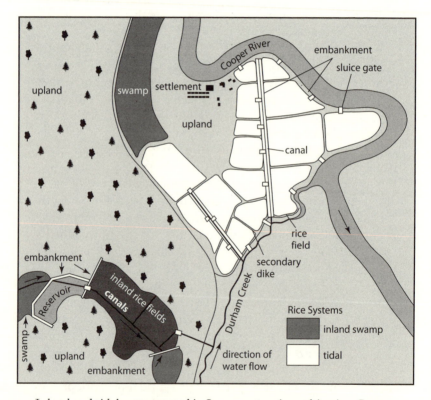

Inland and tidal systems used in Lowcountry rice cultivation. Image after Richard Porcher, reproduced in Judith Carney, *Black Rice: The African Origins of Rice Cultivation in the Americas* (Cambridge, MA, 2002).

the dried stalks. Next, they removed the outer husk that surrounded the grain without damaging the rice inside. Slaves initially did this by hand, following the West African practice of using a mortar and pestle. "Pounding" rice required great skill and endurance, as slaves often stood for hours raising and lowering the ten-pound pestle. Planters developed a number of different kinds of mills that sped up the process by the middle of the eighteenth century, but pounding by hand continued. After pounding, rice was winnowed in baskets to rid the grains of any chaff. The end product was clean, white rice ready for export. Planters kept any damaged rice for domestic consumption or fed it to slaves.

There is a good deal of scholarly debate about the origins of rice agriculture in South Carolina. Many historians argue that enslaved Africans were responsible for introducing rice to the

Mortar and pestle used to pound rice, c. early nineteenth century. Courtesy of the South Carolina State Museum.

Lowcountry. These scholars note that the English had no experience growing rice, but many slaves came from parts of West Africa, where rice was central to diets and cultures. Moreover, the techniques for growing and processing rice in Carolina, including the use of water to flood the fields, mirrored those employed by farmers living along what became known as the Rice Coast of West Africa (present-day Senegal south to Liberia). Other scholars recently have challenged this argument, arguing that English colonists possessed knowledge and experience in draining fields and manipulating water and that they used this knowledge in the development of rice plantations. Moreover, there is no evidence that slaves from rice-growing regions formed a significant proportion of the Lowcountry's slave population in the early decades of settlement.

Regardless of its origins, it is clear that the Lowcountry rice complex that developed by the middle of the eighteenth century represented a mixture of African and European methods. Flooding rice fields was common along the Rice Coast, for example, but the development of reservoirs and the use of hanging gates reflected European practices. Likewise, the process of sowing rice in the ground, winnowing it in distinct baskets, and milling it using mortars and pestles all had West African origins, but colonists in Carolina developed newer, mechanized mills to speed up part of the work. Overall, the production of rice in the Lowcountry is perhaps best characterized as a hybrid process, one that combined Old World practices with New World innovations.

Once colonists mastered the art of growing rice, production increased rapidly. Planters exported one barrel in 1695 to Jamaica. By the early 1710s, production averaged 1.7 million pounds per year, and output increased dramatically in subsequent decades. Production stalled and profits dropped in the 1740s from a combination of factors, including a major slave rebellion in 1739 and war with Spain and France from 1739 to 1748, but conditions improved again in the mid-1750s, when South Carolina plantations produced on average over 37 million pounds per year. By that time, Governor James Glen wrote, "the only Commodity of Consequence produced in South Carolina is Rice, and they reckon it as much their staple Commodity, as Sugar is to Barbados and Jamaica, or Tobacco to Virginia and Maryland."[9] Britain's Navigation Acts required planters to ship their rice to England, but little was consumed there. A good deal of Carolina rice was reexported to northern Europe, Holland and Germany in particular, where it served as an alternative to other inexpensive cereals. A significant market existed in southern Europe as well. Lowcountry planters received a special exemption from the Navigation Acts for this market when they gained the right to ship directly to Spain, Portugal, and ports in the Mediterranean after 1730.

Expanding production required a steady supply of labor. Some indentured servants came to the Lowcountry from England and the West Indies with hopes of acquiring land and improving their economic conditions, but by the 1680s improving economic conditions in England caused fewer servants to seek opportunity in the colonies. At the same time, the creation of new colonies in New York, East and West Jersey (later combined), and Pennsylvania meant increased competition for those who did. In either case, the number of available servants was relatively small. Native American slaves performed labor on some Lowcountry plantations in the early decades of settlement, but the Yamasee War in 1715 brought an end to the trade in Native American slaves, and their numbers diminished rapidly in the following years.

Rice planters instead increasingly relied on the labor of enslaved Africans. This is hardly surprising, given that colonists from the Caribbean sought to replicate the plantation model that had developed on Barbados and had brought slaves with them when they migrated to the Lowcountry. Africans formed at least 25 percent of the colony's population in its first years of settlement, but as rice cultivation expanded, so did the number of slaves. Planters imported approximately 2,200 enslaved Africans in the 1710s, more than 7,800 in the 1720s, and almost 28,000 during the 1730s. As one eighteenth-century visitor noted, "Rice is raised so as to buy more negroes, and negroes are bought so as to get more rice."[10] Slaves outnumbered English colonists as early as 1708, and by 1720 the roughly 12,000 African slaves outnumbered the 6,500 whites almost 2 to 1. South Carolina became the only mainland colony with a slave majority during the colonial period. Moreover, enslaved Africans outnumbered whites in some Lowcountry parishes by ratios as high as 9 to 1, a demographic profile similar to many of the sugar islands.

Rice plantations were large operations by the standards of colonial agriculture. By the middle of the eighteenth century, the average plantation measured 500 acres, smaller than the average landholding in St. Andrew parish, Jamaica, at the same time but dwarfing the 30 or so acres that many Massachusetts farmers worked. As was the case in the sugar islands, the wealthiest rice planters owned huge estates and hundreds of slaves. In one parish, St. James Goose Creek, heads of households owned on average 2,400 acres of land and 43 slaves. The three wealthiest owned, on average, over 11,000 acres and 220 slaves, although such large estates were sometimes divided into separate holdings. A diverse mixture of lowland swamps and higher dry lands characterized these plantations. Planters grew rice on only about 40 percent of this land. The rest served as pasture for animals, forests for firewood or lumber exports, provision grounds, and later, indigo fields. Such large tracts required a large number of laborers. Most contemporaries believed that planters needed at least 30 slaves to operate a rice plantation. By the 1740s, 3 out of every 4 enslaved Africans in Carolina lived on plantations with 20 or more slaves, and over half lived on plantations with 30 or more. By contrast, fewer than 1 in 5 slaves in the Chesapeake lived on plantations with 21 or more slaves.

Rice became the Lowcountry's signature crop during the eighteenth century, but as the pattern of land use in St. James Goose Creek suggests, the region's economy remained diverse. Colonists continued to export other goods in significant amounts, including deerskins, forest products, and provisions. They also developed a major new crop, indigo, the leaves of which produced a blue dye important to England's growing textile industry. Colonists had experimented briefly with indigo in the seventeenth century, but the resulting dye was inferior to that produced in the Caribbean, and when rice emerged as a major staple planters abandoned efforts to develop the crop. The outbreak of war with Spain and France in 1739, however, generated renewed interest in indigo production. Increased freight and insurance charges depressed the rice market, and planters eagerly sought another means to generate profits. Indigo, less bulky than rice and in high demand, became an ideal solution.

Indigo was a relatively easy crop to grow, but processing the dye was difficult and unpleasant work. The process began by placing the leaves of the indigo plant in a large vat, covering them with water, and allowing them to ferment. After several hours, the mixture was drained into a second, adjoining vat where slaves beat it with poles. At a certain point in the beating, when the mixture had obtained a certain color—timing was of great importance—lime was added. Having formed into a paste-like substance, the indigo was then placed into a third vat to drain. After this, the paste was placed into a cloth for further straining, then shaped into two-inch square cakes and left to dry for several weeks before shipment to England. As processing continued, the stench of the fermented mixture grew worse and worse, attracting swarms of mosquitoes. Not surprisingly, planters located the indigo works some distance from their main residences.

Eliza Lucas (later Eliza Lucas Pinckney), the daughter of an Antiguan sugar planter and official who moved to South Carolina in the summer of 1739, often gets credit for the emergence of indigo in the Lowcountry. When military concerns called her father back to Antigua, the sixteen-year-old Eliza took control of his plantations. Using seeds of the West Indian indigo plants sent by her father, Eliza, and later her husband, Charles Pinckney, experimented for several years before perfecting the process of growing the plant and producing the dye. Eliza deserves some credit for indigo's introduction in the 1740s, but she was not the only planter interested in the crop and she later recalled that several French prisoners held in the Lowcountry also shared important information about indigo production. Moreover, enslaved Africans likely played a key role in the successful cultivation of indigo. Eliza's father apparently tried to get a slave from Montserrat who was familiar with indigo sent to Carolina, and slaves themselves often supervised the production process. Lowcountry planters placed great monetary value on slaves skilled in indigo production, often two or three times that of field hands.

Once planters and their slaves perfected the process, indigo production soared during the 1740s, rising from about 5,000 pounds in 1746 to over 138,000 pounds the following year. The industry received a further boost when Parliament granted a bounty on the dye in 1749 to ensure a steady supply within the confines of the British mercantilist system. By the late 1750s,

Carolina was exporting some 531,000 pounds per year, much of it from Lowcountry plantations, although production of the crop had spread into the Backcountry. Even when the rice market rebounded, indigo continued to serve as an "excellent colleague Commodity" to rice, because it was grown on drier lands and the work of processing the dye occurred during slack times in the rice schedule.

Together, rice and indigo generated tremendous wealth during the eighteenth century, and Lowcountry planters became the richest men in the mainland colonies. Per capita wealth in the Lowcountry in the period 1757–62 was £303, low by West Indian measures but far higher than anywhere else on the mainland. Indeed, among mainland colonists who died and whose estates went through probate court in 1774, planters in Charleston and the surrounding area were the wealthiest by far. The average estate inventory in the Charleston district measured £2,337, three and a half times higher than the next wealthiest region, Anne Arundel County, Maryland. Peter Manigault ranked as the richest Lowcountry planter, leaving an estate of £28,000. If rice and indigo did not produce the same level of wealth as sugar, they nevertheless made the Lowcountry, in the words of one observer, "the most opulent and flourishing colony on the British Continent of America."[11]

THE GREATER LOWCOUNTRY

Rice transformed the South Carolina Lowcountry, and by the early eighteenth century, the region exhibited the key characteristics of the plantation complex that had emerged in the islands: a highly profitable staple crop, large landholdings, wealthy planters, and slave populations that outnumbered European colonists, often by huge ratios. Once established in Carolina, the rice plantation complex spread north and south of its core zone in the middle decades of the eighteenth century.

Expansion occurred first, and only to a limited extent, along the lower parts of the Cape Fear River, a region that became part of the separate colony of North Carolina in 1713. The proprietors initially had prohibited land grants in the Cape Fear region during the early eighteenth century, but as rice took hold in Carolina, a number of Lowcountry colonists eyed the area for development. The low-lying river lands and nearby swamps appeared ideal for rice production and, despite its name, the coast was more accessible to trans-Atlantic shipping than were points farther north. Hoping to expand their fortunes, escape debt and taxes, or possibly both, a small group of colonists from South Carolina led by Maurice and Roger Moore moved into the area in the mid-1720s. The Moores' father, James, had migrated to the Carolina Lowcountry from Barbados in the 1670s, established a plantation in Goose Creek, and served as governor of South Carolina from 1700 to 1703. The sons continued his model of migration and plantation development. Aided by a new governor in North Carolina willing to ignore proprietary directives in the pursuit of profits, the Moores and their allies, a group whose connections by blood and marriage earned them the name "The Family," secured land grants in the Cape Fear region and began settlement in 1725.

As was the case with James Moore and other Barbadian immigrants in the early settlement of the Lowcountry, the Family formed something of a charter group in Cape Fear. Only 24 of the 130 individuals who lived in the region between 1725 and 1740 and whose backgrounds can be traced came from Carolina, but more migrants came from Carolina than from any other place during these years, and they played an important role in economic development. They acquired huge tracts of land, often by dubious means. Just eight Carolinians who arrived before 1730 eventually patented over 91,000 acres and one—Roger Moore—held more land than any other individual in the region before the American Revolution. They also brought a significant number of slaves with them. Slaves soon outnumbered whites, and composed over 60 percent of the population throughout the 1750s and 1760s, the only region of North Carolina with a black majority. Colonists and their slaves soon began to grow rice. Export figures do not exist for these early years, but by 1731 one planter was experimenting with tidal flows to flood his fields. By 1737, another observer noted the rapidly increasing wealth of many of these larger planters. By all these measures, the lower Cape Fear represented an extension of the South Carolina Lowcountry.

In other ways, however, the extension proved incomplete. The Lower Cape Fear represented the northern limit of rice production, but rice never dominated the region's economy. Forest products—pitch, tar, turpentine, and lumber—generated far more exports and wealth than rice or any other agricultural pursuits. Even at its peak in the early 1770s, rice occupied only 500 acres of land. Large slaveholdings, likewise, remained limited, concentrated in the hands of a few individuals. Only thirty-seven planters in the 1760s owned twenty or more slaves, and only twenty colonists held thirty or more. Few, if any, of even these largest slaveowners focused predominantly on rice production. Most, like Benjamin Heron, who arrived from England in the 1750s, engaged in a variety of economic activities. Heron's extant business papers indicate that in the years 1771–73 over 50 percent of his income came from naval stores. Profits from rice provided only 6 percent. Forest products allowed men like Heron to prosper, but they did not result in the great fortunes of rice or sugar. Rice production expanded more significantly in the years after the Revolution, but plantation size, slaveholdings, and output remained small compared to the South Carolina Lowcountry. Thus, while elements of the South Carolina plantation regime emerged in the lower Cape Fear, the region constituted a distinct entity, a blurred border zone, and one that marked the outer edge of the Greater Caribbean.

Expansion occurred to a far greater extent south of the Savannah River in the new colony of Georgia, although the process was delayed for two decades. In 1732, the king granted a charter for Georgia to a group of men known as the trustees, led by James Oglethorpe. Oglethorpe and the other trustees had been active in various enterprises to ease social ills in England and they envisioned Georgia—named to honor King George II—as something of a utopian community that would serve several philanthropic, economic, and strategic ends. First, the new colony would provide a refuge for debtors and others in "decayed circumstances," struggling to support themselves in England. Such men and women would find new opportunities for honest work in Georgia. The trustees also hoped that colonists would produce exotic crops, particularly wine and silk, that would reduce England's dependence on foreign suppliers. Some contemporaries estimated that England spent over £500,000 a year on Italian and French silk. Georgia could help eliminate that trade imbalance, while creating work for thousands of colonists and thousands more in England itself who would turn the raw silk into finished garments. Finally, Georgia would serve as a military buffer between Spanish Florida and the increasingly valuable plantations in Carolina. The new colony would solidify British claims to land that remained contested by Spain, help protect South Carolina from Spanish military advances, and reduce opportunities for slaves to run away, a growing problem, as the Spanish promised freedom to any English slaves who made it to Florida.

The trustees enacted a series of regulations to support these goals. They limited landholdings for charity colonists to 50 acres and no more than 500 acres to migrants who paid their own way. Moreover, colonists could not sell their land freely but were required to pass it on to their sons, a process known as *tail-male*. Such regulations were intended to ensure that Georgia remained a land of small producers rather than large slaveholders. The trustees also banned hard alcohol to promote industriousness among the colonists. Finally, and most importantly, they prohibited slavery, making Georgia unique among the British colonies in America. The ban did not reflect moral objections among the trustees regarding slavery but rather the belief that slavery discouraged white laborers and undermined Georgia's role as a military buffer. Slaves, the trustees argued, could not be counted upon to defend the colony from Spanish invaders.

Led by Oglethorpe, the first colonists arrived in 1733 and established a settlement at Savannah, located ten miles upriver from the coast. Oglethorpe quickly engaged the local Yamacraw Indians in a treaty that ceded land between the Savannah and Altamaha Rivers, stretching inland "as high as the tide flows," about thirty miles. The early settlers on these lands were a diverse group. Most of the 2,831 people who arrived in the first decade were "charity" colonists whose expenses were paid by the trustees, but about 1,000 were "adventurers" who paid their own way. English migrants predominated in the early years, but a sizable number of Scots immigrants arrived in 1734 and 1735, as did a small community of Jewish settlers. In addition, a group of German Protestants known as the Salzburgers arrived in 1734 and established a settlement at Ebenezer, north of Savannah.

Almost no colonists came from Carolina or from the sugar islands. The booming rice economy in the 1730s provided plenty of opportunities for colonists at home, and Georgia's restrictions on landholding and slavery offered few incentives for established planters to migrate. Carolina, nevertheless, played an important role in Georgia's early years. Carolinians contributed money (over £1,200), supplies (in the form of cattle, pigs, and rice), and, ironically, slaves to help clear land and construct buildings at Savannah. Moreover, Carolina dominated Georgia's early economy. All trade in and out of the new colony passed through Charleston in the early years, including the lucrative deerskin trade, which was controlled by Carolina traders.

Despite grand designs and enormous financial support from the British government—Parliament provided over £120,000 for the colony between 1733 and 1749, while the War Office provided additional funds for defense—Georgia struggled to develop. Inexperience and sandy soils undermined colonists' efforts at farm building, and experiments with wine and silk failed to generate significant returns. Relatively few new migrants arrived, and many colonists succumbed to disease. As a result, the colony's population stagnated, growing by less than two hundred a year in the 1740s. Without adequate land and labor, Georgia failed to develop the timber and naval stores industry that played such an important role in early Carolina. By the early 1750s, one observer reported that "everything is still forests, and small plantations have been established only here and there."[12]

Frustrated by the conditions in the colony, a group of colonists mounted a challenge to the trustees in the 1740s, arguing that land restrictions and the ban on slavery were undermining Georgia's, and their own, economic development. These "Grumbletonians" and "Malcontents," as they became known, found allies among wealthy English merchants anxious to open the slave trade to Georgia. They also found support from a small group of South Carolina colonists who had migrated to Georgia in the late 1740s and had brought slaves with them. Local officials "knew and wink'd" at the violation, and the clamor for slaves grew louder.[13] The trustees held firm for a period, but faced with increasing pressure from both London merchants and a growing number of disgruntled colonists they finally relented. In 1750–51, they lifted the ban on slavery and ended restrictions on landholding. The following year the trustees relinquished leadership of the colony entirely and passed control to the Crown.

Changes to policies on land and slavery resulted in what one historian has termed the "recolonization" of Georgia, this time led by colonists from South Carolina. Over 100 Carolina colonists sought land in 1752 alone, roughly double the number during the previous five years combined, and colonists from South Carolina outnumbered all others until the middle of the 1760s. Georgia's new and generous land policy—100 acres of land for the head of a household, and an additional 50 acres for family members, including servants and slaves—encouraged the development of large tracts of land, and many migrants amassed thousands of acres. These Carolina migrants quickly claimed land along Georgia's major rivers, the Savannah, the Ogeechee, and the Altamaha. Some older Georgia colonists living near Savannah complained that they were being pushed aside by "great 500 acre Gentlemen late of Carolina."[14]

One of the new arrivals was Jonathan Bryan. Bryan's family had accumulated a good deal of land and wealth in the southern part of the Carolina Lowcountry near Port Royal in the early eighteenth century. Seeking to expand his operations, and perhaps to advance his political career, Bryan petitioned for land in Georgia in the 1750s. He received his first 500 acres along the Savannah River in 1750, an additional 500 acres along the Little Ogeechee in 1752, an adjoining 500 acres in 1755, and 500 more acres on the Great Ogeechee that same year. All were good rice lands, and, within a few years, Bryan was operating plantations on each. He continued to acquire more lands in the following years, while also expanding his operations in South Carolina. By the 1760s he had acquired some 32,000 acres of land and had 250 slaves laboring on plantations in South Carolina and Georgia. Bryan's political fortunes rose alongside his economic ones. He was appointed to Georgia's council (the upper house of the legislature) in 1755, a position he held for fifteen years.

Not all migrants were as wealthy and powerful as Bryan, but Bryan was one of several Carolina men who reshaped the physical, social, political, and economic landscapes of Lowcountry Georgia between 1750 and 1763, rendering it a literal extension of Carolina's rice plantation zone. Past experience with rice aided Bryan and other Carolinians in their recolonization of Georgia. So, too, did their ownership of significant numbers of slaves. Slaves not only provided essential labor but also served as security for credit, enabling Carolina planters to borrow money more readily. This, in turn, allowed them to expand land-holdings and agricultural operations more quickly than other colonists. With slave labor available, they also began to export more timber to the islands, along with provisions and livestock, as well as naval stores to England. Profits from these industries, in turn, supported the further development of plantations.

A small but significant group of planters from the West Indies also migrated to Lowcountry Georgia in the 1750s. Several came from St. Christopher, where the steady expansion of the sugar industry over the course of the eighteenth century replicated seventeenth-century developments in Barbados, meaning that many planters found little room for growth. One of the most prominent was Lewis Johnston, a St. Kitts planter who migrated with his family and his slaves. Johnston prospered in Georgia, eventually rising to a seat on the governor's council.

Despite the significant developments of the 1750s, however, Lowcountry Georgia remained a poor and weak periphery compared to its older, wealthier, and more dynamic neighbor to the north. Georgia's population remained small, rising from 1,900 whites and 400 blacks in 1751 to just 6,000 whites and 3,600 slaves a decade later. Rice production, likewise, remained small. The colony exported an average of just 2,602 barrels of rice per year between 1754 and 1759, compared to an average of more than 76,000 barrels produced in South Carolina. Moreover, even as Savannah slowly emerged as a trans-Atlantic shipping point, Charleston remained the region's dominant port. One leading merchant complained in 1756 that Georgia was "little better now in respect to trade than a province to South Carolina."[15]

It was only in the aftermath of the Seven Years War that Georgia boomed. The defeat of the Spanish, as well as a treaty with the Creek Indians in 1763, opened up new lands for settlement. Much of this new land was in the Backcountry, but the treaties also opened up the region between the Altamaha and the St. Mary's River, Florida's northern border. A land rush ensued as colonists from South Carolina and Georgia eagerly sought to claim prime rice-growing lands. A number of prominent Carolinians managed to establish plantations, but conflict between South Carolina and Georgia regarding who had jurisdiction to authorize land titles in the region impeded settlement in the years before the Revolution. Nevertheless, overall rice production in the Lowcountry increased to an average of 13,660 barrels per year between 1764 and 1769 and to more than 25,000 barrels per year in the early 1770s. Specific population figures for the Lowcountry do not exist, but Georgia's slave population, almost all of whom lived and worked in the Lowcountry, expanded from 7,800 in 1766 to over 15,000 by 1773. At the same time, Georgia planters began to import slaves directly from Africa rather than from Charleston and the Caribbean. With the steady growth of rice plantations and slavery, Lowcountry Georgia increasingly mirrored the plantation complex of Carolina and the Greater Caribbean.

FIVE

"In Miserable Slavery"

SLAVERY EXISTED THROUGHOUT BRITISH AMERICA by the middle of the eighteenth century, from Barbados to Boston, but nowhere did slaves and slavery dominate life as thoroughly as in the Greater Caribbean. It was here that enslaved Africans first arrived in significant numbers, and they continued to arrive in huge numbers across the seventeenth and eighteenth centuries. Unlike in other parts of British America, slaves formed the vast majority of the population in these colonies. Everywhere they outnumbered whites by ratios ranging from 2 to 1 to 15 to 1. As one Swiss visitor wrote of the Lowcountry, "Carolina looks more like a negro country than like a country settled by white people."[1] Slaves built the plantations, cleared and cultivated the fields that generated the colonists' great riches, cooked the food and performed skilled tasks that sustained the colonies, and shaped the development of the region's social and cultural life in innumerable ways.

Roughly 1.1 million slaves were transported to the Greater Caribbean prior to 1760, most to sugar plantations in the islands. Enslaved Africans far exceeded the total number of European migrants to all of British America during the seventeenth and eighteenth centuries. Indeed, the number of Africans imported into Jamaica alone prior to 1775 exceeded the total number of European migrants to all of British North America during that period.

Enslaved Africans faced particularly brutal conditions in the Greater Caribbean. Both sugar and rice demanded a great deal of labor, and planters pushed slaves hard to generate profits. The profits came, but at a horrific cost. Production of sugar and rice consumed the lives of millions of enslaved Africans. Slaves perished from malnutrition, disease, overwork, and from physical abuse, as heavily outnumbered whites employed terror to maintain control. Whereas the slave population in the Chesapeake colonies of Maryland and Virginia began to reproduce itself naturally by the 1720s, the Lowcountry required the continued importation of new Africans for population growth until the late 1750s, while the islands relied on the slave trade until the end of the eighteenth century. As a result, the region's population remained more heavily African than African American for much of this period.

Slaves came from a diverse range of societies across the whole of West Africa, from modern Senegal in the northwest to Angola in the south (a few thousand came from Madagascar and parts of East Africa). They spoke different languages, practiced different customs, and worshipped different gods. Thrown together by the experience of enslavement in Africa, the Middle Passage across the Atlantic, and the brutality of coerced labor in the Greater Caribbean, slaves struggled to forge new families, communities, and customs throughout the seventeenth and eighteenth centuries. The continued importation of slaves from West Africa meant that slaves held on to more of the cultural traditions, and African cultures remained more pronounced in the Greater Caribbean than in other parts of British America, but, from the beginning, slaves also had to negotiate with other groups of Africans, as well as Europeans and Native Americans, in the context of new and distinct physical environments. In their music, language, and religion, in their houses, in the crops they grew in their gardens, the food they cooked, and in a variety of other areas, enslaved Africans maintained what they could from their own cultures, borrowed from others, and over time melded these various materials into new forms and practices. Historians label this process of creative adaptation *creolization,* and throughout the Greater Caribbean enslaved Africans merged old and new into distinct, creole cultures. Africans and African

Americans may have lived in what one colonist termed "miserable slavery," but slaves never accepted the planter fiction that they were property, not persons, and their efforts to resist their enslavement helped carve out space in which they could—and did—assert their own humanity.[2]

THE SLAVE TRADE

The slaves' torturous journey to the Greater Caribbean began with their enslavement in West Africa. Unlike much of western Europe, where the institution of slavery had died out over time (even as other forms of servitude persisted), slavery remained an important feature of many West African societies. Slaves in West Africa performed a variety of tasks. Some worked in the fields harvesting crops. Others served in the military or as personal servants. Slaves in the Gold Coast mined gold, the region's primary export throughout the sixteenth and much of the seventeenth century. In addition to labor, some states or groups traded slaves to Arab merchants for textiles, spices, and other goods from North Africa as part of the trans-Saharan slave trade. For many West African groups, trading slaves to Europeans was simply an extension of existing practices.

Individuals in West Africa found themselves enslaved for a variety of reasons and by a variety of means, including punishment for crimes and payment of debts. Slaves from the Bight of Biafra sometimes were kidnapped, including most famously Olaudah Equiano, whose account is perhaps the best-known eighteenth-century slave narrative. Most slaves, however, were captured in wars. West African groups deemed captives from wars waged against "outsiders" as eligible for enslavement, although the definition of an outsider varied across West Africa. In some cases, religion marked the boundary between insiders and outsiders. Muslim groups in Upper Guinea deemed all non-Muslims eligible for slavery, but not fellow Muslims, regardless of ethnicity. In other cases, ethnic and political divisions defined by kin or clan linkages determined an individual's status as an insider or outsider. Such divisions produced constant conflict between groups, which in turn generated an ongoing stream of captives.

The practice of enslaving war captives predated the arrival of Europeans, but the arrival of Europeans and the introduction of European trade goods fueled an expansion of the slave trade.

English ships carried a variety of trade goods to West Africa, but the most important were textiles, gunpowder weapons, and cowrie shells from the Indian Ocean, the latter serving as currency in many parts of West Africa. Textiles, particularly from India, formed almost two-thirds of the cargoes sent from England to West Africa. Gunpowder weapons were less numerous, but by the early decades of the eighteenth century Europeans traded as many as 180,000 guns a year for slaves on the Gold Coast and the Bight of Benin. Access to gunpowder weapons intensified conflicts, and states such as the Asante Kingdom in the Gold Coast and the kingdoms of Dahomey and Oyo in Benin used access to European guns to expand their power at the expense of neighboring groups. Over time, raiding parties ventured deeper into their respective hinterlands to capture more slaves, who in turn could be exchanged for more goods.

Slaves captured in such raids often spent weeks, and sometimes months, in captivity before they reached the coast and were traded to English slavers. An enslaved woman in eighteenth-century Barbados named 'Sibell recalled that her captor "take and carry, carry, carry, carry, carry me all night and all day, all night and all day [a]way from my Country."[3] The long journey to the coast claimed numerous lives. One scholar estimates that as many as one-third of those enslaved died en route from the vast interior of West Central Africa to ports such as Luanda in modern-day Angola. The figure was lower in other regions, but overall perhaps 10 percent of all captives died on forced marches to the coast. Once there, slaves were held in *barracoons* before being loaded onto ships. Some *barracoons* were open-air pens, which offered no protection from the elements. Others were larger structures called "castles," which were basically prisons in which slaves were held in dank, dark cells. An additional 5–10 percent of slaves perished in these *barracoons* before they made it on board a European slave ship.

European traders hoped to purchase large numbers of men and boys, because those groups were most valued by planters in the Greater Caribbean, but Europeans were unable to dictate the terms of trade. Indeed, the English and other Europeans had little physical presence in West Africa beyond the coastal castles and trading factories they established with the consent of local rulers. Social and economic factors specific to various regions in West Africa, rather than European demand, determined the numbers of men and women sold into the Atlantic trade, and as a result, English traders purchased more women than they desired. Far more African than European women crossed the Atlantic during the seventeenth and eighteenth centuries, which in turn had significant consequences for the development of slave communities in the Greater Caribbean.

Africans sent to the Greater Caribbean came from a number of different regions of West Africa, although the relative importance of any one region as a source of slaves changed over time. In the first quarter of the eighteenth century, for example, an estimated 73 percent of slaves transported to the Greater Caribbean came from the Gold Coast (roughly modern Ghana) and the neighboring Bight of Benin (modern Togo, Benin, and parts of Nigeria). Only about 10 percent of slaves came from West Central Africa (Congo and Angola). By the second quarter of

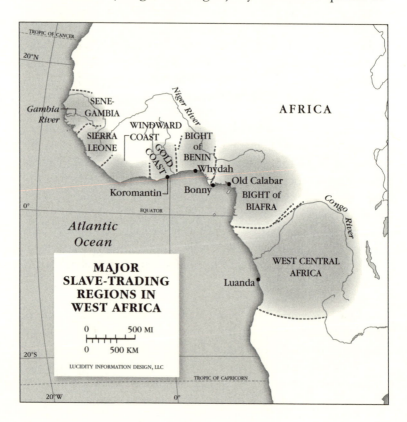

the eighteenth century, however, West Central Africa supplied a quarter of all slaves shipped to the Greater Caribbean, while only 35 percent came from the Gold and Slave Coasts. Senegambia, Sierra Leone, and the Windward Coast (Senegal south and east through the Ivory Coast) accounted for only 11 percent of slaves shipped to the Greater Caribbean from 1726 to 1750, but those regions became more important in the years 1751 to 1760, accounting for 26 percent of all slaves. The slave trade also varied by colony, reflecting changing conditions on both sides of the Atlantic. The Lowcountry, for example, received a far greater

TO BE SOLD, on board the Ship *Bance-Island*, on tuesday the 6th of *May* next, at *Ashley-Ferry*; a choice cargo of about 250 fine healthy NEGROES, just arrived from the Windward & Rice Coast. —The utmost care has already been taken, and shall be continued, to keep them free from the least danger of being infected with the SMALL-POX, no boat having been on board, and all other communication with people from *Charles-Town* prevented. *Austin, Laurens, & Appleby.*

N. B. Full one Half of the above Negroes have had the SMALL-POX in their own Country.

Advertisement of enslaved Africans from Senegambia. Courtesy of the Library of Congress, Prints and Photographs Division.

percentage of slaves from Senegambia (28%) between 1701 and 1760 than did the sugar islands (only 6%).

Once on board ships, African captives faced even more horrific conditions than those in the *barracoons*. They were chained together below deck so tightly that even rolling over required coordination with others. Often they had little more than three feet of space above their heads. Disease, particularly dysentery, spread rapidly in such conditions. One eighteenth-century British sailor stated that decks were so "covered with blood and mucus which had proceeded from them having flux, that it resembled a slaughter-house."[4] Captains of slave ships engaged in a gruesome calculus that sought maximum profits at the border of life and death. They aimed to pack as many slaves as possible onto ships to ensure the highest possible return but slowly learned that too much crowding increased mortality, and thus reduced profits. Through a deadly process of trial and error, traders ascertained the minimum amount of food and water necessary to keep slaves alive for the approximately seventy-day voyage to the Greater Caribbean. Even then, mortality rates on slave ships were appallingly high. Almost 23 percent of slaves died on the Middle Passage during the seventeenth century. Conditions "improved" somewhat during the eighteenth century, but even then almost 15 percent of slaves bound for the Greater Caribbean died en route. As Olaudah Equiano recalled of his passage, "The shrieks of the women, and the groans of the dying, rendered the whole a scene of horror almost inconceivable."[5]

Enslaved Africans did not accept these conditions passively. They rebelled frequently, usually as the ships prepared to depart for the Americas. As many as 1 in 10 voyages experienced some form of revolt during the period from the 1690s to 1807. Slave ship crews brutally suppressed any efforts at rebellion, and most revolts failed, but the efforts themselves had important consequences. Fear of slave resistance forced slave traders to equip their ships with more weapons and more crewmembers than they might have otherwise. More crewmen and guns meant fewer slaves on board ships, and the historian David Richardson estimates that active resistance by slaves reduced the number of Africans shipped across the Atlantic by as many as one million.

Those who survived enslavement in Africa and the trans-Atlantic voyage to the Greater Caribbean faced additional terror when they arrived for sale in Bridgetown, Kingston, Charleston, and other major ports in the region. Slaves were brought on deck and paraded before prospective buyers. Equiano recalled that he and others were divided into small groups and made to jump to display their fitness. Traders tried their best to conceal the physical trauma visible on their human cargoes. Upon arrival they provided slaves with fresh food and water, and sometimes alcohol. They rubbed their bodies with oil. Such efforts may have brought higher prices in some cases, but in the end, demand for slaves was so great that even the weakest slaves found buyers in one colony or another. In many cases local merchants purchased slaves in groups and then resold them to individual planters, subjecting slaves to a second ordeal of separation. For those fortunate few who found themselves purchased alongside "shipmates," that bond remained a powerful one, becoming a form of kinship within slave communities. A Jamaican penkeeper named Thomas Thistlewood, for example, recorded the final wishes of a dying slave who requested that his cow be passed on to his wife's "shipmate." Likewise, children sometimes referred to their parents' shipmates as aunts or uncles. For many individuals, however, the slave markets of the Greater Caribbean sundered whatever links enslaved Africans had formed during the trans-Atlantic voyages, furthering their isolation and alienation.

THE WORLD OF WORK

Planters in the Greater Caribbean purchased slaves as laborers, and work defined the lives of all enslaved Africans. Every spoonful of sugar in a cup of tea and every grain of rice exported to Europe represented the toil of enslaved Africans, and slave labor supported the entire Atlantic trading system. As Daniel Defoe summarized, "No African trade, no negroes; no negroes no sugars, gingers, indicoes etc; no sugars etc no islands, no islands no continent, no continent, no trade."[6] All slaves worked, but specific work routines varied considerably across the region. Differences existed between slaves who worked on sugar estates and those who labored in rice fields, as well as between those who labored on cattle pens, coffee plantations, and various other economic enterprises. The lives of slaves working in towns followed different rhythms from those on plantations. So, too, skilled slaves had different experiences than field slaves. What all shared was that work was the most important factor shaping their lives.

The vast majority of enslaved Africans transported to the Greater Caribbean spent their lives laboring on sugar plantations. From early morning until late in the evening, six days a week, and sometimes seven during harvest time, slaves toiled in sugar fields and mills, performing the difficult and exhausting labor that generated the region's great wealth. Slaves on early nineteenth-century sugar plantations in Jamaica and Barbados worked on average 3,600 hours a year, more than early nineteenth-century factory workers in Britain (3,300 hours) and far more than modern workers in the United States (roughly 1,800 hours).

Slaves on sugar plantations generally worked under what was known as the gang system, a brutally effective labor system that generated large returns but at a tremendous cost in human lives. It is not clear whether the English learned the system from planters in Brazil or developed it themselves during the early transition to sugar, but the system was firmly in place in Barbados by the end of the seventeenth century and soon spread to other islands. Planters usually divided enslaved workers into three gangs, each under the supervision of a driver, another slave. An overseer, usually a young Englishman or Scotsman hoping to advance his fortune, monitored the drivers. The first gang performed the heaviest and most difficult work of digging holes, planting crops, cutting mature canes, and working in the inferno-like mills, feeding the canes into the rollers and maintaining the fires. Interestingly, women often formed a majority of field workers in the first gang. Whatever stereotypes planters may have had about European women and work, they did not hesitate to assign African women to grueling labor in the fields, and because men had access to more-skilled jobs, women predominated in the fields. On William Beckford's Roaring River estate in Jamaica, for example, 70 of the 92 slave women (76%) worked in the fields, compared to only 28 of the 84 men (33%). The second gang, usually comprising older or weaker slaves, performed less difficult tasks such as weeding and carting. Children worked in a third gang, collecting trash and other light tasks. The drivers ensured that slaves, particularly in the first gang, worked at a steady pace. One visitor to the Leeward Islands noted that "every ten Negroes have a driver, who walks behind them, holding in his hand a short whip and a long one . . . [and] you constantly observe where the application has been made."[7]

Sugar production required a host of specialized tasks once the canes were cut, and men occupied most of these positions. The most important was the boiler. He was responsible for deciding when to "strike" the sugar, removing it from the heat after crystallization. A successful crop hinged on a skilled boiler, and the slave who occupied that position received special treatment, but it was also a difficult and dangerous job, one that routinely left boilers burned and scarred. Other slaves worked as coopers, carpenters, blacksmiths, masons, cartmen, herders, and fishermen. These skilled slaves operated with less direct supervision from whites and had greater autonomy. They often occupied positions of status and authority within the slave community.

Women also performed some skilled work, namely, as cooks, nurses, laundresses, and domestic servants. Such occupations placed women in constant contact with planters and their families, for good and ill. Domestics had access to better food and clothes, and the work was less grueling than in the fields, but they were subjected to closer supervision and more intervention from whites, and were more vulnerable to sexual exploitation.

Although most slaves in the West Indies worked in sugar production, slaves also grew coffee, ginger, pimento, and other crops, particularly in Jamaica, where land was more readily available. Others worked on livestock pens, tending cattle needed to operate animal mills. By the middle of the eighteenth century, 4 out of every 10 slaves in Jamaica did not work on a sugar plantation. Cattle pens in particular often had sizable slave labor forces of 100 or more slaves. This labor, although difficult, was far less demanding than that on sugar plantations. Still other slaves worked on the wharves and in the workshops of Kingston, Bridgetown, and St. John's, and other urban centers. Overall, there were few occupations on the islands in which slaves were not employed.

The work regime in the Carolina Lowcountry differed considerably from that in the islands. A task system, rather than gang labor, dominated rice production. Instead of closely monitored and regimented gangs, Lowcountry planters assigned individual slaves a defined task for the day. The standard task for field work in the eighteenth century was a quarter-acre. Each slave was responsible for weeding and tending that piece of ground, after which he or she could pursue his or her own activities.

Rice production lent itself to tasking. Rice is a hardy crop and requires less direct supervision, meaning that overseers did not need to manage enslaved workers as closely. Moreover, the amount of rice grown by an individual worker could be measured easily, ensuring accountability. Finally, the conditions in which the crop was grown encouraged planter absenteeism. The swamplands and tidal rivers that facilitated rice production also served as breeding grounds for mosquitoes carrying yellow fever and malaria. No one understood the relationship between mosquitoes and disease, but planters knew that swampy areas were "sickly," and most escaped to Charleston or more northern colonies during the summer months, leaving control of production to an overseer and enslaved laborers. Tasking suited these conditions more than gang labor.

There is no doubt that tasking provided slaves in the Low-country with a relative degree of autonomy. They worked at their own pace and with little direct supervision, and if they finished the task early, their time was their own. Slaves' output, however, was managed closely by the planter or overseer, and the assigned tasks required a great deal of labor. Moreover, difficult working conditions offset whatever advantages tasking provided in the form of greater autonomy. Standing knee-deep in muddy water and laboring under hot, humid conditions exacted a high toll in human lives. Eighteenth-century commentators routinely wrote that no work was more dangerous to the lives of slaves than working in the rice fields. The author of *American Husbandry* stated that rice production was "dreadful" work, and "a more horrible employment can hardly be imagined, not far short of digging in Potosi," the infamous Bolivian silver mine.[8]

The development of indigo as a secondary crop in the Low-country during the middle of the eighteenth century increased slaves' workload. Indigo's production schedule generally complemented that of rice; planters could profitably employ slave labor in indigo during the slack times in the rice production schedule. Added profits for planters, however, meant more work for slaves, who found themselves pushed to produce more throughout the year. Moreover, planters generally organized slaves into gangs for work in indigo fields, meaning that slaves lost some of their autonomy.

Most enslaved Africans in the Lowcountry worked in rice or indigo fields, but as in the islands, some occupied more-skilled positions. The number of such positions increased over the course of the eighteenth century, so that by the 1780s 1 out of every 4 male slaves in rural areas worked as a carpenter, sawyer, or cooper or in another trade. As in the islands, a significant number of slaves also labored in urban centers, particularly Charleston and Savannah. Enslaved men and women composed 52 percent of Charleston's population in 1760, and 8 percent of South Carolina's entire slave population. Slaves in these urban areas occupied perhaps an even greater range of skilled positions as blacksmiths, butchers, barbers, and bakers. Many slaves in Charleston worked in the city's shipyards, crewed on trans-Atlantic vessels, and piloted smaller craft on the region's rivers and the coastal waterways that connected the city to its hinterland. Slaves also controlled the fish market in Charleston, to the dismay of some whites who complained about high prices. As in the islands, men most often occupied these skilled jobs, meaning that women played a disproportionate role in field work. Many slaves in the lower Cape Fear region who did not work on rice plantations spent a good deal of time in the forests, burning tar, gathering turpentine, and cutting timber. Most of these likely labored under some form of the task system.

Work on the plantation did not end when slaves finished their time in the sugar and rice fields. Many slaves also grew provisions to feed themselves and to sell in local markets. The production of food varied across time and space. In some places where land was limited, such as Barbados and Antigua, planters imported a good deal of food from North America and Great Britain, which they distributed to slaves, although planters in Barbados also forced slaves to grow additional provisions on marginal plantation lands. A standard allocation was one pint of corn a day, one or two pounds of salted fish a week, and occasional allotments of meat at holidays. Where land was more readily available—in the Lowcountry and Jamaica in particular, but parts of the Leeward Islands as well—planters allocated individual slaves plots of marginal land and required them to grow their own food. Slaves tended these plots on Sundays, their "day off" from working in the fields, and occasionally on Saturday afternoons. The two systems were not mutually exclusive. Planters in Jamaica and the Lowcountry purchased some food for slaves, and slaves in Barbados cultivated small gardens in which they produced vegetables that supplemented provisions from the planters. Indeed, despite the small size of their garden plots, slaves used them to great effect and produced significant quantities of yams, potatoes, corn, and other crops. Everywhere throughout the region, slaves produced some of their own food.

Many of these foods were African crops introduced to the region by slaves and the slave trade. Yams, black-eyed peas, okra, rice, sorghum (also known as Guinea corn), and melons all arrived from Africa. In addition, bananas and plantains, originally from Asia but long cultivated in parts of Africa, arrived in the Caribbean via the slave trade. Yams and plantains became especially important to slave diets, because they required relatively little labor. The kola nut also arrived from Africa. This highly caffeinated stimulant added flavor to water, which grew stagnant on long trans-Atlantic crossings. It is perhaps best known today as an original ingredient in Coca-Cola. Besides providing essential calories and some variety to slave diets, familiar foods provided slaves a link to their homelands and contributed to the emergence of distinct creole cuisines. "Pepper pot" stews such as gumbo (made with okra), callalou (made with a leafy green of the same name), and other dishes served in the islands and Lowcountry today trace their roots to slave provision grounds. In addition to growing crops, slaves in the Lowcountry and Jamaica often supplemented the meager protein allowances granted by planters by hunting and fishing on their own. Indeed, slaves quickly emerged as skilled hunters and fishermen, and planters often relied on them to provide meat and fish.

Growing and gathering food required additional labor, but the system of provision grounds in particular provided significant benefits to slaves. It gave them an element of control over one part of their lives. Some slaves not only produced enough food for themselves but often surplus crops as well, which they sold to planters for cash or in markets in Charleston, Kingston, and other urban centers. One manager on a Barbadian estate in the 1740s reported that nothing could keep slaves from marketing their goods on Sunday. The planter and historian Edward Long claimed that, as a result of such marketing, enslaved Africans controlled 20 percent of the circulating specie in Jamaica by the 1770s. Plantation records in South Carolina provide numerous examples of planters purchasing corn and other provisions from their slaves, often paying in cash. Access to cash, in turn, enabled slaves to purchase items for themselves, including small luxuries such as clothes or tobacco.

Not all slaves benefited from this system, however. The extra labor needed to produce provisions meant that older and weaker slaves struggled to provide enough food to feed themselves. Moreover, although the system provided a degree of autonomy and generated tangible rewards for some, slaves who grew their own food on provision grounds often had a worse diet, one that lacked protein in particular. Planters embraced the system of provision grounds for different reasons. It freed them from a good deal of expense in feeding their slaves. Many also came to believe that it served as a means of maintaining control. According to Bryan Edwards, "The Negro who has acquired by his own labour a property in his master's land has much to lose, and is therefore less inclined to desert his work."[9]

Whether or not they produced surpluses on their lands, slaves throughout the Greater Caribbean generally suffered from malnutrition. One scholar has estimated that slaves consumed roughly 1,500 to 2,000 calories a day but needed something closer to 3,000, given their intense labor. Even if that estimate is a bit low, it is clear that slaves often did not have enough food. Moreover, the food they did consume was monotonous and lacked an adequate amount of protein and a range of essential vitamins. Slaves experienced privation in the best of times, but conditions often became catastrophic in the wake of hurricanes and other disasters. Hurricanes devastated fields and crops, and slaves periodically faced severe shortages throughout the seventeenth and eighteenth centuries. The worst situation occurred in the 1780s, when a series of hurricanes swept across the Caribbean. Jamaica was especially hard-hit. Five storms battered the island between 1780 and 1786, destroying provisions and creating famine-like conditions throughout the island. A committee of the Jamaican assembly determined that 15,000 slaves (out of a population of

256,000) had perished from hunger or disease related to malnourishment during that period. Likewise, drought frequently depleted food supplies and contributed to the death of slaves, particularly in the Leeward Islands. Letters from the Stapleton plantation in Nevis during the 1720s reported, "Many Negroes . . . lost for want of provisions and water," a bland accounting of what must have been terrible suffering.[10]

THE REAPER'S GARDEN

Death dominated the world of enslaved Africans in the Greater Caribbean. Hurricanes, drought, and other disasters contributed at times, but death was an everyday occurrence for slaves throughout the region. Many of those who survived the Middle Passage arrived weakened and quickly succumbed to disease. Half of all slaves sold in the sugar islands died within three years of arrival. One-third of Africans who arrived in the Lowcountry died within the first year. Even those who survived these early years—what colonists called the "seasoning" period—still died quickly and in great numbers. The seventeenth-century Barbadian planter Henry Drax estimated that he needed to purchase ten to fifteen new slaves a year to maintain a labor force of two hundred. The Stapleton estate on Nevis purchased seventeen new slaves in 1731. By 1734, seven had died. Six more died in the next five years, so that by 1739 only four of the original seventeen remained alive.

Slaves died from a variety of interrelated causes. Disease was the biggest killer. Slaves from West Africa often had immunity or some resistance to tropical diseases such as yellow fever and malaria, having been exposed to them as children. Indeed, the fact that these diseases claimed the lives of more Europeans than slaves fueled the perception that Africans were uniquely suited to work in the Greater Caribbean. A range of other diseases, however, including smallpox, pneumonia, tuberculosis, measles, and dysentery, weakened and ultimately killed large numbers of slaves. Such diseases proved so deadly in part because enslaved Africans had little strength to fight off infections. Their diet provided inadequate nutrition, they worked long hours, and they did so under brutal conditions. One eighteenth-century Jamaican planter named Simon Taylor noted that a large sugar crop required running the mill almost constantly for nine months. During that period, Taylor wrote, "the poor wretches of Negroes have not had above six hours of rest for 24, & what with getting their little provisions etc. what time have they had to Sleep." Taylor feared that he was literally "murdering the Negroes."[11] Most planters were not as reflective as Taylor. The enormous profits from sugar and rice provided little incentive to keep slaves alive, and planters simply worked slaves to death and then purchased new ones. Even Taylor noted that during periods of peak production, such as the 1760s, slaves paid for themselves within three years. In some cases, including on the Stapleton plantation, slaves took their own lives to escape the harsh work regime.

Overwork and inadequate provisions also inhibited the ability of slaves to reproduce. The birthrate among slaves was low throughout the seventeenth and eighteenth centuries, while infant mortality rates were horrifically high. On the Worthy Park plantation in Jamaica, 20 percent of pregnancies resulted in a miscarriage or stillbirth during the eighteenth century. The Codrington plantations in Barbados experienced 6 slave deaths for every 1 birth during the first half of the eighteenth century, and similar statistics marked other plantations throughout the region. Most planters showed little interest in taking steps that might improve the birthrate during this period. They forced pregnant women to work until just a few weeks before they delivered and then ordered them back to the fields soon after, preferring immediate profits over the health of their slaves and the long-term reproduction of the labor force. Only toward the end of the eighteenth century did planters take steps to ameliorate living and working conditions for pregnant women in an effort to promote reproduction, and only then in response to mounting pressure to abolish the slave trade.

The combination of high mortality and low fertility rates produced what the historian Richard Dunn characterized as a demographic catastrophe for slaves in the sugar islands throughout the seventeenth and most of the eighteenth century. At no point before the American Revolution did any of the island colonies achieve a naturally reproducing slave population. Slave deaths always outnumbered births, and only the continued importation of massive numbers of new slaves allowed the population to grow. The sugar islands together imported some 800,000 slaves in the period before 1750, but the slave population at that date totaled less than 300,000, grim evidence of the extent to which the production of sugar consumed the lives of African slave laborers.

Conditions were only marginally better in South Carolina. There is some evidence that prior to 1720 the slave population had begun to reproduce itself naturally, but the emergence of rice as a staple crop altered the region's demographic profile. The expanding slave trade brought more men than women to the Lowcountry, while terrible working conditions for both men and women undermined reproduction and increased mortality. Fewer births and more deaths resulted in a negative natural population growth beginning in the 1720s. Rice production thus produced conditions akin to those associated with sugar, and only the importation of slaves from West Africa allowed the Lowcountry slave population to grow for the next few decades. The Greater Caribbean as a whole differed from the tobacco colonies of Virginia and Maryland, where the enslaved population began to grow naturally by the 1720s. It was only in the 1750s that births again began to outnumber deaths in the Lowcountry, a development that did not occur in most of the sugar islands until the early nineteenth century. Even then, the rate of natural reproduction in the rice zone was about half of that in the Chesapeake. These dismal demographic realities separated Lowcountry slaves from their mainland neighbors and reinforced comparisons to their island counterparts.

FAMILY LIFE, CULTURE, AND RELIGION

Despite horrific demographic conditions, slaves did manage to form families and communities. The historian Philip Morgan rightly cautions that when speaking of slave families, "the problem of applying terminology that presupposes freedom to relationships that were grounded in slavery must always be borne in mind."[12] Slave marriages carried no legal standing, and families faced the constant threat of sale and separation. Nevertheless, over time slaves throughout the Greater Caribbean established meaningful relationships as husbands and wives, parents and children, brothers and sisters, and slave families provided something of a refuge from the dehumanizing brutality of the plantation system.

Detailed and systematic information about the structure of slave families is not abundant for the seventeenth and eighteenth centuries, but it is clear that slaves lived in a variety of household units. These included individuals living alone, households with unrelated individuals of the same sex, one parent (usually the mother) living with children, nuclear families with a husband, wife, and children, as well as polygamous households. The particular arrangements on any one plantation varied over time and reflected a variety of factors, including the number of Africans and creoles in a population. More Africans meant an uneven sex ratio, because the slave trade delivered more men to the colonies, while creole populations tended to have relatively even sex ratios. Nevertheless, a shift toward nuclear families occurred throughout the region over the course of the eighteenth century. In the Lowcountry, the percentage of slaves living in families rose from 52 percent in 1730 to 79 percent in 1790. Two-parent households were the most common form among those family units, followed by children living with a single parent, usually the mother. Similar patterns existed elsewhere in the region. Enslaved Africans on Thomas Thistlewood's livestock pen in western Jamaica gradually formed themselves into households based on kin links, most frequently nuclear families. At least a few male slaves engaged in polygamy, a practice common in parts of West Africa. One slave on Thistlewood's pen, for example, a man named Lincoln lived with two wives, five children, and one grandchild. Likewise, an Anglican minister in Carolina felt compelled to remind slaves in his parish that Christianity prohibited multiple wives, which may help explain why so few slaves were interested in missionary efforts. Such examples highlight the persistence of some African cultural forms, but they were not common. Most slaves lived in nuclear families or family units of a mother and her children.

Slave families were simultaneously fragile and strong—fragile because they were subject to constant disruption, but strong because they proved resilient in the face of such challenges. Although planters gradually recognized that families created a degree of stability, many did not hesitate to break them apart when they deemed it economically beneficial to do so. The Price family, for example, owned numerous estates in Jamaica, and they often shifted slaves from one plantation to another with little concern for family life. The Prices separated children from their mothers at age six to put them to work in the fields. On one estate in 1744, several children already had worked previously at two other Price plantations, suggesting a high level of disruption to familial bonds. Individual planters who expanded operations by buying or establishing plantations in new territories such as Jamaica, Antigua, or Georgia threatened familial ties that slaves had established on older properties. So, too, the death of an owner created uncertainty about the future as slave families faced the prospect of separation or sale to satisfy creditors or heirs. One Lowcountry slave, Charles Ball, recalled "with painful vividness" the terror he experienced as a young boy when his mother, brothers, and sisters were all sold in one day to different owners to pay off debts following the death of the planter in 1785.[13] Such separations occurred frequently, and at great cost to slave families. Indeed, the importance of "shipmates" as a form of fictive kinship is a reminder that death and forced separation created huge obstacles for the growth of family life in the Greater Caribbean.

Nevertheless, there is also abundant evidence that family ties remained strong despite such obstacles. Slaves solemnized marriages with as much ritual and celebration as was possible under the constraints of enslavement. Marriages took place at night, away from the eyes of masters and overseers. Some slaves appear to have exchanged a brass ring or other object as a symbol of their union, and the event was cause for much "eating and drinking, singing, dancing, and roaring," according to one Lowcountry overseer.[14] Slaves tried to create kin links by naming children after themselves, particularly sons after fathers—a pattern common in both Barbados and the Lowcountry—or after extended kin. It is also clear that such links were not severed easily. Slaves went to great lengths to maintain connections with family members when they had been separated. Some 30 percent of South Carolina runways whose intentions were known left home to reconnect with a relative, sometimes a parent, a child, or a sibling, but most often a husband or wife. One manager of a plantation in Barbados informed the absentee owner that "a Negro man will run after his wife to the other end of the island and be back next morning to his work."[15]

Families formed elements of larger communities, and as was the case with individual families, enslaved Africans faced considerable obstacles in their efforts to re-create familiar African cultural forms in the new world of the Greater Caribbean, including, not least, the violence and dislocation caused by the slave trade itself. Indeed, basic ideas about ethnicity and how slaves defined themselves changed in response to the realities of the slave trade and the plantation system. Entirely new ethnic identities emerged over time and across space. No individuals in Africa, for example, referred to themselves as "Igbo" or "Coromantee." Slave traders affixed such labels to individuals coming from certain regions—Igbo for those from the Bight of Biafra, Koromanti (Coromantee) for slaves from the Gold Coast—often borrowing the name of a particular port from which slave ships sailed. The Koromanti, for example, came from the Gold Coast port of Kormantine. One slave ship trading at Old Calabar in the Bight of Biafra in 1790 purchased 150 slaves who came from fourteen different ethnic groups, but all of them became known as "Calabars." Once in the New World, slaves adopted these labels to refer to themselves. Slavery and the slave trade literally created new ethnicities.

The extent of cultural retention among enslaved Africans has been the subject of a vigorous scholarly debate. Some scholars suggest that because the slave trade often drew heavily from only one or two regions of West Africa at different times, enslaved Africans from those regions often formed something of a charter group who maintained significant elements of their culture and shaped subsequent cultural development in certain colonies. Between 1658 and 1713, for example, about 6 out of every 10 slaves in Barbados and Jamaica came from either the Gold Coast or the Slave Coast. The coastline of the two adjoining regions measured only two hundred miles, and although slaves came from different ethnic groups and spoke different languages, those languages and larger cultures often shared common elements that facilitated communication and cultural retention. As a result, some scholars argue that slave culture in Barbados and Jamaica during this period was recognizably Akan (from the Gold Coast) in the same way that colonists' culture was recognizably English. Scholars exploring the Lowcountry have posited a similar role for slaves from Angola and Senegambia at different times during the eighteenth century.

Other scholars challenge this interpretation. They argue that the slave trade itself caused a great deal of cultural mixing and that few slaves lived and worked with others from the same ethnic group. The slave trade, and the British trade in particular, involved numerous West African regions. These broad regional divisions included dozens, if not hundreds, of different ethnic groups, often speaking distinct languages. West Central African ports, for example, drew from a hinterland that in total encompassed some 2.5 million square kilometers, and individual slaves often found themselves thrown together with strangers as they marched, in some cases, hundreds of miles from the interior. As a result, only rarely did enslaved Africans encounter slaves from the same ethnic or linguistic background. The process of selling slaves in the colonies further increased cultural mixing as merchants purchased groups of slaves whom they then resold to planters, and planters often purchased individual slaves from more than one African region. During the early 1680s, for example, the privateer and planter Henry Morgan purchased 67 slaves: 14 from the Gold Coast, 20 from the Bight of Benin, 28 from the Bight of Biafra, and 5 from an unspecified region. Analyzing the purchases made by 22 Jamaican planters from the Royal African Company between 1674 and 1708, the historian Trevor Burnard found that all 22 acquired slaves from at least two different African regions, and most—17 out of the 22—bought slaves from at least three regions. The cultures that emerged in the region were thus hybrid ones that drew from a variety of traditions.

There is evidence to support both interpretations. Olaudah Equiano recalled that when he arrived in Barbados, some slaves informed him that he and others would "see many of our country people . . . and sure enough, soon after we were landed, there came to us Africans of all languages," suggesting both that slaves in the Greater Caribbean encountered peoples from familiar backgrounds but also from a diverse range of African cultures. Likewise, when Thomas Thistlewood observed "Negro Diversions—odd Music, Motion, etc." in the streets of Kingston, he noted "the Negroes of each Nation by themselves."[16] Conversely, the planter-historian Bryan Edwards maintained that although slaves came from different parts of Africa, the conditions of plantation slavery erased cultural differences that separated "one nation from another in Negroes newly imported" and created a creolized identity marked by a "similitude of manners, and a uniformity of character" among the enslaved.[17] Clearly some slaves maintained some form of ethnic identity at various times in various colonies—although notions of such ethnicity were often recent creations—but it also is clear that even when particular groups appeared numerically dominant—such as the slaves from the Gold Coast in seventeenth-century Barbados or Jamaica—they still needed to negotiate with sizable numbers of slaves with different traditions and practices. Throughout the Greater Caribbean, slaves drawn from diverse parts of West Africa had to find common ground on a wide range of cultural issues.

Music provides one example of these cultural negotiations. When the natural philosopher Hans Sloane visited a plantation in Jamaica in 1688, he witnessed a dozen or so enslaved Africans perform three songs using various instruments, including rattles tied to their hands and ankles, drums made from gourds, and a lute. The plantation overseer informed Sloane that the first piece was an Angolan song (from West Central Africa), the second a Popo (from the Bight of Benin), and the third a Koromanti (from the Gold Coast). What the overseer termed a Koromanti piece of music, however, employed rhythms and instruments, particularly a wooden board with keys called a *sansa* (or *mbira*), widely used in Congo but not common in the Gold Coast. In other words, the slaves from different parts of West Africa observed by Sloane maintained their own distinctive musical practices but also borrowed from one another to create a new, hybrid form. Likewise, while slaves re-created familiar West African instruments such as the banjo, over time they also incorporated European instruments into their music, most notably the violin, or fiddle.

A similar process occurred with language. Africans arrived speaking a variety of languages and dialects but gradually developed a pidgin language by merging different languages, including English, into usable speech. In some cases, enslaved Africans made use of a secondary, trading language such as Akan that was employed by different groups and the secondary language

The Old Plantation. A contemporary painting of enslaved Africans dancing on a Lowcountry plantation. Courtesy of the Abby Aldrich Rockefeller Folk Art Museum, The Colonial Williamsburg Foundation. Gift of Abby Aldrich Rockefeller.

became a primary language over time. One advertisement for a runaway in Jamaica, for example, noted that the Mandingo woman had arrived only five months earlier but already knew enough Akan, and some English, "to be understood."[18] Over time, this pidgin became a creole language, meaning it served as the speaker's primary language. The development of pidgin and creole languages occurred throughout the region. In Jamaica, Akan speakers from the Gold Coast along with Ewe speakers from the Bight of Benin provided the linguistics foundation for a creole language. In the Lowcountry, Gullah developed from a mixture of English and languages spoken in Angola and Senegambia. The ongoing importance of African languages and the distinct creole languages that emerged over time was yet another factor distinguishing slave culture in the Greater Caribbean from the Chesapeake.

Religious practices among enslaved Africans, likewise, exhibited continuities with African traditions as well as adaptations to new circumstances in the Greater Caribbean. Enslaved Africans came from a variety of religious backgrounds. Some from Senegambia were Muslim, and had been for centuries before the

Atlantic slave trade developed. A few who came from the Kingdom of Kongo were Christians (rulers of Kongo had converted to Catholicism in the fifteenth century), or at least had some exposure to Christian beliefs and practices before their arrival in the Greater Caribbean. The vast majority of slaves, however, embraced traditional belief systems. These varied widely across West Africa, but they shared some basic elements, including a belief that supernatural forces acted in the world and that sacred leaders mediated with such forces, helping to heal the sick, avenge wrongs, and resolve disputes by uncovering the truth. Another similarity concerned the afterlife. Most traditional West African religions held that the spirits of the dead traveled to another world but that they also remained involved in the lives of the living. Worship of ancestors figured prominently among groups throughout West Africa.

Slaves transported to the Greater Caribbean struggled to maintain their religious beliefs, but the new and alien physical environment of the region and the harshness of the plantation regime created major challenges. It is unlikely that most Muslim slaves, for example, could stop work to pray several times a day, although scattered evidence of fasting, prayer mats, and Muslim names, including "Mahomet," testify to efforts by some to maintain their Islamic faith. Likewise, those slaves who followed traditional practices found themselves cut off from sacred sites and from the plants and animals that helped mediate between natural and supernatural forces. Nevertheless, slaves managed to recreate many aspects of their former religious life in the Greater Caribbean. As one Anglican minister in eighteenth-century Barbados noted dismissively, slaves "are very tenaciously addicted to the Rites, Ceremonies, and Superstitions of their own Countries." Even creole slaves, the minister maintained, "cannot be intirely weaned from these Customs."[19]

One such ceremony involved burial of the dead. Ideas about the proper length and necessary rituals for funerals varied among slaves from different parts of West Africa and from different religious backgrounds. So did the actual place of burial. Some groups, particularly those from the Gold Coast, buried the dead under their houses, while others employed special burial grounds outside their villages. Slaves literally had to find common ground on such questions. Slave burials often involved a boisterous procession to the grave site. Charles Leslie observed that slaves in Jamaica "scream out in a terrible Manner" during burials. This was "not the Effect of Grief but of Joy," Leslie wrote, as the mourners believed that the dead would soon return to Africa, a belief that developed in the context of plantation slavery and was present throughout the region.[20] Mourners followed the West African practices of placing various goods in the grave—sometimes on top of the coffin, sometimes inside it—that the deceased would need on his or her journey to another realm, including food, clothing, rum, and tobacco. Such offerings also sought to appease the dead so that they would not haunt the living. The amount and variety of goods depended on the status of the individual. The practice had West African roots, but the goods themselves often reflected the economic integration of the Atlantic world and beyond. The grave of a prominent healer on the Newton plantation in Barbados included a pipe whose design mirrored those from the Gold Coast as well as a necklace fashioned from cowrie shells from the Indian Ocean basin, glass beads manufactured in Europe, fish bones, dog teeth, and one large bead from India. Slaves sometimes borrowed—or attempted to borrow—European funeral practices as well. In the middle of the eighteenth century, for example, the legislatures in both Antigua and South Carolina banned slaves from wearing funeral "scarfs," sashes worn at Christian funerals, suggesting that slaves had started to adopt the practice.

Beliefs about the role of supernatural forces in the world also survived the Middle Passage from Africa and played a prominent role in the lives of enslaved Africans. *Obeah* (or *obi, obia,* and other variations) served as the general term for a range of rituals and practices that involved harnessing supernatural forces for good or evil. Slaves from many parts of West Africa believed that such forces influenced events in the world. Such beliefs were not all that different from colonists' ideas about Providence, witchcraft, and astrology, to cite three early modern European answers to questions about why things happened, but West Africans afforded greater latitude for the operation of supernatural forces in everyday affairs. *Obeah* men and women combined the role of doctor, diviner, protector, and sorcerer.

Individuals who were sick or injured, who had lost valuable goods, who sought to know the future, who feared that someone had cast a spell on them, or who sought revenge on enemies turned to *obeah* men and women for help. These spiritual leaders in turn employed a variety of plants and objects—bones, blood, glass, animal bones, teeth, and feathers—to create medicines and charms to heal and to protect. Although the transfer of various plants from West Africa meant that slave healers at times could turn to familiar sources for medicines, they also had to learn about new plants and their properties, knowledge they gained over time from native informants and by a process of trial and error. In addition, they gradually incorporated European materials such as rum into traditional recipes and practices. Such adaptations allowed *obeah* to remain vibrant and vital.

Plants and charms could heal, but they also could be used to poison or bewitch others. Indeed, most whites tended to equate *obeah* with diabolical ends, and beginning in the 1760s they took steps to limit the practice (an anti-*obeah* law is still on the books in Jamaica). *Obeah* certainly involved casting spells on enemies, but it more frequently served to ease individual suffering, to mediate social conflicts, and to protect individuals from evil. Not surprisingly, *obeah* men and women occupied prominent places within slave society, their powers both respected and feared.

Although planters occasionally stepped in to limit—or attempt to limit—religious practices among enslaved Africans that they viewed as threatening, they generally paid little attention to slave religion, and they made almost no effort to convert slaves. Indeed, Christianity exerted only a minimal influence on the lives of slaves for most of the seventeenth and eighteenth centuries. It was only in the second half of the eighteenth century that serious missionary activity began in the region. Prior to that, missionaries like the Anglican Francis Le Jau in the Lowcountry encountered indifference, if not outright resistance, from enslaved Africans, who had little interest in what one historian has called "the thin spiritual gruel of the Protestant liturgies."[21] They also faced hostility from white planters, who had little interest in lessening the cultural divide that separated them from their slaves. The series of religious revivals in North America during the 1740s known as the Great Awakening, and the arrival of Moravian and Methodist ministers in the British islands during the 1750s and 1760s, helped spark new interest in Christianizing slaves. Still, only a small percentage of the enslaved population converted to Christianity during this period. It was only later—in the 1780s and 1790s and, most powerfully, in the nineteenth century—that Christianity emerged as a significant force in the lives of many Africans and African Americans in the Greater Caribbean. Even then, the continuing power of African practices and beliefs encouraged slaves to merge elements of Christianity into existing cosmologies rather than simply replacing one set of beliefs with the other.

Housing provides yet another example of cultural continuity, adaptation, and change. Planters determined where slave houses were built, setting aside specific tracts of land for slave quarters, but slaves across the region generally built their own houses. Most were one- or two- room, rectangular, wattle-and-daub structures that were grouped together into what were essentially small villages. Sticks provided a loose framework (wattle) for the walls, which were then covered (daubed) with mud or wet clay. Seashells were sometimes mixed with the clay to form what were known as tabby walls. Roofs were made of thatch. Most early structures did not have fireplaces. Instead, cooking and other activities took place in the yard. Many of these basic construction techniques were common in Europe as well as in many parts of West Africa, and tracing specific influences is difficult, but certain elements clearly reflected West African practices. The doors of slave houses in Jamaica and elsewhere, for example, often were located on the short end of the building, not the long side as was common in Europe. Likewise, steeply pitched thatched roofs with low-hanging eaves resembled West African styles, although the actual thatching sometimes incorporated Native American techniques. Slaves also gradually incorporated European features, including internal chimneys and wooden or stone walls, so that by the end of the eighteenth century slave houses represented an amalgamation of various African, European, and Native American building practices. In housing as in other areas, slave culture throughout the Greater Caribbean displayed ongoing creative adaptations to new peoples and to new environments.

Heavily outnumbered by their slaves throughout the Greater Caribbean, colonists attempted to control the lives of slaves and to limit any activities that threatened the security of the plantation system. As individuals and as a group, colonists drafted informal guides and formal laws that addressed all aspects of slave life—what slaves could eat, what they could wear, when they could leave the plantation, what social activities they could engage in—and they punished violations brutally. One slave caught stealing a pig in seventeenth-century Barbados was whipped repeatedly for the offense. The owner then cut off the slave's ear, roasted it, and forced him to eat it. Another visitor to Barbados noted that individual colonists "beat [slaves] mercilessly for the least fault" in order to "intimidate the others and to impress fear and dutifulness upon them."[22] Formal laws sanctioned such brutality as the only means of controlling what slave codes termed a "dangerous kind of people," and individual planters devised an array of brutal measures to punish slaves and assert their power. Colonists mixed rewards with punishments, but at base violence and terror supported the plantation system.

On one level, such techniques succeeded. The plantation system in the British Greater Caribbean survived for two centuries, as slavery was not abolished in Britain's Caribbean colonies and in the United States until the 1830s and 1860s, respectively. On another level, however, colonists never achieved the degree of control they desired. Despite the violence employed against them, slaves actively resisted efforts to dominate and dehumanize them. Doing so forced planters to recognize their basic humanity, as well as certain rights and privileges that slaves claimed—for example, the right to market food from their provision grounds, the right to the property that they had accumulated, and the right to pass on that property to their children. The actions of slaves thus helped define the limits of planter authority and ensured that the master-slave relationship involved ongoing negotiation rather than simple domination.

Slave resistance in the Greater Caribbean took a variety of forms. Individual and group actions existed on a continuum that ranged from theft, damaging equipment, and running away to arson, poison, and ultimately armed rebellion. Most common were everyday acts of defiance such as feigning illness, setting sugar fields ablaze, breaking mill equipment, and other forms of work-related sabotage. Such acts did not threaten the plantation regime, but they undermined the functioning of individual plantations, and thus planter profits. Poisoning represented a more direct assault on individual planters. Slaves periodically employed their vast knowledge of plants and the natural world to fashion poisons that were used against planters. Eight slaves were executed in Antigua between 1722 and 1763 for poisoning. A rash of poisoning in South Carolina resulted in the execution of six slaves in 1751.

A far more common form of resistance was running away. Slaves ran away constantly throughout the Greater Caribbean, and did so for a variety of reasons. Some sought to connect, if only briefly, with husbands, wives, or children. Others sought to escape punishment for some infraction. Still others escaped plantations to avoid onerous tasks, and not surprisingly, the number of runaways waxed and waned according to seasonal labor demands. Lowcountry slaves ran away most frequently during the summer months, especially June, when slaves began the grueling work of hoeing rice fields and in the winter months, when they engaged in the arduous work of pounding rice. Sugar island slaves ran away most often at the end of the harvest, when provisions ran low. In most cases these runaways traveled only short distances and were gone only for a short period of time. Nevertheless, this *petite marronage,* as scholars term it, provided some temporary respite from hard labor.

Less common but more serious for planters were slaves who managed to escape permanently and establish themselves in independent communities. The prospects for this *grand marronage* depended heavily on geography, specifically having a place where runaway slaves could find shelter and live beyond the reach of colonial authorities. Small, flat, and deforested Barbados offered no such places, and no Maroon communities developed on that island or in the Leeward Islands, beyond a few small groups in the seventeenth century.

The Lowcountry offered greater possibilities, and some slaves managed to escape into the interior and establish small Maroon communities, but their ability to survive depended on relations with Native Americans, and Carolina planters sought to enlist natives as slave catchers, particularly after the Yamasee War. As a result, although some slaves found refuge among Indians, no large, permanent Maroon communities developed in the Carolina Backcountry. A more important sanctuary for Lowcountry slaves was Spanish Florida. As early as the 1690s, but most notably in the 1730s, the Spanish king issued edicts granting freedom to any English slave who made it to Florida. Hundreds of slaves took up the offer and made their way south. In 1738, the Spanish established a separate town of freed slaves, Garcia Real de Santa Teresa de Mose. Spanish authorities envisioned the town's free black militia as a first line of defense for nearby St. Augustine as well as a beacon to encourage more Carolina slaves to flee, which it proved to be: at least seventy slaves escaped to Florida in 1738 alone. Lowcountry colonists, led by James Oglethorpe, struck back in 1740, leveling the fort and the town, but it was rebuilt in 1752 and remained a free black town until the British gained possession of Florida at the end of the Seven Years War.

The largest and most important Maroon communities formed in Jamaica, as groups of slaves who rebelled against the English sought refuge in the mountains. One group of Koromantis set up a Maroon community in the western mountains of Jamaica in 1673, where they were joined by more Koromantis following a 1690 rebellion. The initial leader was a slave named Cudjoe, and when he died, his son, also named Cudjoe, took over and ruled the community until the 1760s. An earlier group of Maroons established themselves in the Blue Mountains in eastern Jamaica. An *obeah* woman named Nanny became their most important eighteenth-century leader, and the settlement became known as Nanny Town. Colonial officials waged a series of wars against the Maroons in the seventeenth and early eighteenth century but failed to defeat them. Unable to dislodge the Maroons, the British signed a treaty with them in 1739. Jamaican and British officials recognized the existence of both communities, and Maroons secured the right to hunt, to move freely around the island, and to trade with colonists. In exchange, the Maroons promised to return runaway slaves and to aid colonists in suppressing any slave rebellions.

The most significant form of resistance was armed rebellion. Rebellions were relatively infrequent events, although they occurred far more frequently in the Greater Caribbean than they did in other parts of British America. Groups of slaves in Jamaica rose up in 1673, in 1675, and again in 1678, each time killing numerous colonists and destroying property. A larger rebellion occurred in 1685–86, when hundreds of slaves in several parishes in Jamaica rebelled, seized guns, and waged war for a year before Jamaican colonists managed to defeat them.

Other colonies also experienced the threat of rebellion at various points in time. Enslaved Africans led by several Koromantis in Barbados plotted in 1675 to overthrow the planters, seize control of the island, and create a Koromanti state, but a female slave revealed details to authorities and the plot was crushed violently. Six slaves were burned alive and eleven others beheaded. Despite such horrors, some slaves remained defiant until the end. One leader of the plot, a man named Tony, refused to name fellow conspirators, declaring to his torturers, "If you Roast me today, you cannot Roast me tomorrow."[23] An even more elaborate plot was discovered in Antigua in 1736. Slaves planned their rebellion around a grand ball celebrating the anniversary of the coronation of George II. The plan called for a skilled carpenter named Tomboy, hired to build chairs for the celebration, to plant gunpowder in the building. After elites gathered for the celebration, the slaves planned to blow up the residence and seize control of the island. As happened in the Barbados plot, an informant revealed details of the conspiracy and officials quickly and violently executed eighty-eight slaves—seventy-seven were burned alive, six were gibbeted (left in cages to starve to death), and five broken on the wheel. Forty-seven others were banished from the island, most to nearby Spanish islands, but some went to British North America. Some scholars have questioned whether such plots really existed or whether they simply reflected the fears of a besieged white minority, but whether they were real or imagined, hundreds of enslaved Africans perished in the wake of these events as panicked whites sought to repress brutally any threat to their power.

Enslaved Africans took up arms in the Lowcountry in September of 1739. The exact origin and goals of the Stono Rebellion—named after a nearby river—are murky. Most scholars suggest that the rebellion was planned and that slaves sought freedom in Spanish Florida, but more recently Peter Hoffer has argued that the rebellion was a spur-of-the-moment action by slaves on a work crew tasked with digging trenches. Regardless, a slave named Jemmy emerged as the leader. Jemmy and the core group of rebels were among the thousands of slaves from the Angola-Kongo region who had arrived in the Lowcountry during the 1730s. Many may have been former soldiers. They also may have been Catholic, another factor that might explain a march to St. Augustine. Regardless, on the morning of September 9, 1739, a small group of slaves broke into a storehouse, killed the storekeeper, seized weapons, and began a march south. They were joined by dozens more slaves attracted by drumming, dancing, and colorful banners, common elements of Kongolese warfare. By midafternoon their numbers had grown to about a hundred when they halted the march, perhaps hoping more recruits would join them. Instead, the South Carolina militia arrived, and a pitched battle ensued. The militia eventually managed to defeat the slaves, although dozens escaped and small skirmishes continued for days. In the end, some twenty whites and forty slaves were killed in battle or executed thereafter. Militiamen cut off the heads of several slaves and placed them on posts alongside the road into Charleston as a warning to others. In the wake of the rebellion, local officials took steps to tighten restrictions on slaves, passing a new slave code in 1740, and, more significantly, placing a high tax on slave imports. The tariff worked, and the importation of Africans into the Lowcountry fell dramatically during the 1740s, but increasing planter confidence and a strengthening economy led to a repeal of the tariff by the end of the decade and slave imports quickly returned to prerebellion levels.

The largest slave rebellion in the Greater Caribbean occurred in Jamaica in 1760. The leaders of Tacky's War were Koromanti slaves who, echoing the 1675 plot in Barbados, hoped to destroy the white population and then divide the island into a series of small states based on West African polities. The rebellion broke out on April 7, shortly after British troops were redeployed from the island during the Seven Years War. Enslaved Africans often had knowledge of troop movements and took advantage of the perceived weakness to strike. Fighting began in St. Mary parish on Jamaica's north coast, but it spread quickly across the island. Thousands of slaves—perhaps as many as 30,000—rose up and attacked plantations. The fighting lasted for months, generating tremendous panic among whites. Jamaican officials called on the Maroons to aid British troops and local militias in putting down the rebellion, and although some questioned their loyalty, the Maroons played a key role in the fighting. One was credited with killing Tacky himself, weakening the rebellion. The combination of forces defeated most of the slaves by October but not before slaves had destroyed over £100,000 worth of property, killed at least sixty whites, an equal number of free blacks, and sent shock waves through the planter class. Roughly four hundred slaves died in the fighting. Another one hundred were executed, and five hundred were exiled from the island. Because planters feared that *obeah* had played some role in the rebellion, they quickly passed a law mandating death, imprisonment, or exile for any slave caught practicing it. Despite such measures, neither *obeah* nor rebellion ceased, and Jamaican slaves revolted again in 1765 and 1766.

That Tacky's War and numerous other instances of armed revolt took place in Jamaica is noteworthy. That colony experienced more frequent, and more violent, rebellions than any other in the region. Demography was one factor, as slaves outnumbered whites by a large ratio, but geography, again, played a significant role. The same conditions that allowed Maroon communities to form, namely, rugged, mountainous terrain, also supported slave insurrections. Slaves in Barbados and the Leeward Islands faced the prospect of having to secure the entire island in open conflict. Lowcountry slaves had a smaller numerical advantage against whites, and colonists could draw additional support from neighboring colonies and from Native Americans. Slaves in Jamaica, by contrast, could rebel and seek sanctuary in the interior while they regrouped. Such conditions likely encouraged slaves to strike out for freedom and to strike back against whites.

Slaves never managed to overturn the plantation regimes of the Greater Caribbean, but their efforts to resist planter control had important consequences. In the long term, slave resistance undermined planter efforts to defend slavery as an institution that benefited "heathen" and "uncivilized" Africans. Several slave rebellions in the Caribbean in the early nineteenth century highlighted the violence at the foundation of the plantation system and heightened calls for abolition. In the immediate context of the seventeenth and eighteenth centuries, slave resistance forced planters to recognize that their power over slaves had limits. Despite the absolute power planters held in law, the actual functioning of plantations required that they not exercise that power fully. Even when they wanted to assert their power, planters at times faced strenuous opposition from slaves determined to maintain practices and traditions that they increasingly claimed as rights.

Ultimately, the variety of means by which enslaved Africans resisted their enslavement created enough social space to enable slaves to pursue activities that gave meaning to their lives. Slaves independently formed families, celebrated births, weddings, and deaths, built houses, tended their own fields, sold the products of that labor in markets, and purchased goods with the profits. None of these activities and customary rights were secure. Planters could interfere with any or all of them, but doing so risked undermining the workings of the plantation, and therefore their profits. Slave resistance thus checked, at least to a small degree, the unbridled power of planters and secured a small degree of autonomy for themselves. Amidst the death and brutality that defined slavery and the plantation system in the Greater Caribbean, slaves used that autonomy to create distinct and vibrant cultures. They did so by drawing upon diverse African beliefs and practices, adapting them to the particulars of the American environment, and selectively borrowing from Native American and European traditions. The result was a rich culture whose legacy in language, food, music, religious beliefs, and countless other ways is visible today throughout the region— and beyond.

SIX

Creole Societies

IN THE FALL OF 1751, George Washington and his older half brother Lawrence set sail from Virginia for Barbados. Lawrence suffered from what contemporaries called consumption, now known as tuberculosis, and he hoped that travel to the warmer climate of the islands would help alleviate his suffering. Having survived a difficult five-week voyage across a storm-tossed ocean, Washington arrived in Bridgetown in early November. Washington's terse diary entries provide only fleeting glimpses of his thoughts, but it is clear that the island struck him, as it did many others, as a wondrous garden. Everywhere he turned, Washington wrote, the island presented "beautiful prospects" with "fields of Cain, Corn, Fruit Trees, &c in a delightful Green." The gently rising slopes provided views of the shimmering Caribbean Sea on one side and the swells of the Atlantic on the other.

Within days of their landing, the Washingtons found themselves inundated with invitations from local planters. Gedney Clarke, a merchant originally from Massachusetts but with connections to Virginia, asked them to join his family for dinner and to watch the fireworks on Gunpowder Day, the anniversary of the foiled Catholic plot of 1605 to blow up Parliament celebrated throughout the British Empire. A few days later, George and Lawrence dined at the home of Judge Satus Maynard. After a sumptuous dinner, the table was filled with "the greatest Collection of Fruits I have yet seen," including pomegranates, oranges, lemons, apples, guavas, and pineapples. The other gentlemen at the table invited the brothers to dine with them in the near future, and Maynard and his wife insisted that the brothers "spend some Weeks with him and promis'd nothing should be wanting to render our stay agreeable," but Lawrence demurred, citing his health. Instead the brothers rented rooms at an inn a mile above Bridgetown for what George thought an expensive rate of £15 a month, not including laundry or alcohol.

During the next several days, Washington attended church services, likely at St. Michael's Anglican Church in Bridgetown. Several planters invited him to dine with the island's Beefsteak and Tripe Club, a local version of an eighteenth-century English club whose motto proclaimed "Beef and liberty." On November 15, Washington attended a popular contemporary play, *The London Merchant: Or, the History of George Barnwell,* likely his first theatrical performance. Two days later he came down with smallpox and spent the next month in bed. Fortunately for Washington, the experience left him with only a few minor scars, and more importantly, immunity to a disease that plagued the Continental army during the American Revolution. George recovered, but Lawrence's consumption continued, and he determined to try his luck in Bermuda, this time alone. On December 22, George set sail for Virginia, ending his one and only sojourn outside the North American mainland.[1]

Although his stay was brief, Washington's experiences and observations highlight some of the central features that defined life for European colonists in the Greater Caribbean by the mid-eighteenth century, including its great wealth, generous hospitality, dangerous disease environment, and a culture that was simultaneously exotic and thoroughly English. Like new arrivals in all parts of British America, colonists in the Greater Caribbean desired to replicate the world they had left behind. For British migrants, this meant re-creating British institutions, social mores, and cultural practices as best they could—a process often termed *Anglicization.*

At the same time, colonists in the Greater Caribbean, like those elsewhere in British America, had to adapt to the novel social and environmental conditions they encountered, and such adaptations produced new and distinctive cultural forms. Colonists, in other words, became creoles. This dynamic between change and continuity, between creolization and Anglicization, occurred in all colonies, but conditions in the Greater Caribbean exaggerated both processes. On the one hand, the region's climate required significant adaptations to what English colonists considered proper types of food, clothing, and architecture, while the presence of massive slave majorities produced distinctive social relations among whites. On the other hand, those same realities caused colonists to place particular emphasis on the re-creation of traditional English forms, institutions, and practices as evidence of their success in establishing what they viewed as settled and productive societies. Moreover, the wealth generated by sugar and rice enabled colonists to indulge their desires for English goods, English manners, and English education more fully than their counterparts elsewhere. Some even succeeded in retiring permanently to England while still collecting profits from their plantations. Ultimately, these competing forces produced colonial societies that appeared thoroughly British in some ways, yet distinctly creole in many others.

SOCIAL DIVISIONS

One of the first things that struck young George Washington as he traveled around Barbados was the extreme wealth of its inhabitants. Unlike in Virginia, there were "few who may be call'd midling people" on the island. Residents, Washington wrote, were either "very rich or very poor." Washington exaggerated, and colonial society was more complex than he described, but he was not wrong in his essential observation. Planters and merchants in the Greater Caribbean had amassed huge fortunes by the middle of the eighteenth century, and their wealth far exceeded that of elites in other colonies. When Peter Beckford the younger died in 1735, his estate included ownership or part ownership of seventeen plantations and five livestock pens as well as 1,669 enslaved Africans. One report valued the total estate at nearly £300,000. During periods of high sugar prices, Beckford's slaves produced crops worth £28,600 annually, while the estates of another Jamaican planter, Simon Taylor, generated over £17,000 of income during peak years later in the century. Wealthy English landlords received a healthy £5,000–£10,000 from their properties during this period. A prosperous Virginia tobacco planter like Daniel Parke Custis, by contrast, earned roughly £1,300 a year. Overall, the average wealth of a white West

Indian colonist in 1774 was an astonishing £1,042, compared to just £38 for New Englanders, £45 for those residing in the Middle Colonies, and £92 for colonists in the mainland plantation colonies. Lowcountry planters did not approach the wealth of the West Indian sugar grandees, but their wealth far exceeded that of other mainland elites. Based on estate inventories, nine of the ten richest men in mainland America in 1774 were Lowcountry rice planters.

Some planters amassed large enough fortunes to escape the region and return to England as absentees. These absentees maintained ownership of their estates and collected the profits, but they left the day-to day management in the hands of attorneys and overseers who remained in the colonies. As early as the 1670s and 1680s, many wealthy Barbadians removed themselves to England, among them Henry Drax, whose father, James, had introduced sugar to the island forty years earlier. The trend continued in Barbados and elsewhere during the eighteenth century, although the level of absenteeism varied among the different islands. Absentees owned 50 percent of all plantation land on St. Kitts by 1745. By contrast, absentees owned only about one-quarter of lands in Jamaica and numbered only about 10 percent of the island's landowners in the decades before the American Revolution. Ironically, Barbados, the colony that led the transition to sugar and produced the first absentees, always had a greater proportion of resident owners than other islands, the result of less fertile soil, smaller plantations, and thus smaller profits.

West Indian absentees occupied a prominent place in English social, cultural, and political life. Often derided as social upstarts with poor manners and worse taste, absentee planters nevertheless had enough wealth to purchase respectability. Some married into noble families. Others built or purchased country estates and set themselves up as members of the local gentry. Among the most impressive estates were Harewood House, country seat of the Lascelles family of Barbados, and Fonthill Splendens, a 5,000-acre estate belonging to the Jamaican absentee William Beckford. One official noted that by the end of the eighteenth century, "there were scarcely ten miles together throughout the country where the house and estate of a rich West Indian was not to be seen."[2] Their wealth and social position provided entry into British politics, and a number of West Indian absentees were elected to the House of Commons. These planters, along with merchants trading to the islands, formed the foundation of a West India lobby powerful enough to influence British colonial policy at various moments during the eighteenth century.

Absenteeism occurred less frequently among rice planters, as the profits from rice generally did not reach the same dizzying heights as those from sugar. Nevertheless, the Lowcountry was the only part of North America where the practice developed to any significant extent, and more than one visitor noted that Lowcountry elites were "more attached to the Mother Country, than those [from] Provinces which lie more to the Northward."[3] By the 1770s, as many as fifty Lowcountry colonists, including the Middleton, Fenwick, and Izard families, were living in England while maintaining ownership of their Carolina plantations. Numerous other members of the Lowcountry elite, including Henry Laurens, spent some considerable time abroad for business or schooling. Carolinians clustered together in the expanding residential neighborhoods of London's West End, sometimes with several families living on the same street. West Indian absentees often lived nearby, and members of both groups socialized frequently.

Lowcountry planters also engaged in a more limited form of seasonal absenteeism, as planters and their families routinely abandoned their rice plantations for several months each year. Many moved to Charleston for the summer season, where fresh sea breezes provided a healthier environment. Still others traveled to northern cities. Newport, Rhode Island, became a favorite in the middle of the eighteenth century and a sizable community of Lowcountry absentees formed there each year. Regardless of where they went, planters turned over the day-to-day management of the plantations to overseers for months at a time. Whether seasonal or permanent, absenteeism distinguished the plantation societies of the Greater Caribbean.

Wealthy planters and merchants who remained in the colonies lived lives of extravagance and luxury. They traveled about in fancy imported carriages and coaches. They filled their houses with expensive imported goods—fine mahogany furniture, silverware, china sets, books, paintings, musical instruments.

Josiah Quincy from Massachusetts marveled at the house owned by Charleston merchant Miles Brewton. "The grandest hall I ever beheld," Quincy wrote, "azure blue satin window curtains, rich blue paper with gilt . . . most elegant pictures, excessive grand and costly looking glasses."[4] Elite men like Brewton and Gedney Clarke engaged in elaborate displays of hospitality, treating neighbors and visitors such as Quincy or the Washingtons to great feasts. Some spent small fortunes creating idyllic landscapes on their plantations. Peter Manigault's Lowcountry estate featured Chinese temples and bridges, while his fellow Lowcountry planter Henry Laurens employed an English gardener to tend his alpine strawberries and French pears. The Jamaican planter Sir Charles Price constructed a 2,000-acre rural retreat in the hills of St. Mary parish that featured imported deer, an octagonal salon, and a series of walks shaded by coconut and cabbage trees culminating in a grand arch overlooking the northern Caribbean Sea.

Not all visitors were impressed by such extravagances. Several criticized planters as lazy, wasteful, and pampered tyrants whose lifestyle deviated from accepted English norms. Thomas Tryon, who spent several years in Barbados in the seventeenth century, issued one of the most stinging critiques of the planter's social life. "Luxurious masters stretch themselves on soft Beds and Couches," he wrote. "They drink Wine in overflowing Bowls, and set their brains afloat without either Rudder or Compass, in an Ocean of other strong and various Drinks, . . . and vomit up their Shame and Filthiness."[5] Others throughout the seventeenth and eighteenth centuries decried the planters' casual brutality toward slaves (even if they stopped short of condemning slavery itself), their base materialism, their self-interest, and their self-importance. Whether they marveled at or condemned planter lifestyles, all commentators emphasized the huge fortunes that permitted such excess.

Wealthy elites dominated social, political, and economic life in the Greater Caribbean, but not all colonists were rich planters or merchants, George Washington's observations notwithstanding. A significant number of "midling" people found economic opportunities as bookkeepers, overseers, and attorneys for plantations, especially on sugar estates owned by absentees. Others worked as artisans or shopkeepers in Charleston, Bridgetown,

Kingston, and other urban areas. Many of these colonists earned significant wages, enough to allow them to purchase slaves, who could be hired out to provide additional income. Still other whites managed to carve out space as small planters, growing provision crops for domestic markets or producing smaller staple crops such as coffee, pimento, and ginger for export. Thomas Thistlewood is one example of the possibilities for upward mobility for such men. Thistlewood arrived in Jamaica in 1751 with limited resources. He worked for a time as an overseer on a sugar estate, managed to save enough to purchase a slave, and several years later had enough money to acquire a livestock pen. He steadily expanded his operations and purchased more slaves, who in turn generated more income. Thistlewood never became a sugar planter, but at his death in 1786, he owned thirty-four slaves and had amassed an estate valued at £2,408. Opportunities for small planters and penkeepers like Thistlewood were greatest in Jamaica and the Lowcountry, where land was more available, but even Barbados and Antigua offered some space for small farmers and middling artisans.

These prospects for advancement ensured a steady supply of new immigrants, approximately 89,000 during the eighteenth century. A significant number of these migrants came from Scotland. Prior to 1707, Scots had limited access to England's American colonies, but the Act of Union that created "Great Britain" also opened up the colonies to Scots. Pushed out by limited economic opportunities at home and pulled in by the prospects of riches abroad, some 17,000 Scots, mostly young men, migrated to the islands during the eighteenth century. Most went to Jamaica and the Leewards, where the still-developing sugar economies held out the promise of economic advancement. A number of these Scottish migrants worked as doctors on plantations. Scotland offered some of the best medical training in the world during the eighteenth century, but with limited prospects at home, many doctors sought opportunities in the wealthy—and sickly—Greater Caribbean. Two-thirds of the doctors in Antigua were Scots. Likewise, 60 percent of doctors in the Lowcountry between 1725 and 1780 were either Scottish or educated at Scottish universities.

Many of these Scottish immigrants achieved a good deal of success. Walter Tullideph was one. Tullideph had trained as a surgeon in Edinburgh, but with limited prospects he migrated to Antigua in 1726. He operated briefly as a small merchant, importing and selling Scottish linens and other goods, but he quickly began treating sick planters and slaves on numerous plantations. His medical practice provided a good income, and, as his wealth grew, so did his social standing. In 1736 he married a young widow with a sizable estate and set himself up as a planter. He soon found himself appointed or elected to a variety of political offices on the island. Tullideph steadily expanded his plantation operations, so that by 1757 he owned 536 acres of land and 271 enslaved Africans. At that point, Tullideph returned to Scotland, eventually purchasing an estate there for £10,000 while maintaining ownership of his Antigua property. Tullideph had achieved what so many sought in their ventures to the Greater Caribbean; land, wealth, and reentry into British society with enhanced social and economic standing. He even married one of his daughters into the Scottish aristocracy.

Not all migrants fared as well as Tullideph. The plantation economies of the Greater Caribbean provided fabulous fortunes for many colonists and good opportunities for others, but a significant number of colonists lived in poverty. Governor James Glen reported in midcentury that roughly 20 percent of Carolina's population had only "a bare subsistance."[6] Many congregated in and around Charleston, receiving support from the city's parish vestries. Even on smaller islands with limited land, numerous poor whites scraped out a living by fishing, manufacturing cotton hammocks, and hiring themselves out as laborers. Others worked as tenant farmers, renting small plots of land from larger planters. In Barbados, their physical appearance earned them the derisive nickname "redlegs."

Although vast differences in economic condition separated the lives of rich planters from those of the overseers they employed and from the poor living on the edge of urban centers, the presence of overwhelming numbers of enslaved Africans in all of the colonies ensured that class divisions remained muted. A shared sense of racial identity helped unify whites of different economic status. According to the eighteenth-century Jamaican planter and historian Bryan Edwards, "A conscious equality, throughout all ranks and conditions" pervaded white society. "The poorest White person seems to consider himself nearly on a level with the richest, and, emboldened by this idea, approaches his employer with extended hand, and a freedom, which, in the countries of Europe, is seldom displayed by men in the lower orders of life."[7] Even while working as an overseer, Thomas Thistlewood found himself welcomed into the homes of elite planters in Jamaica, and his experience was common throughout the region. Moreover, the limited size of the white population meant that nonelite whites occupied important posts in a variety of local institutions, serving on juries, in parish vestries, and in the militia. Shared service in such institutions further strengthened the bonds between elite and ordinary whites.

Ethnic differences also mattered less than in Britain. Scottish immigrants like Tullideph faced relatively little discrimination from English planters. Instead, they were welcomed into communities desperate for more white inhabitants. French Huguenots prospered in South Carolina, many eventually assimilating into the Anglican Church. Even Irish Catholics found acceptance in the region's social hierarchy, as long as they did not flaunt their religion. Numerous Irish Catholics on Montserrat occupied positions of social and political authority, and Irish residents openly celebrated St. Patrick's Day well into the eighteenth century.

Jewish migrants also found a place in the colonies of the Greater Caribbean. Jewish settlers fleeing Brazil after the Portuguese reconquest in the 1650s aided the development of the sugar industry in Barbados and formed the vanguard of the small but significant Jewish populations that emerged in all the colonies during the seventeenth century. Jewish colonists established synagogues and burial grounds in Bridgetown; Port Royal and later Spanish Town, Jamaica; in Charleston, South Carolina; and in Charlestown, Nevis, which also boasted a Jewish school. A young Alexander Hamilton, whose status as a bastard prevented enrollment in Nevis's Anglican school, learned to read and write at the school. Jewish colonists faced significant discrimination from English officials. They were prohibited from holding office and serving in the militia and often had to pay hefty additional taxes to local governments. Nevertheless, shared whiteness softened some of the worst anti-Semitism, and Jews often established social and economic relationships with prominent English colonists.

The small size of white populations in the region further contributed to this unity. Charleston, the center of Lowcountry life, contained only 5,000 whites on the eve of the American Revolution, meaning a South Carolina official could plausibly claim that he was "well acquainted with the Circumstances of most of our Inhabitants."[8] Such a statement was even more applicable in most of the islands. None of the Leeward Islands contained more than 4,000 whites by the 1750s. Jamaica was home to roughly 13,000 in 1774, many of whom resided in Kingston or in nearby Spanish Town. Barbados had the largest white population among the island colonies, but no more than 18,000 lived on the small island (21 miles by 14 miles) in the 1760s.

In addition to Europeans of diverse ethnic backgrounds and wealth, the colonies were also home to a small population of free blacks. No exact figures exist for this group, but estimates for the later eighteenth century suggest that about 500 free blacks lived on Barbados, about the same number in South Carolina, while fewer than 400 lived on St. Kitts. Jamaica had the largest free black population, 4,093 in 1774. Many lived in the region's urban centers. In the Carolina Lowcountry, about 200 of the region's 500 free blacks lived in Charleston. Although free, these individuals had few rights in the slave societies of the Greater Caribbean. Eighteenth-century laws prohibited them from voting, from serving on juries, and generally from testifying against whites in court. By the 1760s, Jamaica took steps to limit the amount of property they could inherit. The necessity of such a law arose because many freed blacks were the offspring of planters and slave women, and fathers often endowed their mixed-race offspring with sizable estates. In other cases, hard work, skill, and determination enabled some free blacks to accumulate significant wealth. Thomas Jeremiah, for example, used his skills as a harbor pilot and fisherman in Charleston, South Carolina, to amass an estate worth an estimated £1,000 by the 1770s, including ownership of several slave laborers. But Jeremiah's story also illustrates the precarious position of free blacks in the Greater Caribbean. Accused of working with the British to incite a slave rebellion in 1775, Jeremiah was tried under provisions of the South Carolina slave code and, despite a lack of evidence, was found guilty and executed.

Regardless of social rank, colonists in the Greater Caribbean shared a desire to get ahead. Religion played a role in the migration of some colonists, but most colonists focused their energy on advancing their material interests as quickly as possible. As more than one commentator noted, colonists exhibited a "great haste to be rich."[9]

A major reason for that haste was the threat of an early death. The Greater Caribbean became a graveyard for European colonists, who died at even higher rates than enslaved Africans during the seventeenth and eighteenth centuries. Conditions in Jamaica, the best-studied island, were especially bleak. Perhaps as many as 50,000 Europeans migrated to the island in the first half of the eighteenth century, but the white population grew by only 5,000 during that period. Deaths greatly outnumbered births throughout the island. St. Andrew parish recorded 1,921 births between 1667 and 1750, but 4,025 burials. Those born in St. Andrew and elsewhere faced dismal prospects. Life expectancy at birth in Jamaica was less than ten years. Those lucky enough to survive until age twenty could expect to live only another sixteen to eighteen years. Only 1 percent survived past age sixty. Immigrants fared even worse. Most died within twelve to thirteen years of their arrival. Kingston was especially deadly. One-third of infants born in the city did not live to celebrate their first birthday. The death rate in the city during the eighteenth century approximated that of London during the Great Plague, but whereas the plague was an extraordinary disaster, horrific mortality in Kingston was part of everyday life. Although data for other islands is less abundant, the general picture was the same: European colonists on all the islands died quickly and in great numbers.

Conditions were only marginally better in the Lowcountry. Despite early efforts to paint the region as an earthly paradise perfectly situated between the tropics and colder climates farther north, it soon became clear that, as one contemporary proverb had it, "they who want to die quickly, go to Carolina."[10] In Charleston's St. Philip parish, burials outnumbered baptisms by a rate of 3.5 to 1, roughly the same ratio as Bridgetown's St. Michael parish. In rural Christ Church parish, 86 percent of individuals with known birth and death dates died before age twenty. Among men, some 12 percent perished before their first birthday. Of those who made it to age twenty between 1680 and 1720, 41 percent died before their fortieth birthday. Only about 6 percent lived past age sixty. Women died at similarly high rates, with one-third dying before the age of five. High mortality rates undermined the ability of the population to reproduce itself, and in some Lowcountry parishes, as in the islands, population growth required continued immigration. Indeed, the white population of the Lowcountry as a whole stagnated during the middle decades of the eighteenth century, as immigration slowed to a trickle, and those whites who did arrive in the region moved quickly to the Backcountry.

The dismal demographic realities of the Greater Caribbean contrasted sharply with other parts of British America. Most colonists in New England lived into their sixties, and many survived a good many years more. Even those living in the seventeenth-century Chesapeake, often portrayed as a charnel house, survived into their forties, and conditions improved significantly by the eighteenth century. The Greater Caribbean, by contrast, remained what one Barbados governor called, without exaggeration, a "Region of Death."[11]

The main cause of early death was disease. Colonists in the Greater Caribbean died from a number of different diseases, including smallpox, influenza, and dysentery, but malaria and yellow fever claimed the greatest number of lives. Both likely arrived in the region on slave ships from West Africa, and both were transmitted from one individual to another by mosquitoes, for which the region's tropical and semi-tropical conditions and abundant pools of standing water provided ideal breeding grounds. Malaria, known as "ague" or "fever" at the time, existed throughout the region but was especially threatening in Jamaica and the Lowcountry. Deaths from the disease often followed a seasonal rhythm, with most occurring between August and November. In Christ Church, South Carolina, for example, 43 percent of all deaths recorded between 1700 and 1750 occurred in those few months.

Yellow fever epidemics broke out more sporadically, but with even more horrific results, as huge numbers perished in a relatively short time. An outbreak of yellow fever on Barbados in

1647 claimed so many lives that survivors struggled to bury the dead. More than 6,000 colonists perished, approximately one-seventh of the island's population. Barbados experienced another epidemic in the 1690s. The disease did not appear in Jamaica or the Lowcountry until the 1690s, but it made repeated appearances throughout the course of the eighteenth century. The 1699 epidemic in Charleston killed 200 people, including one-third of the colonial assembly.

Yellow fever and malaria were present in other parts of British America, but these diseases exacted a particularly heavy toll on human lives throughout the Greater Caribbean. In doing so, they reinforced contemporary perceptions that linked the Lowcountry to the islands. As one British naval surgeon wrote, diseases in the Lowcountry appeared "more obstinate, acute, and violent" than in colonies to the north, but very similar to "those distempers which are so fatal . . . in West Indian climates." In sharp contrast to most of British America, ill health remained a defining feature of life in the Greater Caribbean.[12]

WOMEN AND FAMILY LIFE

The combination of high mortality rates and skewed gender ratios undermined the stability of family life in the region. Drawn by the hopes of making their fortunes, far more men than women migrated to the Greater Caribbean during the seventeenth century, and men outnumbered women in all the colonies, often by a sizable margin. Such gender imbalances meant many men were unable to find wives. Even those fortunate enough to marry faced the prospect of losing a spouse quickly to disease, so that couples had very little time to form families. High infant mortality rates in turn ensured that few children survived into adulthood.

The gender imbalance improved in most of the colonies during the eighteenth century, so much so that women came to outnumber men in Barbados and several of the Leeward Islands. Nevertheless, families still struggled. The steady arrival of new migrants, most of them young men, meant that marriage-age populations often remained skewed, while disease continued to exact a heavy toll on colonial populations. In 1715 in Barbados women outnumbered men in the general population, but between the ages of twenty and forty, men outnumbered women.

Likewise, in the parish of St. Peter, almost one-quarter of all households included only a single person, usually a male. Among family units, more than a quarter had no children and the average number of children was less than two. Similar conditions characterized the Lowcountry. High infant mortality rates meant that in many parishes the population failed to reproduce itself. One Lowcountry couple, Henry and Mary Ravenel, had sixteen children, including seven daughters, between 1750 and 1779, when Mary died. None of the daughters lived past the age of twenty, and overall Henry and Mary buried ten of their children.

Conditions for family formation remained bleakest in Jamaica. The island attracted the greatest number of new immigrants, most of whom were men, so that, unlike other colonies in the region, men continued to outnumber women by a ratio of almost 2.5 to 1 in 1730. In addition, mortality rates remained horrific during the eighteenth century, with disastrous consequences for marriages and families. Marriages in St. Andrew parish lasted little more than eight years on average before one spouse died, and fewer than one-third of all marriages lasted more than a decade. Some, like that between George Somerville and Elizabeth Roger, lasted only a few days before one spouse died. Overall just over one-third of marriages produced surviving children, and only one-third of those children survived to adulthood. In Jamaica and elsewhere in the Greater Caribbean, parents and children, husbands and wives, sisters and brothers all faced the prospect of losing family members to an early grave. The European population never achieved the dramatic rates of population growth that occurred in other parts of British America, including, eventually, the Carolina Backcountry.

The sexual exploitation of enslaved African women by European men also influenced family life among colonists. The lack of white women ensured that many white men sought relationships with African women, but European men also believed that sexual access to African women was a fundamental part of owning slaves, and they acted on that belief. Everywhere in the region, white men forced themselves on black women, who faced severe punishments if they resisted. Thomas Thistlewood's diary records nearly 4,000 sexual assaults upon enslaved women under his control between 1750 and 1786, acts perpetrated both by

Thistlewood and by other visiting planters. Thistlewood may represent an extreme example, but violence against enslaved women was all too common.

In some cases, exploitation evolved into more complex, longer relationships. Thistlewood repeatedly raped slaves he owned, but he also maintained a long-term relationship with a slave woman named Phibbah, with whom he had a son, John. Many European men like Thistlewood never married, or never remarried, preferring instead to live with slave mistresses. Such open relationships often shocked visitors to the region but carried little social stigma among colonists. Josiah Quincy reported to his wife in Massachusetts that "the enjoyment of a negro or mulatto woman is spoken of as quite a common thing," among Low-country planters. "No reluctance, delicacy or shame is made about the matter."[13]

The sexual freedom afforded white men by the slave system of the Greater Caribbean did not extend to white women. Some early colonists worried that the region's climate disposed women to greater sensuality, but by the eighteenth century most commentators portrayed white women as paragons of modesty and virtue amidst a sea of licentiousness. To ensure they remained so, colonists closely monitored the sexual behavior of white women. The gravest threat was the possibility of white women having sexual relations with African men, which threatened to dilute racial boundaries and challenged white male control over female bodies. Relations between black men and white women did occur, but if discovered, women faced social ostracism.

One eighteenth-century case that achieved considerable notoriety involved Elizabeth Manning, the wife of the wealthy Jamaican merchant and politician Edward Manning. Rumors had circulated that Elizabeth was having an affair with another white man, Ballard Beckford, but in 1741, Elizabeth's maid accused her of sleeping with a slave as well. Edward petitioned for divorce, a rare occurrence in the British Atlantic world, one that required a special legislative act (Manning's request was approved by the Jamaican legislature, but was denied by Parliament). The accusations embarrassed Edward Manning, but he maintained his position in society, eventually becoming speaker of the House of Assembly. Likewise, Manning's later relationship with a free woman of color, with whom he had two children, carried no social stigma, even though they never married. The accusations against Elizabeth Manning, by contrast, made her a social pariah, and, despite her prominent background, she disappears from the historical record entirely.

White women like Elizabeth Manning generally lived within the confines of patriarchal households, their lives circumscribed by law and custom. Most women in the region married in their twenties, although in the parish of St. Andrew, Jamaica, 80 percent married under the age of twenty-one and 58 percent under eighteen. Many were significantly younger than their husbands. The relatively small size of white populations in the Greater Caribbean and the desire to maintain plantations meant that marriages fostered tight connections between families. Cousin marriage and exchange marriage (marriage between multiple siblings of two families) appear to have occurred more frequently in the Lowcountry than other parts of the mainland. Two daughters of Lowcountry planter James Reid, for example, married the sons of Robert Pringle, and the third daughter married Pringle's stepson. When the Lowcountry planter Ralph Izard married Rebecca Blake, he became the brother-in-law of his two nieces, both of whom had married one of Rebecca's brothers.

As was the case throughout the British Atlantic world, married women had no legal identity apart from their husbands. English laws of coverture dictated that married women could not vote, own property, write a will, or engage in any business transaction in their own names. Instead, women were responsible for raising children and running the household, although even those functions decreased in importance over time as the rise of slavery freed many white women from performing essential domestic labor and rendered their economic functions increasingly insignificant. "As mistresses of families they are unimportant," wrote one visitor to Antigua, "almost every domestic concern being left to the management of their negroes and mulattoes."[14]

The particular demographic conditions in the Greater Caribbean, however, created some unusual circumstances for women. The frequent early death of a husband meant that many women became widows at a young age and sometimes inherited sizable estates. English common law required that widows receive one-third of a husband's estate after his death, but in the Lowcountry men who wrote wills frequently granted their wives more property than required by law. Moreover, they often appointed wives as executors of their estates, signaling a high degree of trust that women would make good decisions regarding their husbands' property and the welfare of any children. This did not hold true across the region, however. Jamaican men did not grant their wives the same control over property. Instead, even men who had no children more often gave control of their property to friends or business relations rather than to their wives. Certainly rich widows existed in Jamaica, but in general, they appear to have controlled less property than their Lowcountry counterparts.

Most widows eventually remarried, and property passed to their children or the new husband, but some women remained *femes sole* (married women were *femes covert*), managing plantations or businesses on their own. Mary Elbridge took over her husband's sugar estate in Jamaica following his death in the early eighteenth century. The estate was in financial trouble, but Elbridge returned it to profitability within a few years. Likewise, Esther Pinheiro, a Jewish woman in Nevis, continued her husband's mercantile operations after his death in 1710. Many nonelite women ran boardinghouses or taverns in the region's urban centers or earned income by hiring out slaves. An Antiguan census from 1753 reveals that almost 25 percent of the island's households were headed by women, a disproportionate share of whom resided in the capital, St. John's. Similar figures characterized midcentury Jamaica. Independent women living in Kingston ran taverns, taught school, and worked as seamstresses and washerwomen, among other occupations. At other times, women stepped in when husbands or fathers left the colonies for some period of time. Sixteen-year-old Eliza Lucas took charge of her father's three Lowcountry plantations when he returned to Antigua in 1739, at the outbreak of war with Spain. What little evidence exists suggests that women operating plantations or managing slaves in urban centers did things no differently from men, including treating their slaves harshly. The brutality of some female slaveowners at times shocked contemporaries who viewed women as a more tender sex, but such incidents highlight the pervasive influence of slavery on all aspects of life in the Greater Caribbean, including gender roles.

Many eighteenth-century commentators offered bleak assessments of social and cultural developments in the Greater Caribbean. They decried the haste with which colonists sought material advancement, suggesting that in their frenzied quest for riches colonists neglected religion, education, and cultural life. Moreover, living in a deadly disease environment, and one subject to existential threats in the form of hurricanes, earthquakes, and other disasters, many colonists had become, in the words of one observer, quite "careless of Futurity."[15] Many sought only to make their fortunes and escape back to Britain. Such observations have considerable merit, especially given the increasing practice of absenteeism over the course of the eighteenth century and the all-too-real threat of an early death for those who remained. Nevertheless, the colonies of the Greater Caribbean were not spiritual and cultural wastelands. Colonists in the region participated in the same process of Anglicization that occurred throughout British America during the eighteenth century. Indeed, heavily outnumbered by the diverse Africans they enslaved and facing a dangerous and volatile environment, colonists placed particular emphasis on replicating familiar British institutions and practices, and they trumpeted their success in doing so, even as novel social and environmental conditions forced them to make significant cultural adjustments.

Although material advancement rather than spiritual concerns motivated most migrants to the Greater Caribbean during the seventeenth and eighteenth centuries, religion remained a cornerstone in the lives of individuals and a central force in colonial society. Migrants to the Greater Caribbean came from diverse religious backgrounds, especially during the seventeenth century. Groups settling in the region included Puritans, Quakers, Catholics, French Huguenots, Jews, Presbyterians, and later in the eighteenth century, Moravians and Methodists. Nevertheless, Anglicans increasingly dominated religious life in the region over time, particularly in the islands, and despite the Carolina proprietors' efforts to promote religious toleration, the Church of England became the established church everywhere by the middle of the eighteenth century—meaning that all colonists paid taxes to support it, whether they worshipped there or not.

From the beginning of settlement, colonists laid out parish boundaries and slowly built churches. The process took some time, in part because church buildings suffered repeated destruction from disasters and required frequent rebuilding, but by the eighteenth century, a number of impressive church structures graced the landscape of the Greater Caribbean. Finding ministers for the churches, however, at times proved difficult. Anglican ministers had to be ordained by the bishop of London, and few welcomed a posting to colonies marked by low salaries, high living costs, and a reputation as a graveyard. Barbados had only 11 ministers for 20,000 people in 1680, and governors in Jamaica and the Leewards routinely complained about a lack of ministers. The establishment of the Society for the Propagation of the Gospel in Foreign Parts in 1701 helped ease the situation, but some parishes remained without ministers. Such shortages, however, were not unique to the Greater Caribbean. Outside of New England, many colonies struggled to find ministers.

Colonists often had little regard for those who mounted the pulpits. One seventeenth-century Lowcountry lay minister reportedly became so drunk that he baptized a bear, while preachers in Jamaica were dismissed as better qualified to sell fish than preach the Gospel. The ministers, in turn, had little good to say about their congregations. They railed against planters' vulgar materialism, their sinful lifestyles, and their lack of financial support for churches (and, by extension, for the ministers). Other observers echoed such charges. One visitor commented that planters in Jamaica "love a Pack of Cards better than the Bible."[16]

The Greater Caribbean generally remained untouched by the evangelical movement known as the Great Awakening, which swept across much of the mainland during the middle decades of the eighteenth century. No itinerant ministers challenged island colonists to see themselves as sinners in the hand of an angry God, and no schisms rocked established congregations on the various islands. Moravian and Methodist ministers arrived in midcentury, but they generated little enthusiasm among most colonists. One Antiguan planter who had converted to Methodism complained that slaves and free blacks proved far more receptive to evangelical missionary efforts than whites.

The Lowcountry briefly experienced the Awakening's fires, but they burned out quickly. One of the central figures in the Awakening, the Anglican minister George Whitefield, arrived in Lowcountry Georgia in 1738 with plans to establish an orphanage. Seeking to raise funds, Whitefield began traveling throughout the colonies, and he made several trips to Charleston. His charisma and fervor found a ready audience among the city's numerous dissenters, as well as others who viewed the colony's spate of recent troubles, notably a yellow fever epidemic and the Stono Rebellion, as signs of God's displeasure. Among Whitefield's disciples was Hugh Bryan, a wealthy planter who took to heart Whitefield's desire to spread Christianity to slaves. Bryan's enthusiasm, however, went too far when he predicted that God would send another slave rebellion to destroy an unreformed Charleston, and officials quickly sought to arrest him. Bryan's subsequent failed effort to walk on water (he nearly drowned) led him to renounce his previous statements. More importantly, his actions discredited Whitefield, and the revivals more broadly, and allowed the Anglican ministers to regain control of the discourse. Whatever interest some colonists may have had in the revivals, the mixture of evangelical Christianity and slavery proved too explosive for most.

Despite ministerial criticisms and either indifference or outright hostility to revivals, colonists in the Greater Caribbean were not as irreligious as they were sometimes portrayed by contemporaries or by some later historians. Colonists turned to the church to baptize their children, to celebrate marriages, and to mourn and bury the dead. Although it took time, they built impressive churches, both in urban centers and in rural parishes. Individuals and organizations established parish libraries and donated books and money to maintain them. Like their counterparts throughout the British Atlantic world, colonists celebrated special events with days of thanksgiving and called for public fasting during periods of distress. Colonists adapted such rituals to the particularities of the region's environment. Annual fast days became common at the start of hurricane season in hopes of avoiding the great storms, for example, while days of thanksgiving celebrated the end of seasons in which no hurricane struck. The form of such rituals, however, mirrored those held throughout the British Atlantic world. These rituals, in turn, reinforced colonists' sense of British identity. As the governor of the Leeward Islands reported following a day of thanksgiving celebrating English victories against the French in 1706, "We did as heartily rejoice as any other H[er] M[ajesty's] subjects."[17] Religion did not dominate public life in the Greater Caribbean to the same extent as it did in New England, but that was true for most of British America. Overall, religion, and the Anglican Church in particular, played a central role in the lives of colonists throughout the region.

Colonists were slower to build schools than churches, and educational opportunities in the region remained limited, even into the eighteenth century. Planters in Barbados established several schools, including Harrison College in 1733 and the Alleyne School in 1785, both of which remain in operation today. A burst of interest in schooling in eighteenth-century Jamaica led to plans for the establishment of numerous private academies, but not all of these efforts came to fruition, and even some that did took decades to gain adequate funding. A free, or charity, school opened in Charleston in 1712, and several Lowcountry parishes had privately funded schools, but nothing comparable to the tax-supported schools in many of the northern colonies. Likewise, the only effort made at developing a university in the region, Codrington College in Barbados, proved far less successful than Harvard, William and Mary, or the other mainland colleges. The planter Christopher Codrington had provided an endowment for the school when he died in 1710, but it took thirty years for the school to open and fewer than fifty students enrolled before it closed during the American Revolution. Charleston eventually boasted a fine college, but it was not chartered until 1785.

The relatively few schools in the region did not reflect a lack of interest in education among colonists but rather that colonists had access to different educational opportunities. Instead of establishing and supporting local schools, wealthy colonists in the Greater Caribbean employed private tutors for a period of time and then sent their children to England for more formal schooling, often at a young age. Seven times as many children from the sugar islands attended Eton College (for what we would now call high school) than children from North America in the

Codrington College in Barbados, the only institution of higher learning in the region prior to the 1780s. Detail from William Mayo, *New and Exact Map of Barbadoes* (London, 1722). Courtesy of the John Carter Brown Library at Brown University.

two decades before the American Revolution. In addition, large numbers attended Oxford, Cambridge, and Edinburgh for university, or studied law at the Inns of Court or medicine at Leiden and elsewhere. Highlighting the links between the islands and the mainland perceived by contemporaries, many of these students identified themselves as "of the island of Antigua, in America," or "of the island of Jamaica, in America."[18]

Lowcountry planters also sent their children abroad by the middle decades of the eighteenth century. Despite a far smaller population, the number of Lowcountry boys at Eton roughly equaled those from Virginia between 1753 and 1776, and after 1760 far more Carolinians than Virginians enrolled at Oxford and Cambridge. John Moultrie, Peter Manigault, Thomas Heyward, William Henry Drayton, and Charles Cotesworth Pinckney (son of Eliza and Charles Pinckney) were among the prominent Carolinians educated in England. Worried that London offered too many opportunities for drinking and socializing, Henry Laurens sent his son to Geneva instead.

Colonists invested relatively little in formal schools, but they established and endowed a number of other cultural institutions throughout the region during the eighteenth century. Spanish Town, Charleston, and Bridgetown all boasted library societies, housing extensive and wide-ranging collections of literary, historical, philosophical, and scientific texts. Individuals kept impressive private libraries as well. In rural western Jamaica, Thomas Thistlewood maintained a library of hundreds of volumes, including works by Chaucer, Milton, and the collected works of Voltaire, as well as numerous histories and scientific texts. Despite their relatively small populations, West Indian colonists purchased nearly 25 percent of the books exported to all of British America.

In addition, a number of theaters operated in the region. Charleston's Dock Street Theater opened in 1735 and hosted occasional performances by traveling troupes in the subsequent years. Jamaica had a theater as early as 1682, and others appeared over the course of the eighteenth century. Charles Leslie, writing in 1739–40, noted the opening of a new playhouse in Spanish Town that employed "a Set of extraordinary good Actors." The smaller Leeward Islands do not appear to have supported a troupe of professional actors until 1770, when advertisements for the "Leeward Island Company of Comedians" first appeared. Instead, resident amateurs took to the stage. In addition to his duty as solicitor-general for the Leeward Islands, for example, John Baker acted in local productions of *Othello* and *King Lear*.[19]

Baker rehearsed, and sometimes performed, in a Freemason's lodge, one of three on Antigua. The Masons and a variety of other ethnic and fraternal organizations appeared in all the colonies. By the latter part of the eighteenth century, Charleston claimed some twenty clubs, including the St. Andrew's Society (for Scottish colonists), the St. George's Society (for English colonists), and the Friday-Night Club (for "elder substantial gentlemen"), as well as the St. Cecilia Society, which hosted regular concert performances in the town. As was the case with the Beefsteak and Tripe Club encountered by Washington on his trip to Barbados, many of these clubs were aligned with or modeled after English organizations. Beyond serving as social outlets and providing services, such as lending money at interest or aiding those in financial need, these organizations reinforced a sense of common British identity among colonists living on the far reaches of the British Atlantic world. The 1762 bylaws of the Charleston Library Society made plain such aims. By "handing down the European Arts and Manners to the latest times" and supporting "improvements in the finer as well as in the inferior arts," the society sought to render the colonists "worthy of their Mother-Country."[20]

These theaters, clubs, and societies developed mostly in the region's major urban centers: Bridgetown, Kingston, St. John's,

Basseterre, Charleston, and Savannah. Ironically, the plantation colonies of the Greater Caribbean included some of the largest towns in British America and the largest percentage of urban residents. By the middle of the eighteenth century, Kingston and Charleston each boasted populations of roughly 5,000–7,000, while Bridgetown had between 10,000 and 11,000 inhabitants. Only Boston, New York, and Philadelphia among early American cities had larger populations. A disproportionate share of whites in the Greater Caribbean lived in these urban centers. In Jamaica, whites composed 11 percent of the total population in 1730, but they formed one-third of Kingston's population. Other whites lived in Jamaica's smaller but vibrant capital, Spanish Town, and some of its smaller outports such as Savanna-la-Mar, and the diminished but still functioning Port Royal. A similar percentage of Lowcountry whites lived in Charleston and Savannah. Even in the cities, however, whites remained the minority, outnumbered everywhere (except Savannah) by Africans and African Americans, mostly slaves, but some free blacks as well.

In addition to cultural attractions, the cities were vibrant commercial centers, home to numerous merchants, shopkeepers, and artisans. Kingston boasted some ninety stores and workshops in 1745, many of them crowded onto Port Royal Street facing the harbor. Large mercantile firms importing and selling goods from Britain and slaves from Africa sat alongside sailmakers, silversmiths, and taverns. On Charleston's East Bay Street, blacksmiths, goldsmiths, and milliners offered their services, as did a dancing instructor. Janet Schaw reported that colonists in Antigua "have the fashions every six weeks from London, and London itself cannot boast of more elegant shops than you meet with at St. Johns."[21] Charleston merchants and artisans advertised their ability to provide goods and services—furniture, clothing, even haircuts—that followed "the newest taste now in London." Numerous visitors noted that devotion to English styles appeared particularly pronounced in the Lowcountry, especially compared to the other mainland colonies.

Colonists increasingly knew about the latest European fashions and trends because of the growth of newspapers in the eighteenth century. The region's first paper, and the second in all of the British colonies, appeared in Jamaica in 1718. The

Barbados Gazette began publication in 1731, whereas the *South Carolina Gazette* appeared the following year. Benjamin Franklin dispatched an associate to Antigua to set up a paper in 1748. The newsprints helped integrate the scattered colonies of the Greater Caribbean with one another, and with the wider British Atlantic world, keeping colonists abreast of the latest political, economic, and cultural developments in neighboring colonies and in Europe.

As much as colonists sought to emulate English practices, however, the challenges of the region's environment necessitated significant adaptations in how they lived their lives. In the early decades of settlement, colonists remained wedded to traditional English clothing. Despite the climate, they wore woolen clothes, and the caps worn by poorer whites often lacked brims to protect their faces from the sun. Shops in seventeenth-century Port Royal even advertised beaver fur hats. Such choices made life miserable, and over time, colonists increasingly embraced new materials and styles that made more sense in the tropics. Eighteenth-century island elites, for example, wore relatively little clothing compared to their counterparts elsewhere, often just basic stockings, linen breeches and a vest, and a hat. Formal attire such as wigs appeared only during special events. The more variable climate in the Lowcountry meant that traditional English clothes remained useful, at least in the winter months, but colonists there also turned to lightweight alternatives during most of the year. By the eighteenth century, linens and cotton clothing formed the largest percentage of textiles imported from Britain. Even as they adapted to the region's climate, colonists throughout the region continued to place great emphasis on the quality and style of their clothes. One visitor from Massachusetts reported that Lowcountry gentlemen dressed with a "richness and elegance uncommon with us."[22]

Colonists likewise maintained a taste for traditional English foods, but they also came to appreciate a wide range of local delicacies. Green turtles quickly became popular in the islands. They were captured in the Cayman Islands and kept in open sea pens in port cities, and turtle meat became a staple in colonists' diets. Colonists also embraced various local fishes, fruits, and vegetables, reserving particular praise for pineapples, the nectar of the gods in the words of one visitor. One eighteenth-century visitor to Barbados claimed that colonists preferred bread made from cassava over that made from flour. Even when colonists consumed traditional English provisions, they often prepared them in new ways. Because meat went bad quickly in the tropical heat, colonists adopted the technique of barbecuing and jerking, particularly of pork. The smoky fires flavored and preserved the meat. Both techniques were native in origin, but European colonists soon made them their own. Colonists likewise learned to prepare "escovitch" by frying fish until it dried, then marinating it in various citrus juices, salt, and spicy peppers.

The diet of colonists in the Lowcountry overlapped with that of the islands in several ways. In some cases, the climate allowed for the growth of tropical fruits and plants, but proximity to the islands also allowed for easier importation of such items. Lowcountry colonists ate a significant amount of turtle meat, which they imported from the nearby Bahamas. The Bahamas and other islands provided a plentiful supply of pineapples, as well as a variety of citrus fruits, some of which were also grown locally. Neither Lowcountry nor island colonists produced any decent beer, so both drank large quantities of sangria, rum punch, and Madeira wine. Nevertheless, while Lowcountry cuisine featured island flavors, the greater availability of land and the slightly cooler climate meant colonists could also maintain more traditional English dishes. Venison, poultry, and fowl were widely available, as was fresh beef, although as one English visitor to Charleston in the 1770s noted, only in the winter months.

Climate influenced English diets throughout the region, but so too did the presence of huge numbers of enslaved Africans. The similarity in climate between the Greater Caribbean and large sections of West Africa allowed many African plants to thrive in the Americas. Many foods made their way from slave garden plots into colonists' kitchens and dining rooms. One wealthy Jamaican planter, for example, hosted a feast for a new governor and his wife that featured local delicacies such as jerked pork and a land-crab pepper pot stew made with okra. African cooks prepared meals that incorporated African foods to serve English planters.

Other plants, some native, some introduced from Africa, served medicinal purposes, and both Native Americans and enslaved Africans made key contributions to colonists' medical knowledge. Colonists frequently turned to African healers for help, especially as European medical experts often had little success in healing various ailments. Colonists only rarely acknowledged such contributions, but in 1749, officials in South Carolina granted freedom and a pension of £100 to a man named Caesar, who had developed a successful cure for snake venom and other poisons. Likewise, the Majoe plant in Jamaica was named after a slave woman who had remarkable success with the plant in alleviating yaws as well as venereal diseases. Far more frequently colonists simply incorporated such knowledge into their everyday lives without fully crediting its source.

Enslaved Africans influenced white society in other ways as well, most of them negatively in the opinion of visitors and some locals. Several observers noted that colonists had a distinct form of speech that mirrored that of slaves in certain respects. George Washington wrote that many European women on Barbados "affect the Negro style" in their speech.[23] Edward Long likewise complained that too much time spent in the company of domestic slaves had a detrimental impact on how European women spoke and on how they carried themselves. Another commentator noted that white women carried children on their hips, rather than on their forearms, a practice copied from enslaved Africans. Contemporaries decried such developments, but they highlight the extent to which European society had become creolized in ways large and small. Europeans may have held political power in the Greater Caribbean, but African cultures played a major role in shaping the region's social landscape.

In addition to what they ate and how they dressed, colonists gradually made adjustments to their houses and other buildings. Early colonists to the Greater Caribbean made few concessions to the region's environment. Many seventeenth-century visitors observed that the multistory, brick buildings found in Port Royal and other towns resembled those in London. Such structures may have reminded colonists of home, but they were often cramped and hot, and they proved vulnerable to the various disasters that routinely struck the region. This became especially clear in Jamaica, where the shorter, squatter buildings built by the early Spanish colonists often withstood hurricanes and earthquakes far better than the newer buildings built by the English.

By the early eighteenth century, experience with the environment led colonists to rethink their designs. Basic English architectural forms remained the ideal throughout the region during the eighteenth century, but colonists made a number of adaptations to the region's climate, including lowering the profile of their houses by building fewer stories, employing hipped rather than gabled roofs (to better withstand hurricanes), and constructing verandas or piazzas to provide shade. Shutters, rather than glass, covered the windows. The Assembly House in Spanish Town, Jamaica, for example, followed the prevailing eighteenth-century Georgian styles, but the relatively short, two-story building with a front arcade to provide shade differed significantly from the much taller, more ornate statehouses in Boston and Philadelphia. Many visitors also commented that streets in the towns were noticeably wider and more open than in Europe, to better facilitate the movement of cooling breezes.

A distinct church architecture likewise appeared in the islands. The threat of hurricanes and earthquakes meant that many churches did not have tall steeples. Cruciform churches—those

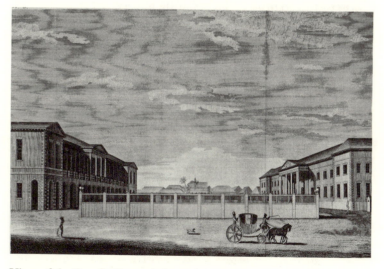

View of the Parade Ground, Spanish Town, Jamaica. The Assembly House is on the left, the governor's mansion on the right. From Edward Long, *The History of Jamaica* (London, 1774), vol. 2. Courtesy of the James Ford Bell Library, University of Minnesota.

built in the form of a cross—and some with thick walls became common in Jamaica, likely because that design provided greater stability. Some colonists in the Leeward Islands and Jamaica constructed special "hurricane houses"—short, squat structures designed to withstand storms.

Architectural alterations appeared more pronounced in the tropical islands than in the semi-tropical Lowcountry. Occasional frosts ensured that Lowcountry buildings had chimneys, whereas most houses in the islands did not, and fewer hurricanes encouraged colonists to crown St. Philip's and St. Michael's Churches with tall steeples. The result was a built environment that mirrored English styles and trends closely. Nonetheless, colonists also adapted to the region's climate. Colonial builders in Charleston took a traditional English house design, turned it on its side to accommodate the city's narrow lots, and then added piazzas facing the sea to catch the fresh breezes. The result was the city's distinctive single-house. Likewise, houses in Charleston often had more space between them than in some other colonial cities, which allowed for more cooling breezes. By the early nineteenth century, some Lowcountry planters built storm towers to protect slaves during hurricanes.

Overall, such adaptations to the striking sights, sounds, smells, tastes, and feel of life in the tropical and subtropical Greater Caribbean provided constant reminders to colonists and newcomers alike that, as one wrote, "this part of the new World [was] new indeed in regard of ours, for here I find every Thing alter'd."[24] Despite the best efforts of colonists to re-create British culture and institutions; despite their expensive mahogany furniture, elaborate tea sets, and riding carriages; despite the churches they built and the theaters and clubs they established, the combination of the environmental forces they encountered and the socioeconomic institutions they developed resulted in the emergence of distinctive creole societies. Significant differences distinguished the various colonies within the region, but the heat, humidity, hurricanes, diseases, and, perhaps most of all, the presence of massive slave majorities, also created a good deal of social and cultural overlap across the region's vast expanse. Visitors and commentators found much to admire in these societies—great wealth, generous hospitality, exotic foods, beautiful landscapes, elements of British high culture—but also much to condemn—rampant greed and self-interest, a base materialism, sexual license, and excessive brutality. Whether they offered praise or denunciations, however, all commentators agreed that despite the trappings of British society, colonists had created a distinct world in the Greater Caribbean.

SEVEN

Trade, Politics, and War in the Eighteenth Century

ONE OF THE MEN WHO HOSTED several dinners for George and Lawrence Washington on their trip to Barbados was Gedney Clarke. Clarke was born in Salem, Massachusetts, in 1711, the son of Francis Clarke and Deborah Gedney. Both the Clarke and Gedney families traced their ancestry to the Great Migration of the 1630s, when roughly 24,000 Puritans migrated to the Bay Colony. Both families had prospered in Salem, but in 1733, seeking new adventures and economic opportunities, twenty-two-year-old Gedney Clarke left Salem and migrated to Barbados. It is not surprising that young Clarke turned his attention to Barbados. Direct trade between Massachusetts and Barbados had begun in the 1630s, and the two regions remained tightly connected by numerous social and economic links. Clarke established himself as a merchant in Bridgetown and used his contacts in Salem to begin a lucrative trade, exchanging sugar and rum for fish and whale oil, the latter used for lamps. At the same time, his sister Deborah married William Fairfax of Virginia, thus connecting Clarke to the Virginia elite, including the Washingtons (George's half brother Lawrence married one of William Fairfax's daughters from his first marriage).

As Clarke prospered in Barbados, he began to diversify his activities. He developed relationships with South Carolina merchants, sending sugar and rum to Charleston and bringing back rice, naval stores, and lumber. He used the profits from that trade to pay for imported goods from London. In the 1740s and 1750s, he became involved in the slave trade and shipped slaves to planters in Charleston, among other places. He also became a sugar planter. Clarke purchased thousands of acres of plantation land in nearby Demerara and Essequibo, Dutch colonies on the northern coast of South America (what is now Guyana) in the late 1740s, and he acquired the 500-acre Belle plantation in Barbados in 1752. Finally, Clarke profited from the frequent wars that played out in the region between the 1730s and 1760s. He organized privateering ventures against French and Spanish ships, and he secured commissions to victual British naval ships in the region. In many of these activities, Clarke partnered with, or drew on the financial resources of Lascelles and Maxwell, one of London's preeminent merchant houses with deep ties to all parts of the British Atlantic world.

Clarke's growing economic prominence soon resulted in greater political power. In 1748, he was appointed customs collector for Bridgetown, a position he passed on to his son, Gedney Clarke Jr., when he died in 1764. Both father and son served on the Barbados council, the upper house of the legislature, and both held senior ranks in the Barbados militia.

Even as Gedney Clarke Sr. established himself in Barbados, he maintained close ties to Massachusetts. He paid £25 to rent a pew in the new Anglican church in Salem. He donated bells to Boston's North Church in 1744. Clarke also assisted family members who had experienced hard times in Massachusetts, helping several struggling nephews establish themselves on Barbados. Family connections to England also deepened. Clarke's son, Gedney Clarke Jr., eventually settled in London and married Frances Lascelles in 1762. When George Maxwell died in 1763, Gedney Jr. became a partner in the London firm the following year.

Gedney Clarke's story illustrates the central position occupied by the colonies of the Greater Caribbean in the economic and political life of the British Atlantic world. The tremendous expansion of sugar and rice exports during the eighteenth century generated great riches, not only for colonists in the region, but for the empire as a whole. Some individuals like Clarke migrated to the region, but many others prospered by trading with the colonies, supplying both essential materials and a wide range of luxury goods. The fortunes of fishermen in Massachusetts, merchants in Rhode Island, wheat farmers in Pennsylvania, gun manufacturers in Birmingham, textile makers in Manchester, and bankers in London all became increasingly linked to the plantations of the Greater Caribbean. For good reason, the Trinidadian historian Eric Williams called the West Indies the "hub of the British empire," and his comments may be extended to the Lowcountry as well. With spokes radiating out in all directions, the Greater Caribbean linked disparate parts of the British Atlantic world into a shared commercial empire.

The wealth of planters and merchants in the Greater Caribbean was matched by their political power and influence, within individual colonies and, in the case of absentee sugar planters, within Great Britain itself. The structure of government in the region mirrored other parts of British America, and colonists shared many of the same political beliefs as their counterparts elsewhere. However, the centrality of slavery and the region's peculiar geographic and demographic conditions created particular issues and resulted in a distinctive form of politics, one dominated by the interests of the great planters and with relatively little participation by nonelites. Most significantly, absentee sugar planters exercised a degree of political influence in imperial politics unmatched by any other group of colonists.

Not surprisingly, the great riches that flowed from the Greater Caribbean generated great rivalries as well. The Greater Caribbean became the "cockpit of European nations," the scene of almost constant warfare between England, France, Spain, and the Netherlands during the seventeenth and eighteenth centuries. Gedney Clarke and some others found ways to profit from these conflicts—one colonist on Nevis wrote that "warr time is money time here"—but for many colonists, wars destroyed plantations, interrupted shipping, and produced social and economic turmoil.[1] For all their destruction, however, frequent conflicts did little to alter the region's map, as final peace treaties often stipulated a return to the *status quo ante bellum*. That changed in 1763. The end of the Seven Years War transformed the political boundaries of the Greater Caribbean. Britain gained significant territory in the Lowcountry and the islands, unleashing a new wave of plantation expansion, but the costs of war and the unintended consequences of territorial acquisitions created issues that eventually led to the American Revolution.

A GRAND MARINE EMPIRE

Sixteenth- and seventeenth-century promoters of colonization emphasized trade as one of the primary benefits of establishing new settlements. Men like Richard Hakluyt argued in the 1580s that colonies would provide England with valuable staple crops, serve as outlets for English manufactured goods, and employ thousands of sailors to ship the materials back and forth across the Atlantic. That was the ideal, but in practice England took few steps to control colonial trade during the first decades of colonization, generally leaving affairs in the hands of proprietors, private companies, and the colonists themselves. As a result, a good deal of the products and profits from the English colonies ended up on Dutch ships and in Dutch towns, particularly Amsterdam, Europe's preeminent trading center at the time. Concerned that they were losing the benefits of the increasingly valuable sugar and tobacco trades, English officials passed a series of Navigation Acts designed to regulate trade in and out of the empire. The first act in 1651 aimed simply to eliminate Dutch shipping from English colonies. A larger and more expansive act passed in 1660. It stipulated that certain enumerated items, including sugar and tobacco, had to go directly to England, where they could be taxed and either consumed or reexported to European markets. Rice was added to the list of enumerated commodities in 1704. The act also required that all goods going into and out of the colonies had to go on English ships, defined as any ship built in England or the colonies and manned by crews that were three-quarters English or colonial subjects. A 1663 law prohibited direct trade between Europe and the colonies, requiring all European goods shipped to the colonies to pass through England. Although these acts placed restrictions on colonial commerce, they also guaranteed colonists a protected market, as commodities produced in foreign colonies faced high tariffs in England. The goal of these mercantilist policies was simple: to keep the wealth of the colonies within the English empire.

Sugar planters initially reacted to the Navigation Acts with howls of protest. Eliminating Dutch traders and access to Dutch markets promised higher costs for essential goods and lower prices for their sugar, and colonists lobbied vigorously for free trade throughout the seventeenth century. By the middle of the eighteenth century, however, planters had changed their tune. Increased competition from the French islands, where newer and richer soils yielded bumper crops at lower costs, rendered British planters increasingly dependent on their protected home market. Even a successful lobbying effort to gain direct access to European markets in 1739 was more about keeping prices high in England than about trading to Europe, where English sugars remained too expensive to be competitive.

Sugar exports from the islands to England grew considerably during the eighteenth century, although production varied from island to island. Jamaica witnessed the greatest transformation during this period, and by the 1770s, Jamaica was producing more sugar than the other British islands combined, as well as small but significant amounts of pimento, ginger, cotton, and coffee. St. Kitts, with its rich volcanic soil, emerged as the second great sugar producer during this period, exporting more sugar than the larger islands of Barbados or Antigua. Exports of muscovado from Barbados's worn-out soils actually declined during the first half of the eighteenth century, but planters responded by increasing their use of manure, by shifting from cattle mills to more efficient windmills to process cut canes, by distilling more molasses into rum, and by producing more clayed sugar, a whiter and higher grade of sugar that fetched higher prices. Overall, planters in Barbados and elsewhere never matched the fantastic profits of the so-called golden age of the mid-seventeenth century, when sugar remained an exotic luxury item and commanded high prices, but increasing consumer demand in Britain kept prices relatively high and stable even as production expanded. The result was something of a "silver age" for sugar planters during the middle decades of the eighteenth century.

Planters in the Lowcountry also profited handsomely during the eighteenth century, as rice exports grew substantially. After a slow start during the first two decades, production exploded, increasing sevenfold between 1720 and 1740. Production stalled during the 1740s, the result of war with Spain and France and the decision to limit slave importations following the 1739 Stono

Rebellion, but exports rebounded in the following decade. Georgia began to export rice at the same time. Indigo production also grew significantly, buoyed by a parliamentary bounty.

Sugar, rice, and other plantation crops filled the hulls of ships departing from the region. Ships arriving from Britain and other mainland colonies brought increasing quantities of manufactured goods and assorted provisions to the Greater Caribbean. Plantation operations required a wide range of manufactured goods, including clothing, hats, nails, tools, and boiling equipment. Planters, for example, generally supplied enslaved men with at least one linen jacket and a pair of pants each year and each woman a linen frock, although some planters provided a more generous allotment of clothing. Even at these minimal levels, the number of enslaved Africans in the Greater Caribbean necessitated significant imports of clothing. Likewise, iron hoes were essential for working the fields, and colonists purchased massive quantities of these tools, far more than their counterparts in Virginia—testimony both to the size of the region's slave population and the difficulties of sugar and rice production. Sugar plantations also required a great deal of specialized equipment such as cisterns, pipes, and copper kettles for boiling the cane juice, and British copper exports jumped dramatically beginning in the 1660s.

In addition to essential supplies, planters bought a variety of luxury goods for themselves. Although the colonies increasingly boasted their own local, skilled craftsmen, both free and slave, colonists continued to rely heavily on British finished goods, ownership of which denoted wealth and status. Colonists purchased imported clothing, clocks, mahogany furniture, china sets, tea and coffee sets, chariots and riding chairs, books, billiard tables, playing cards, mirrors, drinking glasses, and a wide range of other items. One woman in Barbados even imported her own tombstone.

Overall, the great wealth generated by sugar and rice allowed planters to import huge quantities of European goods. The total value of exports to the West Indies did not lag far behind those to the mainland, despite the islands' far smaller European populations. The per capita value of imports far exceeded those of their mainland counterparts. Whites living in Barbados in 1700 on average purchased goods from London valued at £3.47.

Per capita consumption in Jamaica, still developing its sugar economy, was £2.06. By contrast, consumption in New England was a paltry £0.59, while colonists in the richer tobacco colonies of the Chesapeake purchased little more, only £0.63 per capita. Such differences were not lost on contemporaries. The seventeenth-century English merchant Josiah Child maintained that one English colonist with ten slaves in Barbados created work for four men in England, whereas ten colonists in New England would not employ one man in England. The growing wealth of Lowcountry planters likewise supported an increasing supply of goods from the mother country. South Carolina's imports rose from 3.3 percent of England's total trade to the mainland colonies in the beginning of the eighteenth century to just under 11 percent by the early 1770s.

Historians have long debated the contribution of the colonies, and the sugar islands in particular, to the Industrial Revolution in England. In the 1940s, Eric Williams, a West Indian historian educated at Oxford, argued that the colonies and colonial trade played a major role in industrial development. Put simply, Williams posited that the sugar and slave trades spurred technological innovation and provided the means to finance industrial development. Numerous scholars since have refuted the specifics of that argument, suggesting that domestic markets and trade with Europe played a far greater role in hastening the onset of industrialization. Nonetheless, the importance of the colonial trade was not negligible. Increased demand for manufactured goods in the colonies, and in West Africa, stimulated English manufacturing. The need for bulk cargoes of shoes, linen jackets, and other items encouraged innovations in production. Colonial demand for finished, dyed textiles, for example, pushed manufacturers to develop new printing methods that could replicate patterns from Indian manufacturers. Hoe manufacturers designed different models for Virginia, Carolina, and Barbados, reflecting the different requirements of tobacco, rice, and sugar cultivation. Likewise, the need for copper kettles promoted the development of copper mining. The sugar and slave trade also fostered important innovations in banking, finance, and insurance. If the sugar islands did not finance the Industrial Revolution, they nonetheless contributed directly and indirectly to England's economic development.

The sugar islands also relied heavily on goods and materials from the mainland colonies, first New England and Virginia, later the Middle Colonies and the Lowcountry. As early as the 1640s, colonists in Barbados looked to Massachusetts for provisions, livestock, timber, and salted fish. They also imported large numbers of cattle and horses, particularly from Rhode Island, to turn the sugar mills. By the 1660s, between thirty-five and sixty-five ships each year docked at Bridgetown from various New England ports, and by the 1680s almost half of all ships in island ports came from New England. Barbados and the other islands also purchased cattle, pork, lumber, corn, and tobacco from Virginia. By the early eighteenth century, Pennsylvania and New York supplied flour and other provisions. The Lowcountry exported a variety of foodstuffs to the islands, including broken rice used to feed slaves. As the Board of Trade reported in 1709, the sugar islands could not "subsist (especially in time of war) without the necessary supplies from the Northern plantations of bread, drink, fish, and flesh of cattle and horses for cultivating their plantations, of lumber and staves for casks for their sugar, rum, and molasses, and of timber for building their houses and sugar works."[2]

Just as the islands depended on the northern colonies for supplies, the mainland colonies depended on the islands for sugar and molasses and as a market for their goods. Colonists throughout the mainland profited from selling their products to the islands. Ships from New England and elsewhere returned home laden with sugar, rum, and most of all, molasses, which they distilled into rum. By 1770, the mainland colonies were home to some 26 sugar refineries and 140 distilleries, mostly in New England. Mainland colonists consumed gallons of rum in their local taverns (21 gallons a year per adult white male, or put another way, 7 one-ounce shots a day), traded it to Native Americans, used it to purchase slaves in West Africa, and shipped it to England to pay for imported manufactured goods. Without trade to the sugar islands, many northern colonies would have been unable to pay their debts to English merchants. Overall, trade between North America and the islands increased dramatically after the 1680s.

The constant flow of goods and ships between the islands and the mainland fostered deep connections between the two.

Bridgetown's public wharf was renamed "New England Row" during the 1670s, and one of the central streets in the town was called "New England Street." Lowcountry elites were not the only ones to own estates on both the mainland and the islands. The New York merchant Philip Livingston used profits from the triangular trade to purchase a plantation in Jamaica. His son would later sign the Declaration of Independence. Likewise, the Quaker merchant Jonathan Dickinson migrated from Jamaica to Pennsylvania a few years after the Port Royal earthquake but continued to own property on the island. Another merchant, Thomas Benson, remained in Jamaica but also owned property in Philadelphia and St. Kitts. Abraham Redwood moved from Antigua to New England in the 1710s but maintained ownership of his plantations on the island. His son, also Abraham, inherited the Cassada Garden plantation in 1729 and managed it from his home in Newport, Rhode Island. The two hundred slaves on the plantation produced profits of £2,000–£3,000 a year for the son, who owned two impressive mansions in Newport, one with iron gates imported from England. Atop the gates sat carved stone pineapples, the symbol of West Indian hospitality.

Over time, the trade in provisions and commodities between the islands and the mainland expanded into the trade in human beings—in both directions. The first Africans in New England had Caribbean roots. New England officials sent several Native Americans captured in the Pequot War of 1637 to Barbados in exchange for enslaved Africans. A similar exchange occurred after King Philip's War in 1675. Some slaves were acquired by trade, but others arrived with colonists who migrated between regions. Among the best-known of those migrants was Samuel Parris, who moved from Barbados to Massachusetts in 1680, accompanied by an enslaved native woman named Tituba. Both became central actors in the Salem witch crises of 1692.

Over time, colonists in the Greater Caribbean also began to receive slaves from northern traders. John Winthrop reported in 1645 that a ship had just returned from Barbados laden with tobacco, which it had received in exchange for slaves. Such voyages occurred sporadically during the seventeenth century, but beginning in the 1730s northern merchants organized hundreds of voyages to Africa. The developing triangular trade sent rum distilled in New England from molasses produced in the Caribbean to purchase slaves in West Africa, who were sent to labor in the Caribbean producing sugar and molasses, thus starting the cycle again. Rhode Island merchants in particular played an active role in the slave trade. Among those engaged in the buying and selling of slaves were the brothers John and Moses Brown. They used some of the profits acquired in the trade to establish the university that now bears their name.

Although trade between the northern colonies and the sugar islands generally worked to the benefit of colonists in both regions, tensions developed during the early decades of the eighteenth century. Specifically, sugar planters complained that northern merchants increasingly traded provisions, timber, and other supplies to the French sugar islands of Guadeloupe and Martinique, purchasing cheap molasses in return. France restricted importation of molasses and rum to protect domestic brandy producers, meaning that French planters had plenty of molasses to sell at low prices. Moreover, neither France nor the French colonies in North America supplied their sugar islands with adequate provisions and lumber. As a result, planters in Guadeloupe and Martinique offered high prices for these essential items, and New England merchants were happy to provide them. The effect for planters in the British islands was to drive up the cost of essential items and to lower the price of their molasses.

The sugar planters, led by absentee planters in London, turned to Parliament to protect their markets. Their lobbying resulted in the passage of the Molasses Act in 1733. The act allowed northern colonists to sell their provisions and timber to the French islands, but it placed heavy taxes on imports of foreign sugar, rum, and especially molasses. The Molasses Act, however, turned out to be a hollow victory for the sugar planters. New England merchants found all sorts of ways to evade the regulations, including bribing customs officials, and the act never was enforced effectively. Sugar planters complained bitterly for the next decade, but efforts in the late 1740s to tighten control of colonial trade foundered with the outbreak of renewed war with France in 1754. When British officials eventually cracked down on illegal trade in the 1760s, New England merchants and distillers protested vigorously, unleashing the opening volleys in the debate about colonial rights that culminated with the outbreak of war between Britain and the mainland colonies in 1775.

PLANTERS AND POLITICS

Although it did not succeed in curtailing trade between the French islands and New England, passage of the Molasses Act highlighted the growing power and influence of absentee planters from the islands in British political affairs. As early as the 1730s, absentees established the informal Planters Club in London, which met regularly at Rose's Coffee House, the Jamaica Coffee House, and others to discuss plantation affairs and imperial policies. They were joined at times by merchants trading with the islands. Such informal meetings later developed into a more formal lobbying organization during the American Revolution, the London Society of West India Merchants and Planters. In addition, many islands also appointed formal agents to lobby Parliament on their behalf. The most influential of these agents represented Jamaica, reflecting the island's position as the wealthiest colony in British America.

More importantly, absentees from the islands gained a more direct voice in political affairs by standing for election to Parliament. By the middle of the eighteenth century, several dozen absentee sugar planters held seats in the House of Commons, while several members of the House of Lords had direct or indirect connections to the plantations. Among the most prominent of these absentee politicians was William Beckford. Born in Jamaica, Beckford served continuously in the Commons between 1747 and 1770, as well as two terms as lord mayor of London. Beckford and other absentees did not formally represent their home islands—no American colony sent representatives to Parliament—but they provided the sugar islands with a voice in imperial affairs unmatched by any other group of colonists. Benjamin Franklin discovered this during the imperial crises of the 1760s, observing, "The West Indies vastly outweigh us of the Northern Colonies" in London's corridors of power.[3] Whereas relatively few members of Parliament had any experience in or knowledge of the mainland colonies, the numerous absentee owners living in England had vested interests in the welfare of the sugar islands, and they acted repeatedly on behalf of those interests during the eighteenth century.

While absentees gained influence in London, wealthy planters and merchants resident in the colonies dominated local politics. The political structures of the colonies resembled one another and most other British colonies. Following an initial period of proprietary or trustee governance, all the colonies eventually came under direct royal control. The king appointed a governor or lieutenant governor to represent his interest in each colony. In the case of the Leeward Islands, the king appointed a governor-general for all four islands, while each island had its own lieutenant governor. The governors had the power to call and dismiss legislative assemblies and had veto power over legislative acts. They served as the head of the colonial militia as well as of the Anglican Church. Governors also nominated individuals to the council, subject to approval by English officials. The council served as advisors to the governor and, with him, formed the highest civil and criminal court in the colony. When meeting without the governor present, the council formed the upper house of the legislature and played a role in shaping laws.

Most importantly, each colony contained an assembly of elected officials who represented the interests of the "people." (The Leewards experimented briefly with a general assembly of representatives from all four islands, but it met only sporadically between 1681 and 1710, when the plan was abandoned, except for a brief revival at the end of the eighteenth century.) The assembly voted on all questions of taxation and expenditure. Indeed, the right not to be taxed without their consent was widely viewed as the foundation of British liberty, and elected assemblies, in Britain and the colonies, served to protect that right and to check the power of the monarch or his representative, the governor. Even in Barbados and the Leewards, which agreed to a 4.5 percent tax on exports as part of the settlement following Charles II's Restoration, and in Jamaica, which voted to provide the Crown a permanent revenue in 1728, such funds were never enough to cover the normal operating costs of government, to say nothing of extraordinary expenses during wartime. As a result, governors had to negotiate with assemblies to fund many government operations and to get anything accomplished. One Leeward Island governor complained bitterly about the "constant practice of these Assemblys to keep their Governours dependent on their favours from year to year."[4]

These representative assemblies were not representative in the modern sense of the term. As was the case in other parts of the British Atlantic world, only those who held a minimum amount of property qualified to vote in elections. Jamaica, Barbados, and St. Kitts limited voting to adult men who owned ten acres of land or a house worth £10 and who were Christians, thereby disfranchising Jews on the islands. South Carolina required fifty acres of land or payment of 20 shillings in taxes. Georgia, not surprisingly, adopted a similar land requirement when it gained a representative assembly in the 1750s. Such requirements resembled those in other colonies, but whereas the widespread availability of land in most mainland colonies ensured a large percentage of colonists met the property requirement to vote, the small size of most colonies in the Greater Caribbean limited political participation. The Lowcountry was an exception to this, as more land allowed a large majority of the adult male population to vote. By contrast, only 20 to 25 percent of the adult white men could vote in Barbados. In the small Leeward Islands, property requirements sometimes created absurd situations. In St. Kitts, the single vote of one man, Samuel Crooke, at times determined who represented St. Mary Cayon parish in the island's legislature. Crooke was the only freeholder among the parish's forty-six white residents who met the property requirement.

Property requirements also limited who could serve in local offices. South Carolina required that members of the Commons House of Assembly own five hundred acres of land and ten slaves. Georgia had a similar property standard. Jamaica required a total wealth of at least £3,000. Requirements were lower in the Leeward Islands. Candidates in St. Kitts, for example, needed only forty acres of land or property valued at £40, but given the small size of the islands, these rules remained prohibitive to most colonists, so much so that they were often ignored. Such requirements ensured that all political affairs remained firmly in the hands of planter and merchant elites. The percentage of South Carolina assemblymen with estates valued at more than £2,000 more than doubled between the 1720s and 1750s, from 30 percent to 63 percent. An even smaller group dominated the colony's council: between 1720 and 1762, more than one-third of council seats were occupied by members of six interrelated families.

Needless to say, governments controlled by planters ensured that planter issues dominated government business. What one visitor from Massachusetts observed about political affairs in South Carolina was true for the entire region. "'Tis true they have a house of Assembly: but who do they represent?" asked Josiah Quincy. "The laborer, the mechanic, the tradesman, the farmer, husbandman or yeoman? No. The representatives are almost if not wholly rich planters. The Planting interest is therefore represented, but I conceive nothing else (*as it ought to be*)."[5] The dominance of planters was such that few men challenged their position. Even in Jamaica and the Lowcountry, with their relatively large white populations and more land, elites generally agreed among themselves who should stand for election, and often just a handful of votes determined the election. One election in St. Bartholomew parish, South Carolina, in 1748 had only 23 voters, although there were 120 households in the parish. The winning candidate received 11 votes.

Colonists in the Greater Caribbean, like those throughout British America, believed that they held the same rights as native-born Englishmen. They considered their local assemblies equivalent to the House of Commons, even if many met in taverns or private homes until the middle of the eighteenth century, and modeled their actions accordingly. Many went so far as to purchase maces, the symbol of Parliament's authority. Following British practice, the Carolina assembly laid its mace before the speaker of the House at each session. Members also wore their hats in the chamber because that was the practice in England.

Colonial assemblies jealously guarded their power and privileges and sought to extend their influence in myriad ways, much to the frustration of governors appointed to rule them. (The governor-general of the Leeward Islands had the unwelcome task of dealing with four assemblies.) Regular efforts by the Crown, working through the governors, to assert more control over colonial affairs met firm resistance from the assemblies. The Jamaican assembly rebuffed attempts to generate a permanent revenue, one that would not require an annual vote by the assembly, for decades. They also forced the Crown to back off a plan to apply

Poyning's Law to the island in the 1670s. That law, which governed the Irish Parliament, would have prohibited meetings of the assembly unless called by the king and required royal approval of all laws before they went into effect. Outraged assembly leaders rejected the proposal, declaring that as Englishmen, they had the right to live under the laws of England or to make their own laws through the assembly, and English officials withdrew the plan. Jamaican officials eventually agreed to provide a permanent revenue for government in 1728 but only in exchange for the Crown's recognition of their local laws.

Colonists elsewhere engaged in similar battles against governors who sought to enlarge the power of the Crown at the expense of the assembly. Governors frequently found themselves caught between their orders from London to curtail the powers of local assemblies and opposition from assembly leaders determined to maintain them. Frustrated, many governors requested leaves or new postings in other parts of the British political or military establishment.

Given the region's disease environment, not all governors lived long enough to be recalled. In the middle of writing a sentence reporting on the "bleeding fever" that struck the island in 1702, Jamaican governor William Selwyn became "indisposed." He was dead within days. The administration of one of his successors, the hard-drinking Henry Cunningham, lasted only seven weeks. In one case, a governor's death came at the hands of his political opponents. A native Virginian, Daniel Parke began making enemies soon after his arrival as governor of the Leeward Islands in 1706. Parke's appointment resulted more from powerful connections, a rakish charm, and the good fortune of personally delivering news of a key military victory to Queen Anne than from any administrative abilities. Shortly after arriving on Antigua, he challenged the most powerful man in the colony, former governor Christopher Codrington Jr. Parke charged Codrington with smuggling, confiscated his estate on St. Kitts, and raided his plantations on Barbuda. Codrington had his enemies, but attacks on private property worried all colonists, and they rallied to Codrington's defense. Parke also sought to control appointments to various offices and to build a new governor's mansion and new barracks for troops he had brought from England, both at taxpayer's expense. Living up to his scandalous reputation, he began sleeping with the wives and daughters of several prominent planters, and he fathered a child with the wife of the official in charge of regulating Antigua's slave trade.

The combination of Parke's personal and political actions enraged colonists in Antigua, who petitioned for his removal. British officials eventually recalled Parke, but not before he sent armed troops to break up a 1710 meeting of the Antigua assembly, which refused to provide defense funds he had requested. This was the final straw for Antiguans, and hundreds of men besieged Parke's residence in December 1710. When Parke refused to leave and fired on his attackers, the colonists stormed the house and killed the governor. Parke's murder ultimately went unpunished. Despite the involvement of hundreds of men, colonists all claimed they knew nothing of the matter. Unable to punish the entire colony, the new governor issued a general pardon.

Political conflict, and even violence, was not unique to the Greater Caribbean, but Parke's murder was an extreme, indeed treasonous, act. It was also an exceptional one. Colonists in the Greater Caribbean generally had reason to seek consensus in the political arena. As the Jamaican planter and historian Bryan Edwards observed, "In countries where slavery is established, the leading principle on which government is supported, is *fear*," and that was especially true in the Greater Caribbean, where enslaved Africans outnumbered whites so heavily.[6] Planters knew that they lived with "enemies in their own households," and the constant threat of rebellion meant that they remained on guard at all times. It also meant that colonists could ill afford deep divisions amongst themselves, lest they provide an opening for slave resistance.

This is not to say that political conflict did not exist. Political factions formed in many of the colonies. Ironically, some of the strongest divisions existed in Jamaica, home of the largest slave population in the region and scene of frequent rebellions. During the seventeenth and early eighteenth centuries, disagreement over the Spanish trade gave rise to factions termed Whigs and Tories, after the two dominant parties in England (although at least some contemporaries questioned such labels, given Jamaica's relatively small population). Later, in the middle of the eighteenth century, planters and merchants divided over a plan to move the island's capital from Spanish Town to Kingston, which at times led to violence. At one assembly meeting, a motion to adjourn resulted in a near riot, during which three members of the Spanish Town faction were held in their seats by sword-wielding Kingston supporters.

All of the colonies had their share of "Grumbletonians" ready to do battle over particular issues, and political disputes erupted periodically throughout the region at various times. Observers described Barbados as "miserably divided into Factions" and "perplexed with Parties and Animosities."[7] Disputes regarding the establishment of the Anglican Church, the rule of the proprietors, and the use of paper money fostered divisions and promoted discord within South Carolina's political society.

By the middle of the eighteenth century, however, political conflicts had become less pronounced in much of the region. A combination of factors, including rising economic prosperity; the absence of major religious schisms; the continued danger posed by neighboring Spanish, French, and Native American groups; and perhaps most importantly, an ever-expanding slave population—or, in Georgia's case, the introduction of slavery—muted political discord, resulting in relatively harmonious relations among local elites. Colonial officials remained ready to battle royal governors, and fierce debates concerning rights and privileges continued within the halls of the new assembly buildings that appeared in many of the colonies by the middle of the eighteenth century, but such disputes rarely spilled over into broader social relations. Jamaica proved something of an exception, but even there elites maintained firm control and resolution of the Spanish Town–Kingston debate eased (although did not end) political discord among colonists. In the end, the overwhelming number of enslaved Africans made serious and prolonged political conflict simply too dangerous to consider.

WARFARE

In addition to slave rebellions, colonists in the Greater Caribbean faced the constant threat of attack from enemies in neighboring territories throughout the seventeenth and eighteenth centuries. At first, conflicts among European colonists played out as side-shows to the main action in Europe, but over the course of the eighteenth century, events in the American colonies occupied an increasingly central role in larger European conflicts. Island colonists found themselves pitted against the French in particular, as each side sought to dominate sugar production in the region by destroying its rival's plantations.

A number of factors influenced warfare in the region during the seventeenth and eighteenth centuries. Geography played a significant role in determining the vulnerability of individual colonies to attack. Situated far to the windward of the other islands, Barbados was relatively isolated from the other islands and difficult to reach, as any attack launched from Guadeloupe or Martinique required sailing against the wind. As a result, Barbados experienced no serious invasions during this period, although colonists remained on guard during times of conflict. Conversely, the Leeward Islands were located close to, and downwind from, Guadeloupe and Martinique, as well as the Carib-controlled island of Dominica. Moreover, St. Christopher remained divided into French and English sections until 1713, rendering it especially vulnerable, while the large and disgruntled Irish Catholic servant population there, and on Montserrat, formed something of a fifth column. Not surprisingly, the Leewards suffered frequent invasions from French and Carib forces (who were at times allied). St. Christopher was captured and recaptured by English and French forces seven times between 1666 and 1713, while the other Leewards each suffered at least one major invasion. Jamaica and the Lowcountry also occupied perilous positions within the region. Spanish and French islands surrounded Jamaica, while Spanish Florida, French Louisiana, and numerous powerful Indian nations (at times allied with the Spanish or French) threatened the security of colonists in the Lowcountry.

Warfare in the Greater Caribbean was a seasonal affair, particularly during the eighteenth century. Most campaigns occurred between November and June to avoid the hurricane season. The Spanish learned this lesson the hard way in 1686, when the expedition they sent out to attack Carolina in early September was crushed by a major storm. Most commanders were unwilling to risk the loss of ships and men, and fleets often evacuated the region during the hurricane months, sailing to Europe, parts of North America, or to the northern coast of South America.

The biggest environmental impact on warfare came in the form of disease. Yellow fever and malaria decimated European soldiers sent to fight in the Greater Caribbean. European soldiers and sailors had no previous exposure to these diseases, and thus no immunity to them, and they died in horrific numbers. Admiral Edward Vernon led an expeditionary force of 29,000 men to attack Cartagena, Colombia, in 1741–42. By October 1742, only 7,000 remained alive; 21,000 of the 22,000 dead had perished from disease. More British soldiers died in the two months following the successful siege of Havana in 1762 than in all of North America during the entire Seven Years War. Spain organized the defense of its territories around the threat of disease, building massive stone fortifications designed to hold off attacks for a few weeks, by which time they assumed that disease would start to take its toll on the invaders. French and British officials anticipated losing three-fourths of their forces to disease, and as a result, they sent out large numbers of men to fight in the region. Soldiers viewed service in the region as a death sentence—with good reason. Few returned alive, even if they never saw any actual combat.

Britain relied on a variety of military forces to defend its colonies. Each colony had its own militia in which all white males were required to serve. The most effective militias emerged in Barbados and in the Lowcountry. The tiny white populations of the Leeward Islands, by contrast, rendered their militias far less effective. In many cases, the crew of a relatively small warship outnumbered the island's militia. The desire among planters for the social status that came from leading a militia troop meant that, in some cases, the number of officers equaled or exceeded the number of soldiers. Moreover, many colonists wanted to protect their own properties, so they often failed to turn out for militia duty or served only briefly. Jamaica had a much larger white population than the Leewards, but it was spread out over a large island and some commentators suggested that the militia performed better on the parade grounds than in battle.

Relatively small colonial militias meant that colonists sometimes resorted to arming slaves to help fight off foreign invasions, or in some cases, slave rebellions. Colonists hesitated to take this step, both because they were so heavily outnumbered by their slaves and feared that armed slaves would turn against them and because having slaves fight undermined arguments that they were inferior to whites. Necessity at times outweighed these concerns, however. Colonists in Barbados armed slaves when threatened with a French invasion in 1707, and slaves formed perhaps one-third of the forces defending the island. Antigua had 1,000 slaves in arms in 1742. The British army and navy utilized thousands of slaves in the region. Some served as "baggage negroes," building forts and trenches, gathering supplies, and maintaining barracks, but others were "shot negroes" who fought in battles. South Carolina also occasionally armed slaves, the only mainland colony to do so. Local officials mobilized slaves to fight in Queen Anne's War (1702–13), the Yamasee War (1715), and the War of Jenkins' Ear (1739–48). The practice of arming slaves declined during the rest of the eighteenth century, most likely because the growth of the white population in the Backcountry reduced the need to take the dangerous step of giving weapons to slaves.

Instead of local militias, most colonies looked to imperial troops for protection. British officials first sent regular troops to the islands during the latter part of the seventeenth century, but the number of troops increased significantly during Queen Anne's War, particularly in Jamaica and the Leewards. Colonists in both places regularly allocated funds for barracks, hospitals, and other military installations. The size of these peacetime garrisons remained relatively small, but the number of troops swelled dramatically during times of war, when Britain sent thousands of men to protect their most valuable colonies. At other times, as the Jamaican planter Edward Long observed, the presence of troops served less to guard against the French and the Spanish than to keep watch on slaves.

Colonists also constructed significant fortifications throughout the region. Port Royal, Jamaica, had the most extensive fortifications in all of English America during the seventeenth century, and it remained one of the most heavily fortified towns during the eighteenth century. Other colonies also boasted impressive batteries, including Brimstone Hill on St. Kitts. Charleston began as a walled city, and although by the early eighteenth century the town had outgrown its walls, the bastions remained in place. Colonists took advantage of the 1752 hurricane to rebuild the fortifications and hired a German engineer to oversee construction, although it took the threat of a French invasion to jumpstart the work.

Of far greater importance for the defense of the colonies was the British navy. As Christopher Codrington Sr. noted in the early part of the eighteenth century, "All turns upon the mastery of the sea . . . If we have it our islands are safe, however thinly populated."[8] Dependent on outside supplies and vulnerable to attacks at numerous coastal points, the islands required vigorous support from the British navy. Likewise, while Lowcountry colonists feared land attacks from the Spanish and Native Americans, French ships also presented a threat.

England periodically sent warships to the region during the seventeenth century, but beginning in the early part of the eighteenth century permanent dockyards were constructed at Port Royal, Jamaica, and English Harbour, Antigua. These facilities enabled the British to maintain a year-round naval presence in the Greater Caribbean and to repair ships locally, giving them a distinct advantage over their French rivals, whose naval operations remained based in Europe.

The size and scale of military operations in the islands expanded dramatically between the seventeenth and eighteenth centuries. The major conflicts of the seventeenth century— particularly the Anglo-French/Dutch War of 1666–67 and the Nine Years War in 1688–97—played out as relatively small-scale affairs in the region. Often a few hundred, or in some cases a few thousand troops, launched raids on nearby colonies. Raiders generally lacked the means and desire to hold territory. Instead, the goal was to destroy the enemies' plantations and to capture their slaves, undermining their ability to produce sugar. One Jamaican sugar planter wrote to another amid invasion rumors in 1745 that he doubted the French could capture the island, but "if you and I are ruined it is the same thing to us."[9]

Raids often resulted in extensive damage. The French captured some 400 slaves during an attack on St. Kitts in 1666 and expelled roughly 5,000 English colonists from the island. (To add insult to injury, a relief expedition sent from Barbados sank in a hurricane.) From there the French moved on to Antigua and Montserrat, and aided by Carib fighters and disgruntled Irish servants, captured 1,000 additional slaves and burned dozens of sugar estates. Such destruction hindered economic development in the Leewards, but the English lost no territory, as the French returned the English section of St. Kitts at the Treaty of Breda in 1667. England did surrender the valuable plantation colony of Surinam to the Dutch as part of the peace settlement, but it gained New Netherland in exchange, soon renamed New York.

Similar violence and destruction marked the Nine Years War and Queen Anne's War. St. Christopher changed hands three times during the former, as the French first expelled the English from the island, the English counterattacked and defeated the French, then returned the territory to France at the Treaty of Ryswick in 1697. French raiders attacked Jamaica's eastern parishes in 1694 and made off with 1,600 slaves, but the Jamaican militia led by Governor William Beeston prevented the French from reaching the most valuable plantation zone on the island's south coast. During Queen Anne's War, the English managed to attack the French first, but French counterattacks resulted in tremendous damage on Nevis, St. Kitts, and Montserrat. Planters on St. Kitts claimed losses of £145,000, while Montserrat reportedly suffered £180,000 in damages.

The Lowcountry also participated in the war. Colonists launched two expeditions against Spanish Florida in 1702 and 1704. The first managed to burn the town of St. Augustine but could not capture the massive stone fort, Castillo de San Marcos, and the Carolinians were forced to retreat when a Spanish fleet arrived. The second destroyed Apalachee Indian and Spanish settlements in northwestern Florida and captured 1,000 Indian slaves. The colonial militia then defeated a Spanish counterattack on Charleston in August 1706, reportedly losing only 1 man while killing 30 Spaniards and capturing another 230.

As in previous conflicts, both sides in Queen Anne's War sought to burn crops, steal slaves, and damage plantations rather than to conquer territory. Indeed, English officials explicitly instructed forces in early 1703 to destroy French plantations on Guadeloupe and Martinique as quickly as possible but then to sail to Jamaica rather than attempt to hold the islands. In the end, despite the serious damages suffered by planters in parts of the Greater Caribbean, the English emerged victorious in the larger conflict. The gains secured by the Treaty of Utrecht in 1713 included winning the *asiento*, the highly prized contract for supplying slaves to Spain's American colonies, as well as complete control of St. Christopher.

MID-EIGHTEENTH-CENTURY CONFLICTS

Queen Anne's War marked a transitional moment in the Greater Caribbean. Although England had sent ships and troops to the region in earlier conflicts, English officials allocated increasing resources and attention to the colonies during this war. The valuable colonies of the Greater Caribbean were no longer minor theaters of action but had assumed ever-greater importance in the conflicts between European powers.

Trade disputes in the warm waters of the Caribbean during the 1730s served as the impetus for the next great imperial conflict, the so-called War of Jenkins' Ear. The war emerged from disputes regarding the *asiento*. The contract allowed English ships entry to Spanish American ports to deliver slaves, as well as the right to send one ship a year carrying 500 tons of manufactured goods to the great market fair at Portobello. This legitimate trade, however, provided all sorts of opportunities for illegal trade, and numerous ships arrived in Spanish colonies carrying a range of goods other than slaves. To suppress this illegal trade, Spain licensed private ships to patrol the coasts. These *Guarda-Costas* often did not distinguish between legitimate and illegitimate British traders, and they confiscated entire cargoes, not just illegal goods. The result was a long-simmering conflict in which both sides violated the rights of the other. One British naval officer stationed in Jamaica complained in a letter in 1731 that "villainy is inherent to this climate, and I should be partial if I was to judge whether the trading part of the island [Jamaica] or those we complain of among the Spaniards are most exquisite in that trade."[10]

Outrage over the Spanish depredations built in England, fueled by merchants eager to expand into new markets. During parliamentary hearings in 1738, a Captain Jenkins reportedly claimed that the *Guarda-Costas* had cut off his ear when they boarded his ship several years earlier, displaying his severed ear in a jar as proof. The story may have been apocryphal—the Jamaican absentee planter William Beckford claimed at the time that anyone looking under Jenkins's wig would find both ears—

but it fanned the flames of anti-Spanish sentiment among the British public, and war broke out the following year. Britain sent thousands of troops to the region, including some 3,400 North Americans, among them George Washington's half brother, Lawrence (who later honored the commander under whom he served, Admiral Edward Vernon, by naming his Virginia estate after him). Vernon won great fame for his seizure of Portobello (Panama) in 1739, but his effort to capture Cartagena in 1741 failed miserably, as disease ravaged his forces. Success proved equally elusive elsewhere. Efforts by colonists in South Carolina and Georgia to attack Spanish Florida in 1740 faltered and led to a good deal of recrimination between James Oglethorpe and officials in South Carolina, although Oglethorpe found some redemption when his forces beat back a Spanish counterattack at Fort Frederica two years later.

The trade war between Spain and England expanded into a larger European conflict involving France and other powers in 1744, although the War of Austrian Succession, or King George's War as it was called in America, witnessed relatively little action in the Greater Caribbean. Both sides sent large forces to the region, and they took turns harassing each other's shipping, but neither side mounted a serious attack on the other's colonies beyond the English seizure of St. Louis, a major fortification on St. Domingue. Colonists in the Lowcountry worried about French activity in Louisiana and about possible alliances between France and the powerful Cherokee and Creek confederations in the Backcountry, but the threats never materialized. French privateers, however, exacted a heavy toll on shipping in and out of the colony, plunging the economy into depression. Carolina's governor reported later that the French war had brought the colony "to the Brink of Ruin."[11]

As happened often, the Treaty of Aix-la-Chapelle in 1748 stipulated a return to conditions at the start of the war and failed even to mention the issues of trade and the *Guarda-Costas* that had triggered the conflict nine years earlier. Peace, however, did not last long. The Seven Years War—often labeled the French and Indian War in North America—began in 1754 as a fight between England and France for control of the Ohio River valley, but it spread quickly to all parts of the globe, and by the time fighting commenced, Britain had developed a greater interest in acquiring territory in the Greater Caribbean. Several factors explain the shift in attitude. High sugar prices assuaged the fears of many planters that adding new sugar colonies would depress prices. In addition, many in Britain felt that their existing islands could not meet the increasing demand for sugar among British consumers, much of which was fueled by the growth of tea and coffee consumption. Finally, some argued that capturing and holding French islands would reduce the seemingly constant conflict in the region, providing greater security for British colonists and fewer disruptions to sugar production.

Britain and France formally declared war in 1756, but British officials, led by Prime Minister William Pitt, hesitated to commit resources to the Caribbean until they had secured control of North America. After a series of victories in 1758 and 1759, culminating in the capture of Quebec in 1759, ended fighting on the mainland, Britain shifted its gaze south. A British force of 6,000 men attacked Guadeloupe in January 1759 and, after several months of fighting, captured the island in April. By early 1762, Britain had seized Martinique as well as four smaller islands—Grenada, Tobago, St. Vincent, and Dominica. Concerned about Britain's growing power, Spain entered the war in January 1762, which soon proved a costly mistake. British officials outfitted a force of some 15,000 men led by the Earl of Albemarle to invade Cuba. The forces landed in June and, aided by unseasonably dry weather, within several weeks had captured Havana, and with it sugar, tobacco, and bullion worth £3,000,000, as well as one-fifth of the Spanish navy. Unfortunately, success took longer than planned. Eventually the rains returned, and yellow fever did what Spanish troops could not. By October Albemarle had lost 4,708 men to disease (as opposed to 560 from combat), while the navy lost at least 3,000 men. England had captured Spain's key to the Indies, but holding it proved costly.

The Lowcountry experienced no armed conflict during the war. The threat of a French invasion in 1757–58 led British officials to deploy 1,700 troops to the region, but the most pressing issue became where to house them, which in turn generated a heated debate between local officials and British commanders. Even the threat of privateers was less pronounced than in earlier conflicts. Governor William Henry Lyttleton proposed an attack on the French in Alabama and Louisiana, but British officials remained focused on events in the north. In 1759, however, conflict erupted in the Carolina Backcountry. Long-simmering boundary issues between colonists and the Cherokee erupted into war when Virginia settlers killed several Cherokee warriors they accused of stealing horses and the Cherokee responded by attacking Backcountry settlements in Virginia, North Carolina, and South Carolina. British and colonial troops from South Carolina launched three campaigns against the Cherokee between 1759 and 1761. The first two had only limited success, but the third, led by Lieutenant Colonel James Grant, pushed deep into Cherokee territory and burned numerous towns and cornfields. Increasingly short of provisions and cut off from trade goods, including ammunition, the Cherokee agreed to a treaty in 1761. That treaty, and a subsequent, larger meeting with other native groups and officials from several colonies, opened up new lands for colonial settlement, and the population of whites in the Backcountry surged.

THE TREATY OF PARIS

Well before the end of the war, but after success in Canada and Guadeloupe, British officials and the British public began to debate which territory might be returned to France as part of a possible peace settlement. In formal speeches, pamphlets, newspaper articles, and coffeehouse conversations advocates laid out the relative merits of each. Several prominent absentee sugar planters, including the powerful Jamaicans William Beckford and Rose Fuller, argued against keeping Guadeloupe, fearing that the addition of a major sugar producer would depress sugar prices, and thus planter profits. North Americans, led by Benjamin Franklin, advocated keeping Canada as well, although for different reasons. Franklin argued that conflict with the French on the mainland had been the prime cause for the war and returning it would inevitably result in renewed conflict. Moreover, the steadily expanding population of North America would provide a growing market for British manufactured goods.

Other voices, however, argued for keeping Guadeloupe and returning Canada to the French. They maintained that eliminating Guadeloupe as a rival promised greater security for Britain's existing sugar colonies, while increased production from the island promised great wealth for the empire. Echoing Voltaire, they dismissed Canada as little more than "a few acres of snow." Proponents for keeping Guadeloupe found powerful allies among English slave traders, who saw a huge new market for enslaved Africans, as France had never been able to meet planter demand from the island. Finally, at least a few prescient commentators suggested that keeping Guadeloupe and returning Canada to the French would provide a means of checking the expansionist tendencies of North American colonists, who many feared were growing too independent of British control. Having an enemy at the back of mainland colonists would ensure their continued military and economic dependence on Great Britain.

In the end, the debates proved somewhat premature, as Britain rolled up even more conquests in the Caribbean and throughout the globe, complicating peace negotiations. At the Treaty of Paris in 1763, Britain returned Guadeloupe to France and kept Canada, along with four smaller islands, the so-called Ceded Islands of Tobago, Dominica, St. Vincent, and Grenada, the last of which governed dozens of smaller islands known as the Grenadines. Britain also agreed to return Havana to Cuba in exchange for Florida, welcome news to Lowcountry planters, who had grown tired of the threat posed by the Spanish colony. Despite these tremendous gains, not everyone approved of the treaty. Many believed Britain had been too generous in returning Guadeloupe, including William Pitt, who railed against the treaty in the House of Commons. In the end, his protests were for naught and the treaty passed by a vote of 319 to 65.

Even with generous concessions to France, the Seven Years War, unlike most previous conflicts, reshaped the political landscape of the Greater Caribbean. The Treaty of Paris removed the Spanish and French presence east of the Mississippi, allowing Britain to proclaim sovereignty over the eastern half of the continent—ignoring, of course, Native American nations who claimed and occupied much of that territory—and opening new lands in Florida and the Backcountry for British colonists. A few Lowcountry planters acquired title to land in East Florida with the hope of extending the Carolina plantation complex south of the St. John's River, but most, including Henry Laurens, were more skeptical of the region's potential, arguing that only a massive investment of time and labor could produce good returns. "Don't encourage people of worth to throw away their Money in that Country," Laurens advised one correspondent.[12] His advice proved prescient. A few plantations producing rice and indigo developed in the new colony before the outbreak of the American Revolution, but several other grand schemes, including one utilizing migrants from Greece and Italy and another engaging London paupers, failed massively as laborers died or deserted in droves.

Britain also expanded its holdings in the Caribbean basin itself for the first time since the conquest of Jamaica in 1655, not counting the addition of French lands on St. Kitts in 1713. The most important of these new colonies was Grenada, which within a few years became Britain's second largest sugar producer. The French had developed plantations on the island, but British colonists quickly expanded operations. By 1773, over 26,000 enslaved Africans labored on 334 plantations growing coffee, indigo, and sugar. Production of sugar and other commodities increased on the other Ceded Islands as well, although at a slower pace. Among the first to develop plantations on Tobago was Gedney Clarke Jr., who sold the family's plantation in Demerara in the late 1760s and purchased four properties on the island, along with a plantation in Grenada.

Britain's great success in the Seven Years War, however, created complicated new issues for British officials. One set of concerns involved the treatment of conquered subjects, including French planters on Grenada and the so-called Black Caribs of St. Vincent. What rights would these new subjects of the British Crown possess? What was their status within the empire? In Grenada, virulent anti-Catholicism and a desire for political power among British colonists overturned metropolitan attempts to extend political rights and religious toleration to conquered French colonists and resulted in what one newspaper called "a kind of civil war."[13] Actual war erupted in St. Vincent in 1772. British plans to push the Black Caribs—descendants of shipwrecked Africans and local natives—off their lands, thereby freeing up land for expansionist sugar planters, encountered forceful resistance from the Caribs and strong criticism from many in England, who argued that the Caribs were rightly fighting to protect their property. Britain sent two regiments from North

America to St. Vincent in 1772, but the Caribs fought them to a draw and forced British officials to sign a treaty the following year guaranteeing them 30,000 acres of land.

And then there was the issue of debt. Britain's national debt had roughly doubled during the course of the war, rising from £75,000,000 in 1756 to £146,000,000 by 1763. Concerned about funding troops who remained in North America, British officials, led by George Grenville, designed a series of measures to raise revenue to cover the costs of colonial administration. The first, the Revenue Act of 1764—better known as the Sugar Act—revised the 1733 Molasses Act and tightened enforcement of trade between North America and the French sugar islands. Its passage was greeted warmly by sugar planters, who had long complained that mainland colonists routinely violated the previous act, but it elicited strong protests from northern merchants, who believed that their interests had been sacrificed to the wealth and power of the West India lobby. Although this was not the first time that the islands and northern colonies had squared off over issues of trade, the Sugar Act represented a new—and increasingly contentious chapter—in relations between the islands and the mainland, a first step on a road that ultimately would divide the colonies of the Greater Caribbean, and the British Empire as a whole.

The Political Crisis of the 1760s

W‌HEN GEORGE GRENVILLE INTRODUCED the Sugar Act to Parliament in 1764, he hinted that more measures would be needed to cover the costs of colonial administration and defense in North America. In February 1765, Grenville brought forward the next step in his plan to raise that revenue. The Stamp Act required that all paper documents in the colonies have stamps of varying values affixed to them. Anyone purchasing a newspaper or a deck of cards, writing a will, buying land, or seeking a marriage license would pay the tax. Unlike the Sugar Act and others that regulated colonial trade, the Stamp Act was a direct tax and threatened to affect the lives of all colonists, not just those who bought and sold imported goods.

Passage of the Stamp Act provoked swift and at times violent reaction in colonies throughout British America, including those in the Greater Caribbean. Like their counterparts elsewhere, colonists in the Greater Caribbean decried the attempt to levy taxes without their consent and invoked their rights as freeborn British subjects in numerous letters and pamphlets. Colonists declared that only elected representatives could raise taxes, and their elected representatives sat in the colonial assemblies, not the House of Commons. As one group of Jamaican planters wrote, the link between taxation and representation was "a Bulwark essential to the very existence of a British Constitution."[1] Although many absentee planters sat in the Commons, colonists rejected the idea that absentees represented the colonies.

Allowing Parliament to tax without actual representation, they claimed, would reduce them to the status of slaves.

Beyond issuing pamphlets and petitions asserting their rights, many colonists took to the streets to halt the landing and distribution of the stamps. Angry colonists in Charleston forced the governor to keep the stamps under armed guard at Fort Johnson on nearby James Island, and later on a British warship. South Carolina's stamp distributor found himself hung and burned in effigy in Charleston, and he quickly resigned his position. Artisans and mechanics calling themselves the Sons of Liberty demanded entry to homes of wealthy elites to search for stamps they thought might be hidden inside. Protestors in St. Kitts burned the stamps that arrived on the island and forced the stamp distributor, William Tuckett, to renounce his commission. Cries of "Liberty, Property, and No Stamps" rang out in the streets of Basseterre. When Tuckett escaped to Nevis and started to distribute stamps there, crowds followed him, destroying the stamps and burning two homes in the process. Colonists in Kingston set ablaze effigies of George Grenville and the local stamp agent during celebrations following the repeal of the Stamp Act in 1766.

Nevertheless, despite the violence in some parts of the Greater Caribbean and the near universal constitutional objections to the Stamp Act, colonists in a number of places complied with the act, at least for a time. Colonists in Antigua paid the duty for a few weeks, as did those in Georgia, the only mainland colony to do so. So too did colonists in Jamaica and Barbados, even though the tax rates were higher in the islands and the money raised was for defense of the mainland colonies, not their own. Jamaicans paid more stamp taxes than the other colonies combined.

The varied and often more muted reaction to the Stamp Act in parts of the Greater Caribbean foreshadowed the response to subsequent British measures and highlighted growing differences between the sugar islands and the Carolina Lowcountry in particular. Colonists in the islands, for example, raised no outcry against the Townshend duties of 1767, which taxed a variety of imported products, including lead, glass, paper, and tea. Unlike South Carolina and most other mainland colonies, no nonimportation movements formed in the islands to protest the taxes. One reason is that the West India lobby successfully secured exemptions for the islands from the new American Board of Customs Commissions and the new mainland Vice-Admiralty courts created in conjunction with the Townshend duties. As a result, while the Townshend Acts escalated tensions in the Lowcountry and other parts of the mainland between 1767 and 1770, the sugar islands remained relatively calm and quiet. Some British officials even suggested repealing the Townshend taxes in Jamaica, Barbados, and the other islands as a reward for their dutiful submission to parliamentary measures.

Island colonists became more involved in the imperial crisis following passage of the Intolerable Acts and the calling of the Continental Congress in 1774. Colonists in Barbados sent support to embattled Bostonians after British officials closed the port of Boston. Several island legislatures, including those in Tobago and Grenada, drafted resolutions supporting the mainland colonists and imploring the king to mediate the escalating crisis between Parliament and the colonists. The most noteworthy of these came from Jamaica. Echoing the language that permeated political discourse on the mainland, as well as the language used in their own struggles against royal governors over the course of the seventeenth and eighteenth centuries, the Jamaican petitioners maintained that they and their North American counterparts "were a part of the *English* people, in every respect equal to them, and possessed of every right and privilege . . . which the people of *England* were possessed of" including "that great right of consenting to the laws which should bind them." They pleaded with the king to protect the rights and liberties of the colonists against Parliament's "plan . . . for enslaving the colonies" by the "unrestrained exercise of legislative power."[2]

The strong rhetoric of the Jamaican petition, however, represented the high-water mark of Caribbean support for their mainland cousins and resulted as much from self-interest as from political principles, as the outbreak of war threatened to disrupt plantation operations. Colonists in the sugar islands may have agreed with many of the constitutional concerns articulated by mainland colonists and disagreed with some of the harsh measures adopted by British officials in response, but few planters were ready to join a revolutionary movement against Great Britain. Colonists in the sugar islands sought to work within the imperial system, to bend it to their needs, not to reject it entirely.

Colonists in the Carolina Lowcountry, by contrast, found themselves increasingly involved with their fellow mainland colonists and increasingly willing to reject the authority of British rule. South Carolina attended the Stamp Act Congress in 1765 and boycotted British goods in response to the Townshend Acts. Assembly leaders clashed with royal governors and British officials over their right to receive the Massachusetts Circular Letter advocating resistance to the Townshend duties and to donate funds to support the British radical John Wilkes. Indeed, royal government in South Carolina effectively ended in the early 1770s as a result of the so-called Wilkes Fund controversy. When a British ship carrying tea arrived in Charleston harbor following passage of the Tea Act in 1773, the Sons of Liberty refused to allow the tea to be sold. To protest the Intolerable Acts, South Carolina sent delegates to the first Continental Congress in 1774 and signed on to the Continental Association, pledging to halt imports from Great Britain immediately and to cease exports to Britain and the West Indies in one year if no resolution was reached, although they forced a concession allowing rice exports to continue.

These divergent responses to the political turmoil of the 1760s and 1770s, and ultimately to the question of independence, reflected three significant differences between the Lowcountry and the islands that, while present earlier in the eighteenth century, had grown more pronounced in the decade before the Revolution. The first concerned the colonies' economic relationship to Great Britain. The Navigation Acts required that both sugar and rice travel first to Great Britain (although rice planters received an exemption for exports to southern Europe in 1731), but Britain never served as the primary market for Lowcountry rice during the eighteenth century. The great majority of rice sent to Britain was reexported to northern Europe. The English market was "insignificant" to Carolina planters, according to Charleston merchant and emerging patriot leader, Christopher Gadsden.[3] Moreover, after 1764 rice shipments to the Caribbean, especially to the French islands, expanded rapidly, providing Lowcountry planters and merchants with new avenues for profit. As the political crisis of the 1770s deepened, in other words, Lowcountry planters could imagine prospering outside the British Empire.

Caribbean sugar planters could not imagine such a prospect. They relied on the British market for their profits. Especially following the rise of St. Domingue (present-day Haiti) as a major sugar producer during the eighteenth century, British planters found themselves unable to compete with French sugars on the open market in Europe. British consumers paid higher prices to sweeten their tea, but older mercantilist arguments about national autonomy and the military benefits of a closed trading system remained influential. Caribbean planters worried about losing the North American provisions trade—the threat of a nonexportation movement by the mainland colonies was a major reason for their increased petitioning in 1774 and 1775—but in the end the protected sugar market proved more important than the provisions trade. Planters could find ways to replace the latter, but not the former.

Vulnerability to internal and external enemies played an equal, if not more important, role in shaping colonists' diverging responses to the imperial crisis. The sugar islands remained far more vulnerable and far more dependent on the British military than the Lowcountry. The expansion of the slave trade in the years after the Seven Years War produced even higher ratios of slaves to whites by the 1770s, meaning island colonists relied all the more on British troops for protection. Unlike their northern counterparts, who questioned the need for a standing army in peacetime and protested the costs associated with quartering troops, the islands welcomed British soldiers and willingly contributed funds to support them. Colonists received a vivid reminder of their dependence when they uncovered a slave plot in western Jamaica in 1776 timed to coincide with the withdrawal of British troops for service in North America. The conspiracy was crushed, but reported plans suggested that slaves were well aware of the fluctuating strength of island defenses. Ultimately, colonists in Jamaica and the other islands could not conceive of existing outside the protective umbrella provided by the British military. The Jamaican petitioners in 1774 underscored this point in their address to the king. Although they expressed strong support for the North Americans and concern about Parliament's actions and the prospect for war, "it cannot be supposed that we now intend, or ever could have intended, resistance to *Great Britain*." The small number of whites and the vast number of slaves rendered Jamaica too "weak and feeble" to do so. Colonists in Jamaica and the other islands could—and did—engage in political and constitutional battles with British officials, but their vulnerability to slave uprisings ensured that such battles never crossed the line into open rebellion.[4]

The prospect of slave revolts haunted Lowcountry colonists as well, but a surging population in the Backcountry reduced the importance of British protection. Slaves continued to outnumber colonists in the Lowcountry in the 1760s and 1770s, in some parishes by ratios as high as 9 to 1, making South Carolina and Georgia the "weakest sisters" among the North American colonies, in the words of Henry Laurens.[5] Reports of enslaved Africans and African Americans marching through the streets of Charleston crying, "Liberty," during protests against the Stamp Act, moreover, no doubt gave considerable pause to many elites as they considered resistance to established British authority. Nevertheless, Lowcountry planters found themselves in a stronger position militarily than their island counterparts, because of the tremendous growth of the Backcountry population during the 1760s. South Carolina's white population doubled between the 1750s and 1770s, and three-fourths of those whites resided in the Backcountry. South Carolina's relatively large white population had always provided a more effective militia than most of the islands could muster, but as one early nineteenth-century historian of the state wrote, the flood of migrants into the Backcountry after the 1750s "added thousands to [Carolina's] domestic strength."[6] Lowcountry whites remained fearful of slave revolts, as well as attacks by Native Americans, but a growing Backcountry population provided greater security against such threats, a security the sugar islands found only in British troops.

The growth of the Backcountry population after the 1750s had additional consequences for the Lowcountry that further distinguished it from the islands. The Backcountry remained a world apart from the Lowcountry in the years before the American Revolution. Although the region was home to the vast majority of white colonists in South Carolina, those colonists remained poor and marginalized. They controlled only 15 percent of the colony's wealth, only 10 percent of the enslaved population, and had almost no representation in the colony's government. As colonists began appropriating lands and building farms in the 1750s and 1760s, however, they increasingly chafed under a political system that remained centered in Charleston and that provided them with little protection against Native Americans and wandering gangs of criminals operating on the frontier. By the later 1760s, groups of colonists known as the Regulators demanded the establishment of local courts that would allow them to engage in legal proceedings without the expense of journeying to Charleston. They also sought greater representation in the assembly, which remained dominated by Lowcountry planters and merchants. Lowcountry elites increasingly realized that they needed to reach some kind of accommodation with Backcountry settlers if they hoped to maintain their power in the colony or exercise any control over the expanding region. Responding to Regulator demands, they created two new western parishes in 1768 and authorized new courts, jails, and sheriffs the following year.

Lowcountry elites faced additional pressure from urban artisans and mechanics in Charleston, for whom the Stamp Act, Townshend duties, and other British measures threatened economic hardship. These men were quick to embrace the nonimportation movement of the late 1760s, because it provided tangible benefits to them—in the form of a "buy American" campaign—as well as a means of resisting British policies and challenging the political monopoly of local merchant and planter elites. Charleston's population of white artisans and mechanics was smaller than those in northern cities, but it was large enough to command attention. The growing assertiveness of the Sons of Liberty forced elites to open up the governance process to ordinary men, so that when a committee was formed to monitor the boycott of British goods in 1769, it included an equal number of planters, merchants, and artisans. As was the case in other mainland colonies, Lowcountry elites increasingly realized that the best means of limiting internal political upheaval was to lead the opposition to unpopular British policies, but doing so required sharing power with artisans, mechanics, and Backcountry farmers.

Planters in the islands faced no such challenges. The islands had no backcountry and few colonists owned enough land to participate fully in the political process. The small size of the white populations meant that artisans, craftsmen, and smaller planters posed no real threat to planter rule. Moreover, such men, regardless of their economic status, occupied an elevated social position, because there were so few whites in the islands. The shared privileges of whiteness helped ease potential economic or political divisions. Political factions did exist on some of the larger islands, particularly Jamaica, but none challenged existing power structures in any meaningful way. The islands remained plantocracies, with local governing institutions firmly in the hands of small groups of planters and merchants and serving the interests of those men. And those interests dictated loyalty to Great Britain.

Other factors also played some role in tempering the opposition to British policies that existed in the islands. Greater absenteeism among Caribbean colonists, for example, reinforced social and cultural ties to Great Britain, as well as providing entry into the world of British politics. Whether as elected officials or effective lobbyists, the political muscle of the West India lobby made sure that island colonists did not feel shut out from debates over colonial policy, nor were they as quick to see conspiracies in the actions of the British government. Their ability to win exemptions from parts of Townshend's program was an example of that power, and it freed the islands from some of the tensions that inflamed opposition to Britain in the Lowcountry.

Colonists in Georgia took longer to join the opposition movement to Great Britain. Georgians had perhaps the strongest ties of any mainland colony to the mother country. Parliament provided massive funding during the 1730s and 1740s, and it continued to provide an annual subsidy of £3,000 to pay Georgia's government salaries into the 1770s. Moreover, Georgia was just starting to prosper in the wake of the Seven Years War, the colony looked to Britain to help protect its frontier from Native Americans, and the colonists had relatively few links to their mainland counterparts, with the exception of South Carolina. Those links, however, would prove important as tensions with Britain mounted. Georgia's governor complained that radical elements in Charleston influenced the emergence of "Liberty people" in Lowcountry Georgia during the Stamp Act crisis and again following passage of the Intolerable Acts. Reports that Britain planned to arm slaves and Native Americans against the colonists had an even greater influence. Rather than protecting colonists, Britain's imperial might now threatened them. By the end of 1775, increasing numbers of Georgians embraced the patriot cause. Like their Carolina counterparts, Lowcountry Georgians slowly found that they could imagine a world outside of the British Empire.

Ultimately, the political crisis in the British Atlantic world during the 1760s and 1770s brought to the fore fundamental issues that distinguished the Lowcountry and the islands. Such differences had always existed, but greater access to land and resources, a subtropical climate that could not support the cultivation of sugarcane, and larger populations of European colonists in particular assumed heightened importance in the tumultuous years after the Seven Years War. These factors shaped colonists' interpretation and response to political developments in those years and gradually pushed them in opposite directions, one group embracing independence, the other remaining loyal to Great Britain.

To focus on such differences at the end of the colonial period, however, risks overshadowing how much these colonies had in common, particularly prior to the 1760s: similar (if not the same) environmental conditions and challenges; shared history and cultural orientation; similar social, economic, and demographic profiles; the powerful influence of African cultures and peoples. Such factors defined the Greater Caribbean as a colonial region, distinguishing these colonies from others in British America. That later developments would pull apart these colonies should not obscure the similarities and connections that led many in the seventeenth and eighteenth centuries to link them together. Indeed, the political revolution that divided the Lowcountry from the islands in 1776 did not sever their shared history nor eliminate continuing cultural similarities. Visitors in subsequent decades often noted that Charleston differed from other cities in North America and that the Lowcountry climate, environment, and society had much in common with the Caribbean. Even as the Lowcountry became an influential part of the "South" within the new American nation, it remained a distinct place, shaped to a large extent by its Caribbean origins. Seeing the seventeenth- and eighteenth-century Lowcountry as part of the Greater Caribbean, and the Caribbean as a central part of early British America, not only restores something of a seventeenth- and eighteenth-century perspective to our understanding of early American history; it also highlights the diverse influences that shaped what became the United States.

Notes

PROLOGUE. Rethinking Regions in Colonial British America

1. Jack P. Greene and J. R. Pole, "Reconstructing British-American Colonial History: An Introduction," in Greene and Pole, eds., *Colonial British America: Essays in the New History of the Early Modern Era* (Baltimore, 1984), 11.

2. Jack P. Greene, "Colonial South Carolina and the Caribbean Connection," in Greene, *Imperatives, Behaviors, and Identities: Essays in Early American Cultural History* (Charlottesville, VA, 1992), 68–69.

3. Eric Williams, *Capitalism and Slavery* (1944; reprint, Chapel Hill, NC, 1994), 52.

4. T. H. Breen, "Creative Adaptations: Peoples and Cultures," in Greene and Pole, eds., *Colonial British America*, 195–232.

5. Harry Carman, ed., *American Husbandry, Containing an Account of the Soil, Climate, Production, and Agriculture of the British Colonies in North America and the West Indies* (London, 1775; reprint, New York, 1939), 265.

6. Thomas Ashe, *Carolina; or a Description of the Present State of that Country* (London, 1682), reprinted in B. R. Carroll, ed., *Historical Collections of South Carolina* (New York, 1836), 2:61.

ONE. Plundering and Planting the Greater Caribbean

1. "An Old Letter," in *Shaftesbury Papers* (Charleston, SC, 2010), 308; Robert Sandford, *A Relation of a Voyage on the Coast of the Province of Carolina, 1666,* in Alexander Salley, ed., *Narratives of Early Carolina, 1650–1708* (New York, 1911), 103.

2. David Buisseret, ed., *Jamaica in 1687: The Taylor Manuscript at the National Library of Jamaica* (Kingston, 2008), 246; *The Laws of Jamaica* (London, 1683), 8.

3. Richard Ligon, *A True and Exact History of the Island of Barbados* (London, 1673), ed. Karen Kupperman (Indianapolis, 2011), 73.

4. Edward Littleton, *The Groans of the Plantations: Or, A True Account of their Grievous and Extreme Sufferings by the Heavy Impositions Upon Sugar* (London, 1698), 17.

5. Quoted in A. P. Thornton, *West-India Policy Under the Restoration* (Oxford, 1956), preface.

6. William Hilton, "A True Relation of a Voyage," in *The Shaftesbury Papers* (1897; reprint, Columbia, SC, 2010), 19.

7. John Archdale, *A New Description of that Fertile and Pleasant Province of Carolina* (London, 1707), reprinted in Alexander Salley, ed., *Narratives of Early Carolina, 1650–1708* (New York, 1911), 285.

8. Maurice Mathews to Lord Ashley, August 30, 1671, *Shaftesbury Papers,* 334.

9. Kenneth R. Andrews, *Elizabethan Privateering: English Privateering during the Spanish War, 1585–1603* (Cambridge, UK, 1964), 16.

10. Quoted in Kenneth Andrews, *Trade, Plunder, and Settlement: Maritime Enterprise and the Genesis of the British Empire, 1480–1630* (Cambridge, UK, 1984), 121.

11. James, King of England, *A Counterblaste to Tobacco* (London, 1604).

12. N. A. M. Rodger, quoted in Philip Morgan, "Virginia's Other Prototype: The Caribbean," in Peter Mancall, ed., *The Atlantic World and Virginia, 1550–1624* (Chapel Hill, NC, 2007), 357.

13. V. T. Harlow, ed., *Colonising Expeditions to the West Indies and Guiana, 1623–1667* (London, 1925), 1.

14. Quoted in Larry Gragg, *Englishmen Transplanted: The English Colonization of Barbados, 1627–1660* (Oxford, 2003), 41, 37.

15. Quoted in J. H. Bennett, "The English Caribbees in the Period of the Civil War, 1642–1646," *William and Mary Quarterly* 24 (July 1967): 366.

TWO. The Sweet Negotiation of Sugar

1. Richard Dunn, *Sugar and Slaves: The Rise of the Planter Class in the English West Indies, 1624–1713* (Chapel Hill, NC, 1972), xv.

2. Jerome Handler, ed., "Father Antoine Biet's Visit to Barbados in 1654," *Journal of the Barbados Museum and Historical Society* 32 (May 1965): 67.

3. J. Edward Hutson, ed., *The Voyage of Sir Henry Colt to the Islands of Barbados and St. Christopher* (Bridgetown, Barbados, 2002), 14.

4. John Winthrop to Henry Winthrop, January 30, 1629, Massachusetts Historical Society, *Winthrop Papers* (Boston, 1931), 2:67.

5. Hutson, *The Voyage of Sir Henry Colt,* 17.

6. Peter Hay, quoted in Dunn, *Sugar and Slaves,* 52.

7. "Extracts from Henry Whistler's Journal of the West India Expedition," in C. H. Firth, ed., *The Narrative of General Venables, with an Appendix*

of *Papers Relating to the Expedition to the West Indies and the Conquest of Jamaica, 1654–1655* (London, 1900), 146–47.

8. Richard Ligon, *A True and Exact History of the Island of Barbadoes* (London, 1673), ed. Karen Kupperman (Indianapolis, 2011), 93–94.

9. Peter Thompson, "Henry Drax's Instructions on the Management of a Seventeenth-Century Barbadian Sugar Plantation," *William and Mary Quarterly* 66 (July 2009): 592.

10. Edward Littleton, *The Groans of the Plantations: Or, A True Account of their Grievous and Extreme Sufferings by the Heavy Impositions Upon Sugar* (London, 1698) 17.

11. Ligon, *A True and Exact History*, 147, 103.

12. Handler, "Father Antoine Biet's Visit," 66.

13. David Eltis, "New Estimates of Exports from Barbados and Jamaica, 1665–1701," *William and Mary Quarterly* 52 (October 1995): 646.

14. Governor Sir Jonathan Atkins to the Lords of Trade and Plantations, July 4/14, 1676, *Calendar of State Papers, Colonial Series* (London, 1860), (hereafter cited as *CSPC*), 421.

15. Richard Vines to John Winthrop, *Winthrop Papers*, 5:172

16. The President and Council of Barbadoes to [Sec. Nicholas?], July 10, 1661, *CSPC*, 45.

17. Quote from Sir George Downing to John Winthrop Jr., August 26, 1645, in *Winthrop Papers*, 5:42–44.

18. Quoted in Dunn, *Sugar and Slaves*, 239.

19. Atkins to Lords of Trade, quoted in Peter Wood, *Black Majority: Negroes in Colonial South Carolina from 1670 through the Stono Rebellion* (New York, 1974), 9.

20. John Cordy Jeaffreson, ed., *A Young Squire of the Seventeenth Century: From the Papers of Christopher Jeaffreson* (London, 1878), 1:215.

21. Ibid., 1:211.

22. Jack P. Greene, "Colonial South Carolina and the Caribbean Connection," in Greene, *Imperatives, Behaviors, and Identities: Essays in Early American Cultural History* (Charlottesville, VA, 1992), 68.

THREE. Jamaica

1. William Byam to Sir Charles Pym, November 8, 1668, Historical Manuscripts Commission 96, *Tenth Report*, Appendix.

2. Quoted in Stephen Saunders Webb, *The Governors-General: The English Army and the Definition of Empire, 1569–1681* (Chapel Hill, 1979), 165–66.

3. Quoted in J. Harry Bennett, "Cary Helyar, Merchant and Planter of Seventeenth-Century Jamaica," *William and Mary Quarterly* 21 (January 1964): 59.

4. "A Summary Prospect of the Advantages and Conveniences Capable to Arise to his Majesty from the Planting of Jamaica," 1670, *Calendar*

of *State Papers, Colonial Series* (London, 1860), (hereafter cited as *CSPC*), 150–51.

5. Quoted in Bennett, "Cary Helyar," 59–60.

6. Sir G. Heathcote and Sir B. Gracedieu to the Council of Trade and Plantations, July 4, 1704, in *CSPC*, 207–8.

7. John Style to Secretary Sir William Morrice, January 14, 1669, *CSPC*, 3–5.

8. Governor Lord Vaughan to Lords of Trade and Plantations, April 4, 1676, *CSPC*, 368–69.

9. John Helyar, quoted in Nuala Zahedieh, "Trade, Plunder, and Economic Development in Early English Jamaica, 1655–89," *Economic History Review* 39 (May 1986): 218.

10. Governor Sir Thomas Modyford to Sec. Lord Arlington, October 31, 1670, *CSPC*, 121.

11. David Buisseret, ed., *Jamaica in 1687: The Taylor Manuscript at the National Library of Jamaica* (Kingston, 2008), 238, 150.

12. Henry Cadbury, ed., "Conditions in Jamaica in 1687," *Jamaican Historical Review* 3 (March 1959): 53.

13. Governor Sir Thomas Modyford to the Duke of Albemarle, November 30, 1669, *CSPC*, 46.

14. Charles Leslie, *A New and Exact Account of Jamaica* (Edinburgh, c. 1740), 355.

15. Ibid., 41.

FOUR. "Carolina in ye West Indies"

1. Quoted in Peter Wood, *Black Majority: Negroes in Colonial South Carolina from 1670 through the Stono Rebellion* (New York, 1974), 33.

2. For the concept of "charter groups," see T. H. Breen, "Creative Adaptations: Peoples and Cultures," in Jack P. Greene and J. R. Pole, *Colonial British America: Essays in the New History of the Early Modern Era* (Baltimore, 1984), 204–5.

3. John Coming to Sir P[eter] C[olleton], c. September 1671, in *The Shaftesbury Papers* (1897; reprint, Columbia, SC, 2010), 347.

4. "The Proprietors to the Governor and Council at Ashley River, May, 1674," in *Shaftesbury Papers*, 436–38.

5. [John Norris], *Profitable Advice for Rich and Poor in a Dialogue, or Discourse between James Freeman, a Carolina Planter and Simon Question, a West Country Farmer* (London, 1712), reprinted in Jack Greene, ed., *Selling a New World: Two Colonial South Carolina Promotional Pamphlets* (Columbia, SC, 1989), 106.

6. Lynch to Lords of Trade and Plantations, February 28, 1684, quoted in Mark Hanna, "The Pirate Nest: The Impact of Piracy on Newport, Rhode Island and Charles Town, South Carolina, 1670–1730," (PhD diss., Harvard University, 2006), 70.

7. Kathryn Braund, *Deerskins and Duffels: Creek Indian Trade with Anglo-America, 1685–1815* (Lincoln, NE, 1993), 88.

8. Wood, *Black Majority,* 13.

9. James Glen, *A Description of South Carolina* (London, 1761), reprinted in Chapman Milling, ed., *Colonial South Carolina: Two Contemporary Descriptions* (Columbia, SC, 1951), 95.

10. Johann David Schoepf, *Travels in the Confederation, 1783–84,* ed. Alfred Morrison (Erlangen, 1788; Philadelphia 1911), 2:182.

11. Robert Pringle, quoted in Robert M. Weir, *Colonial South Carolina: A History* (1983; reprint, Columbia, SC, 1997), 263.

12. Johann Martin Bolzius, "Reliable Answer to Some Submitted Questions Concerning the Land Carolina" (1751?), *William and Mary Quarterly* 14 (April 1957): 246.

13. Betty Wood, *Slavery in Colonial Georgia, 1730–1775* (Athens, GA, 2007), 79.

14. "Petition from the Freeholders of Abercorn," July 13, 1750, in *Colonial Records of the State of Georgia* (Atlanta, GA, 1916), 26:4.

15. Quoted in Kenneth Coleman, *Colonial Georgia: A History* (Millwood, NY, 1989), 203.

FIVE. "In Miserable Slavery"

1. Samuel Dyssli, December 3, 1737, quoted in Peter Wood, *Black Majority: Negroes in Colonial South Carolina from 1670 through the Stono Rebellion* (New York, 1974), 132.

2. Douglas Hall, *In Miserable Slavery: Thomas Thistlewood in Jamaica, 1750–86* (Kingston, Jamaica, 1989; 2nd ed., 1999), 80.

3. Quoted in Stephanie Smallwood, *Saltwater Slavery: A Middle Passage from Africa to American Diaspora* (Cambridge, MA, 2007), 203.

4. Quoted in Emma Christopher, *Slave Ship Sailors and Their Captive Cargoes, 1730–1807* (Cambridge, UK, 2006), 170.

5. Olaudah Equiano, *The Interesting Narrative and Other Writings,* ed. Vincent Carretta (New York, 2003), 58.

6. Quoted in Vincent Brown, *The Reaper's Garden: Death and Power in the World of Atlantic Slavery* (Cambridge, MA, 2008), 24.

7. Janet Schaw, *Journal of a Lady of Quality; Being the Narrative of a Journey from Scotland to the West Indies, North Carolina, and Portugal, in the Years 1774 to 1776,* ed. Evangeline Walker Andrews and Charles Andrews (New Haven, CT, 1922), 127.

8. Harry Carman, ed., *American Husbandry, Containing an Account of the Soil, Climate, Production, and Agriculture of the British Colonies in North America and the West Indies* (London, 1775; reprint, New York, 1939), 277.

9. Bryan Edwards, *The History, Civil and Commercial, of the British Colonies in the West Indies* (Dublin, 1793), 2:124.

10. Edwin Gay, "Letters from a Sugar Plantation in Nevis, 1723–32," *Journal of Economic and Business History* 1 (November, 1928): 156.

11. Simon Taylor, quoted in Brown, *The Reaper's Garden,* 53.

12. Philip Morgan, *Slave Counterpoint: Black Culture in the Eighteenth-Century Chesapeake and Lowcountry* (Chapel Hill, NC, 1998), 499.

13. Charles Ball, quoted in ibid., 514–15.

14. James Barclay, quoted in ibid., 532.

15. Quoted in Barry Higman, *Slave Populations of the British Caribbean, 1807–1834* (Baltimore, 1984; reprint, Kingston, 1995), 369.

16. Equiano, *Interesting Narrative,* 60; Hall, *In Miserable Slavery,* 12.

17. Edwards, *History, Civil and Commercial,* 2:72.

18. Quoted in Michael Mullin, *Africa in America: Slave Acculturation and Resistance in the American South and British Caribbean, 1736–1831* (Urbana, IL, 1992), 30.

19. Griffith Hughes, *The Natural History of Barbados* (London, 1750), 15.

20. Charles Leslie, *A New and Exact Account of Jamaica* (Edinburgh, c. 1740), 325–26.

21. Michael Craton, "Forms of Resistance to Slavery," in Franklin Knight, ed., *General History of the Caribbean,* vol. 3: *The Slave Societies of the Caribbean* (UNESCO, 1997), 235.

22. Neville Connell, ed., "Father Labat's Visit to Barbados in 1700," *Journal of the Barbados Museum and Historical Society* 24 (1957): 168–69.

23. Quoted in Richard Dunn, *Sugar and Slaves: The Rise of the Planter Class in the English West Indies, 1624–1713* (Chapel Hill, 1972), 258.

SIX. Creole Societies

1. John Fitzpatrick, ed., *The Diaries of George Washington, 1748–1799* (Boston, 1925), 1:17–30.

2. Quoted in Andrew O'Shaughnessy, *An Empire Divided: The American Revolution and the British Caribbean* (Philadelphia, 2000), 11.

3. "Journal of an Officer who Travelled in America and the West Indies in 1764 and 1765," in Newton Mereness, ed., *Travels in the American Colonies* (New York, 1916), 398.

4. "Journal of Josiah Quincy, Jr., 1773," *Proceedings of the Massachusetts Historical Society* 49 (1915–16): 444–45.

5. Thomas Tryon, *Friendly Advice to the Gentleman Planters of the East and West Indies* (London, 1684), 122–23.

6. "Governor James Glen's Valuation, 1751," in H. Roy Merrens, ed., *The Colonial South Carolina Scene: Contemporary Views, 1697–1774* (Columbia, SC, 1977), 184.

7. Bryan Edwards, *The History, Civil and Commercial, of the British Colonies in the West Indies* (Dublin, 1793), 2:8.

8. Peter Manigault, quoted in Robert Weir, " 'The Harmony We Were Famous For': An Interpretation of Prerevolutionary South Carolina Poli-

tics," in Weir, *"The Last of American Freemen": Studies in the Political Culture of the Colonial and Revolutionary South* (Macon, GA, 1986), 10–11.

9. James Knight, cited in Trevor Burnard, *Mastery, Tyranny, and Desire: Thomas Thistlewood and His Slaves in the Anglo-Jamaican World* (Chapel Hill, 2003), 19.

10. Quoted in H. Roy Merrens and George Terry, "Dying in Paradise: Malaria, Mortality, and the Perceptual Environment in Colonial South Carolina," *Journal of Southern History* 50 (November 1984): 549.

11. Governor James Kendell, quoted in Susan Dwyer Amussen, *Caribbean Exchanges: Slavery and the Transformation of English Society, 1640–1700* (Chapel Hill, NC, 2007), 84.

12. James Lind, *An Essay on Diseases Incidental to Europeans in Hot Climates* (London, 1768), 37.

13. "Journal of Josiah Quincy, 1773," 463.

14. John Luffman, quoted in Trevor Burnard, "'Gay and Agreeable Ladies': White Women in Mid-Eighteenth-Century Kingston, Jamaica," *Wadabagei; A Journal of the Caribbean and Its Diaspora* 9 (2006): 29.

15. Charles Leslie, *A New and Exact Account of Jamaica* (Edinburgh, c. 1740), 2.

16. Ibid., 38.

17. Governor Parke to Mr. Secretary Hedges, August 29, 1706, *Calendar of State Papers, Colonial Series* (London, 1860), 201.

18. Quoted in Julie Flavell, *When London Was Capital of America* (New Haven, CT, 2010), 21.

19. Leslie, *A New and Exact Account of Jamaica*, 28.

20. *Rules and By-Laws of the Charlestown Library Society* (Charleston, 1762), quoted in James Raven, *London Booksellers and Their American Customers: Transatlantic Literary Community and the Charleston Library Society, 1748–1811* (Columbia, SC, 2002), 43.

21. Janet Schaw, *Journal of a Lady of Quality; Being a Narrative of a Journey from Scotland to the West Indies, North Carolina, and Portugal, in the Years 1774 to 1776*, ed. Evangeline Andrews and Charles Andrews (New Haven, CT, 1922), 115.

22. "Journal of Josiah Quincy, 1773," 442.

23. Fitzpatrick, *The Diaries of George Washington*, 1:28.

24. Leslie, *A New and Exact Account of Jamaica*, 1.

SEVEN. Trade, Politics, and War in the Eighteenth Century

1. Letter from Azariah Pinney to Hester Pinney, May 31, 1704, quoted in Sarah Yeh, "In an Enemy's Country: British Culture, Identity, and Allegiance in Ireland and the Caribbean, 1688–1783" (PhD diss., Brown University, 2006), 56.

2. Quoted in Charles M. Andrews, *The Colonial Background of the American Revolution* (New Haven, CT, 1924; reprint, 1961), 90.

3. Benjamin Franklin quoted in Andrew O'Shaughnessy, *An Empire Divided: The American Revolution and the British Caribbean* (Philadelphia, 2000), 17.

4. John Hart to Council of Trade and Plantations, April 4, 1722, *Calendar of State Papers, Colonial Series* (London, 1860), 36.

5. "Journal of Josiah Quincy, Jr., 1773," *Proceedings of the Massachusetts Historical Society* 49 (1915–16): 454.

6. Bryan Edwards, quoted in Philip Morgan, "British Encounters with Africans and African Americans, circa 1600–1780," in Bernard Bailyn and Philip Morgan, eds., *Strangers within the Realm: Cultural Margins of the First British Empire* (Chapel Hill, 1991), 173.

7. Quoted in Jack P. Greene, "Changing Identity in the British West Indies in the Early Modern Era: Barbados as a Case Study," in Greene, *Imperatives, Behaviors, and Identities: Essays in Early American Cultural History* (Charlottesville, VA, 1992), 45.

8. Quoted in O'Shaughnessy, *An Empire Divided*, 50.

9. Quoted in Richard Pares, *War and Trade in the West Indies, 1739–1763* (Oxford, 1936), 228.

10. Quoted in N. A. M. Rodger, *The Command of the Ocean: A Naval History of Britain, 1649–1815* (New York, 2006), 235.

11. Quoted in Russell Menard, "Slavery, Economic Growth, and Revolutionary Ideology in the South Carolina Lowcountry," in Ronald Hoffman et al., *The Economy of Early America: The Revolutionary Period, 1763–1790* (Charlottesville, VA, 1988), 252.

12. Henry Laurens to James Grant, January 30, 1767, quoted in S. Max Edelson, *Plantation Enterprise in Colonial South Carolina* (Cambridge, MA, 2006), 192.

13. *Westminster Journal*, April 4, 1772, quoted in O'Shaughnessy, *An Empire Divided*, 124.

EPILOGUE. The Political Crisis of the 1760s

1. Charles Price et al. to Stephen Fuller, December 1764, quoted in Andrew O'Shaughnessy, *An Empire Divided: The American Revolution and the British Caribbean* (Philadelphia, 2000), 86.

2. *To the King's most Excellent Majesty in Council, The Humble Petition and Memorial of the Assembly of Jamaica* (1774), in George Bridges, *The Annals of Jamaica* (London, 1828), 2:463–66.

3. Daniel J. McDonough, *Christopher Gadsden and Henry Laurens: The Parallel Lives of Two American Patriots* (Cranbury, NJ, 2000), 105.

4. *To the King's most Excellent Majesty*, 463–64.

5. McDonough, *Christopher Gadsden and Henry Laurens*, 102.

6. John Drayton, quoted in Jack P. Greene, "Colonial South Carolina and the Caribbean Connection," in Greene, *Imperatives, Behaviors, and Identities: Essays in Early American Cultural History* (Charlottesville, VA, 1992), 85.

Essay on Sources

PROLOGUE. Rethinking Regions in Colonial British America

The argument for the centrality of regions to the study of early American history was made by Jack P. Greene and J. R. Pole in "Reconstructing British-American Colonial History: An Introduction," in Greene and Pole, *Colonial British America: Essays in the New History of the Early Modern Era* (Baltimore, 1984), 1–17. A good discussion of the importance of regions to early American history over the past forty years is Michael Zuckerman, "Regionalism," in Daniel Vickers, ed., *A Companion to Colonial America* (Oxford, 2003): 311–33. Also see Trevor Burnard, "A Passion for Places," *Commonplace* 8 (July 2008). Examples of important works that employ a regional model in one form or another include Jack P. Greene, *Pursuits of Happiness: The Social Development of Early Modern British Colonies and the Formation of American Culture* (Chapel Hill, NC, 1998); David Hackett Fischer, *Albion's Seed: Four British Folkways in America* (New York, 1989); John McCusker and Russell Menard, *The Economy of British America, 1607–1789, with Supplemental Bibliography* (Chapel Hill, NC, 1991); D. W. Meinig, *The Shaping of America: A Geographical Perspective on 500 Years of History,* vol. 1: *Atlantic America, 1492–1800* (New Haven, CT, 1988).

Among those scholars who emphasize the existence of smaller subregions, see Lorena Walsh, *Motives of Honor, Pleasure, and Profit: Plantation Management in the Colonial Chesapeake, 1607–1763* (Chapel Hill, NC, 2010); Martyn Bowden, "Culture and Place: English Sub-Cultural Regions in New England in the Seventeenth Century," *Connecticut History* 35 (1994): 68–146; Bradford Wood, *This Remote Part of the World: Regional Formation in the Lower Cape Fear, North Carolina, 1725–1775* (Columbia, SC, 2004); and Robert Gough, "The Myth of the 'Middle Colonies': An Analysis of Regionalization in Early America," *Pennsylvania Magazine of History and Biography* 107 (July 1983): 393–419.

The idea of a Greater Caribbean that encompassed plantation regions from Bahia to Virginia was first articulated by Immanuel Wallerstein (who called it the "extended Caribbean") in *The Modern World System*, vol. 2: *Mercantilism and the Consolidation of the European World Economy, 1600–1750* (New York, 1974), 103. Others who have employed the Greater Caribbean framework include: Peter Hulme, *Colonial Encounters: Europe and the Native Caribbean, 1492–1797* (London, 1986); J. R. McNeill, *Mosquito Empires: Ecology and War in the Greater Caribbean, 1620–1914* (Cambridge, UK, 2010); Christopher Iannini, *Fatal Revolutions: Natural History, West Indian Slavery, and the Routes of American Literature* (Chapel Hill, NC, 2012); and most recently, Edward Rugemer, "The Development of Mastery and Race in the Comprehensive Slave Codes of the Greater Caribbean during the Seventeenth Century," *William and Mary Quarterly* 70 (July 2013): 429–58.

Numerous scholars have emphasized the links between the Caribbean colonies, particularly Barbados, and the Carolina Lowcountry. See the early chapters in Peter Wood's classic book, *Black Majority: Negroes in Colonial South Carolina from 1670 through the Stono Rebellion* (New York, 1974); Richard Dunn, "The English Sugar Islands and the Founding of South Carolina," *South Carolina Historical Magazine* 72 (April 1971): 81–93; Jack P. Greene, "Colonial South Carolina and the Caribbean Connection," in Greene, *Imperatives, Behaviors, and Identities: Essays in Early American Cultural History* (Charlottesville, VA, 1992): 68–86; and most recently, Justin Roberts and Ian Beamish, "Venturing Out: The Barbadian Diaspora and the Carolina Colony, 1650–1685," in Michelle LeMaster and Bradford Wood, eds., *Creating and Contesting Carolina: Proprietary Era Histories* (Columbia, SC, 2013), 49–72. Two recent works that emphasize Lowcountry Georgia's Caribbean links are Paul Pressly, *On the Rim of the Caribbean: Colonial Georgia and the British Atlantic World* (Athens, GA, 2013), and Philip Morgan, "Lowcountry Georgia and the Early Modern Atlantic World, 1733–c. 1820," in Morgan, ed., *African American Life in the Georgia Lowcountry: The Atlantic World and the Gullah Geechee* (Athens, GA, 2010).

ONE. Plundering and Planting the Greater Caribbean

The most comprehensive account of the Caribbean environment is David Watts, *The West Indies: Patterns of Development, Culture, and Environmental Change since 1492* (Cambridge, UK, 1987), although Philip Morgan's forthcoming work will be an important updating. See Morgan, "The Caribbean Environment in the Early Modern Era" (originally presented at the International Seminar on the History of the Atlantic World, 1500–1825, Harvard University, August, 2010). S. Max Edelson's *Plantation Enterprise in Colonial South Carolina* (Cambridge, MA, 2006) provides a fine overview of the Lowcountry environment and the challenges it created for English and African colonists. See also Timothy Silver, *A New Face on the Countryside: Indians, Colonists, and Slaves in South Atlantic Forests, 1500–1800* (Cambridge, UK, 1990). For an excellent discussion of economic activity in the "Caribbean Commons," see Michael Jarvis, *In the Eye of All Trade: Bermuda, Bermudians, and the Maritime Atlantic World, 1680–1783* (Chapel Hill, NC), 185–256.

On the environmental challenges the English faced in colonizing the tropics, see Karen Kupperman, "Fear of Hot Climates in the Anglo-American Colonial Experience," *William and Mary Quarterly* 41 (April 1984): 213–40. The danger of yellow fever and malaria are treated with great skill (and some gallows humor) in McNeill, *Mosquito Empires*. Matthew Mulcahy discusses the impact of hurricanes on the development of the colonies in *Hurricanes and Society in the British Greater Caribbean, 1624–1783* (Baltimore, 2006).

A general overview of the Native Caribbean is the collection of essays edited by Samuel Wilson, *The Indigenous People of the Caribbean* (Tallahassee, FL, 1997), as well as the essays by Louis Allaire and Neil Whitehead in Frank Salomon and Stuart Schwartz, eds., *The Cambridge History of the Native Peoples of the Americas,* vol. 3, pt. 1 (Cambridge, UK, 1999). The standard work on the Taino remains Irving Rouse, *The Tainos: Rise and Decline of the People Who Greeted Columbus* (New Haven, CT, 1992). For a general overview of the Caribs and their encounters with Europeans, see Philip Boucher, *Cannibal Encounters: Europeans and the Island Caribs, 1492–1763* (Baltimore, 1992). An accessible survey can be found in the opening chapters of B. W. Higman, *A Concise History of the Caribbean* (Cambridge, UK, 2011).

There are fewer studies of Native Americans in the Lowcountry compared to their Backcountry neighbors such as the Creek and the Cherokee, but the best place to start is Gene Waddell, *The Indians of the South Carolina Lowcountry, 1652–1751* (Columbia, SC, 1980). In addition, see his essay, "Cusabo," in *The Handbook of North American Indians,* vol. 14: *The Southeast* (Washington, DC, 2004). John Worth has essays on the Guales and the Yamasee in the same volume.

A rich literature details English privateering in the region. Kenneth Andrews has written several excellent works on the topic, but a good starting point is *Trade, Plunder, and Settlement: Maritime Enterprise and the Genesis of the British Empire, 1480–1630* (Cambridge, UK, 1984). A good and very accessible overview of pirates and privateers generally is Kris Lane, *Pillaging the Empire: Piracy in the Americas, 1500–1750* (New York, 1998).

Richard Dunn, *Sugar and Slaves: The Rise of the Planter Class in the English West Indies, 1624–1713* (Chapel Hill, NC, 1972), remains the best book written about English colonists in the seventeenth century and provides an insightful discussion of the establishment of permanent colonies in the Leeward Islands and Barbados. In addition, see Richard Sheridan's *Sugar and Slavery: An Economic History of the British West Indies, 1623–1775* (Kingston, 1974; reprint, 1994); and Carl and Roberta Bridenbaugh, *No Peace Beyond the Line: The English in the Caribbean, 1624–90* (New York, 1972). Susan Dwyer Amussen, *Caribbean Exchanges: Slavery and the Transformation of English Society, 1640–1700* (Chapel Hill, NC, 2007), has a great deal of material on the colonization of Barbados and Jamaica, as well as the impact of slavery and colonization on English life. For Barbados in particular, see Larry Gragg, *Englishmen Transplanted: The English Colonization of Barbados, 1627–1660* (Oxford, 2003).

T W O. The Sweet Negotiation of Sugar

Several studies explore the development and operation of the sugar plantation complex in seventeenth-century Barbados. Along with Dunn, *Sugar and Slaves,* see Russell Menard, *Sweet Negotiations: Sugar, Slavery, and Plantation Agriculture in Early Barbados* (Charlottesville, VA, 2006), and Gragg, *Englishmen Transplanted.* Discussion of the "plantation complex" in Barbados and elsewhere is in Philip Curtin, *The Rise and Fall of the Plantation Complex: Essays in Atlantic History,* 2nd ed. (Cambridge, UK, 1998). On migration to the region, see Alison Games, *Migration and the Origins of the Atlantic World* (Cambridge, MA, 1999). The most complete discussion of indentured servitude is Hilary Beckles, *White Servitude and Black Slavery in Barbados, 1627–1715* (Knoxville, TN, 1989). Environmental issues are discussed in Watts, *The West Indies.*

There is a large literature on sugar. The essential starting point remains Sidney Mintz, *Sweetness and Power: The Place of Sugar in Modern History* (New York, 1985). An important new collection of essays is Stuart B. Schwartz, *Tropical Babylons: Sugar and the Making of the Atlantic World, 1450–1680* (Chapel Hill, NC, 2004). English and American consumption figures and habits are discussed in Carole Shammas, *The Pre-Industrial Consumer in England and America* (Oxford, 1990), 81–83.

For the development of slavery in Barbados, in addition to the works cited above (and several studies cited in chapter 5 below), see David Eltis, *The Rise of African Slavery in the Americas* (Cambridge, UK, 2000); Hilary Beckles and Andrew Downes, "The Economics of the Transition to the Black Labor System in Barbados, 1639–1680," *Journal of Interdisciplinary History* 18 (Autumn 1987): 225–47.

Dunn and Sheridan explore plantation development on the Leeward Islands, but other important works include: Natalie Zacek, *Settler Society in the English Leeward Islands, 1670–1776* (Cambridge, UK, 2010); Elsa Goveia, *Slave Society in the British Leeward Islands at the End of the Eighteenth Century* (New Haven, CT, 1965). Several studies have focused on individual islands. For Montserrat, see Donald Akenson, *If the Irish Ran the World: Montserrat, 1630–1730* (Montreal, 1997). The best study of Antigua is David

Barry Gaspar, *Bondmen and Rebels: A Study of Master-Slave Relations in Antigua* (Baltimore, 1985).

THREE. Jamaica

The history of Providence Island is recounted in Karen Kupperman, *Providence Island: The Other Puritan Colony, 1630–1641* (Cambridge, UK, 1993). On the conquest of Jamaica, see S. A. G. Taylor, *The Western Design: An Account of Cromwell's Expedition to the Caribbean* (Kingston, 1965); Stephen Saunders Webb, *The Governors-General: The English Army and the Definition of Empire, 1569–1681* (Chapel Hill, NC, 1979).

Nuala Zahedieh discusses privateering and illegal trade in a series of articles, including: "Trade, Plunder, and Economic Development in Early English Jamaica, 1655–89," *Economic History Review* 39 (May 1986): 205–22; "The Merchants of Port Royal Jamaica and the Spanish Contraband Trade, 1655–1692," *William and Mary Quarterly* 43 (October 1986): 570–93; and "'A Frugal, Prudential, and Hopeful Trade': Privateering in Jamaica, 1655–1689," *Journal of Imperial and Commonwealth History* 18 (1990): 145–68. The John Taylor manuscript at the National Library of Jamaica has long been used as a source for early Jamaica, including discussions of Port Royal. That manuscript has now been transcribed and edited by David Buisseret, *Jamaica in 1687: The Taylor Manuscript at the National Library of Jamaica* (Kingston, 2008). For Port Royal, see Michel Pawson and David Buisseret, *Port Royal, Jamaica* (Oxford, 1974; reprint, Kingston, 2000).

A good discussion of early planting in Jamaica is J. Harry Bennett, "Cary Helyar, Merchant and Planter of Seventeenth-Century Jamaica," *William and Mary Quarterly* 21 (January 1964): 53–76. Trevor Burnard has done more than anyone to outline social, demographic, and economic conditions in eighteenth-century Jamaica. His findings appear in numerous important articles, but some key information, including population figures, is summarized in Burnard, *Mastery, Tyranny, and Desire: Thomas Thistlewood and His Slaves in the Anglo-Jamaican World* (Chapel Hill, NC, 2003). Vincent Brown's *The Reaper's Garden: Death and Power in the World of Atlantic Slavery* (Cambridge, MA, 2008) explores the impact and meaning of Jamaica's horrific mortality rates for enslaved Africans and planters.

For information about the Maroons, see Michael Craton, *Testing the Chains: Resistance to Slavery in the British West Indies* (Ithaca, NY, 1982). For conditions in St. Andrew parish, see David B. Ryden, "'One of the fertilist pleasentest Spotts': An Analysis of the Slave Economy in Jamaica's St. Andrew Parish, 1753," *Slavery and Abolition* 21 (April 2000): 32–55. A good discussion of the coffee sector is S. D. Smith, "Sugar's Poor Relation: Coffee Planting in the British West Indies, 1720–1833," *Slavery and Abolition* 19 (December 1998): 68–89. For the role of livestock and pens, see

Verene Shepherd, *Livestock, Sugar, and Slavery: Contested Terrain in Colonial Jamaica* (Kingston, 2009).

There are several excellent accounts of individual plantations in Jamaica that explore the lives of enslaved Africans, relations between planters and slaves, and economic production. The specific titles are cited for chapter 5 below. In addition, B. W. Higman explores the management of Jamaican plantations in *Plantation Jamaica, 1750–1850: Capital and Control in a Colonial Economy* (Kingston, 2005). Christer Petley's work focuses on the later eighteenth and nineteenth century but provides an informative analysis of the planter class. Petley, *Slaveholders in Jamaica: Colonial Society and Culture during the Era of Abolition* (Brookfield, VT, 2009).

FOUR. "Carolina in ye West Indies"

The literature on the Lowcountry has grown tremendously in the past thirty years. Robert M. Weir provides a comprehensive account in *Colonial South Carolina: A History* (1983; reprint, Columbia, SC, 1997). Peter Wood, *Black Majority,* remains essential reading. S. Max Edelson's, *Plantation Enterprise in Colonial South Carolina* (Cambridge, MA, 2006) skillfully weaves together environmental and economic history. Other important works include Philip Morgan, *Slave Counterpoint: Black Culture in the Eighteenth-Century Chesapeake and Lowcountry* (Chapel Hill, NC, 1998); Joyce Chaplin, *An Anxious Pursuit: Agricultural Innovation and Modernity in the Lower South, 1730–1815* (Chapel Hill, NC, 1996); Peter Coclanis, *The Shadow of a Dream: Economic Life and Death in the South Carolina Lowcountry, 1670–1920* (New York, 1989); Robert Olwell, *Masters, Slaves, and Subjects: The Culture of Power in the South Carolina Lowcountry, 1740–90* (Ithaca, NY, 1998); L. H. Roper, *Conceiving Carolina: Proprietors, Planters, and Plots, 1662–1729* (New York, 2004); Richard Waterhouse, *A New World Gentry: The Making of a Merchant and Planter Class in South Carolina, 1670–1770* (Charleston, SC, 2005). An older but still very useful account is Eugene Sirmans, *Colonial South Carolina: A Political History, 1663–1773* (Chapel Hill, NC, 1966). In addition, see the essays in Jack P. Greene, Rosemary Bhrana-Shute, and Randy Sparks, eds., *Money, Trade, and Power: The Evolution of South Carolina's Plantation Society* (Columbia, SC, 2001), and, most recently, essays in LeMaster and Wood, eds., *Creating and Contesting Carolina.*

On the Indian slave trade, see Alan Gallay, *The Indian Slave Trade: The Rise of the English Empire in the American South, 1670–1717* (New Haven, CT, 2003), and Paul Kelton, *Epidemics and Enslavement: Biological Catastrophe in the Native Southeast, 1492–1715* (Lincoln, NE, 2007). The Yamasee War has garnered a great deal of attention from scholars in recent years. In addition to Kelton and Gallay, see William Ramsey, *The Yamasee War: A Study of Culture, Economy, and Conflict in the Colonial South* (Lincoln, NE, 2010), and Steven Oatis, *A Colonial Complex: South Carolina's Frontiers in the Era of the Yamasee War* (Lincoln, NE, 2008).

There is a large literature on the development of rice plantations in the Lowcountry. Peter Wood first made the case for the importance of African slaves in the development of rice agriculture in *Black Majority*. Daniel Littlefield provided additional support in *Rice and Slaves: Ethnicity and the Slave Trade in Colonial South Carolina* (Baton Rouge, LA, 1981). The most recent and thorough argument is Judith Carney, *Black Rice: The African Origins of Rice Cultivation in the Americas* (Cambridge, MA, 2001). Carney's interpretation is challenged by Edelson in *Plantation Enterprise in Colonial South Carolina* and by David Eltis, Philip Morgan, and David Richardson, "Agency and Diaspora in Atlantic History: Reassessing the African Contribution to Rice Cultivation in the Americas," *American Historical Review* 112 (December 2007): 1329–58. That article, in turn, generated a forum in the *AHR* with contributions from Edelson, Gwendolyn Midlo Hall, Walter Hawthorne, and Eltis, Morgan, and Richardson. See "AHR Exchange: The Question of 'Black Rice,'" *American Historical Review* 115 (February 2010): 123–71. For analysis of the Lowcountry economy, in addition to works cited above, see Russell Menard, "Slavery, Economic Growth, and Revolutionary Ideology in the South Carolina Lowcountry," in Ronald Hoffman et al., *The Economy of Early America: The Revolutionary Period, 1763–1790* (Charlottesville, VA, 1988), 244–74.

The best and most thorough study of the Cape Fear region is Bradford J. Wood, *This Remote Part of the World: Regional Formation in the Lower Cape Fear, 1725–1775* (Columbia, SC, 2004). See also H. Roy Merrens, *Colonial North Carolina in the Eighteenth Century* (Chapel Hill, NC, 1964), and A. Roger Ekirch, *"Poor Carolina": Politics and Society in Colonial North Carolina, 1729–1776* (Chapel Hill, NC, 1981).

For Colonial Georgia, see Kenneth Coleman, *Colonial Georgia: A History* (Millwood, NY, 1976), and Harold Davis, *The Fledgling Province: Social and Cultural Life in Colonial Georgia, 1733–1776* (Chapel Hill, NC, 1976). Betty Wood's *Slavery in Colonial Georgia, 1730–1775* (Athens, GA, 1997) has a good deal of general information on Georgia's early history, as well as the best discussion of the development of slavery in the colony. A terrific environmental history is Mart Stewart, *"What Nature Suffers to Groe": Life, Labor, and Landscape on the Georgia Coast, 1680–1920* (Athens, GA, 1996). A new study emphasizing Lowcountry Georgia's place in the Greater Caribbean is Pressly, *On the Rim of the Caribbean*.

Several biographies provide good context on early Georgia's politics and economy. See Alan Gallay, *Jonathan Bryan and the Southern Colonial Frontier* (Athens, GA, 1989); Julie Anne Sweet, *William Stephens: Georgia's Forgotten Founder* (Baton Rouge, 2010); Frank Lambert, *James Habersham: Loyalty, Politics, and Commerce in Colonial Georgia* (Athens, GA, 2005); and Phinizy Spalding and Harvey Jackson, eds., *Oglethorpe in Perspective: Georgia's Founder after Two Hundred Years* (Tuscaloosa, AL, 1989).

A rich, and rapidly expanding, literature explores slavery and slave life in the Greater Caribbean. Two recent collections of essays that provide good entries into the recent scholarship on slavery are Gad Heuman and Trevor Burnard, eds., *The Routledge History of Slavery* (New York, 2011), and Robert Paquette and Mark Smith, eds., *The Oxford Handbook of Slavery in the Americas* (Oxford, 2010). Kenneth Morgan, *Slavery and the British Empire: From Africa to America* (Oxford, 2007), provides an accessible survey.

The essential starting point for exploring the slave trade is *The Trans-Atlantic Slave Trade Database* compiled by David Eltis, Stephen Behrendt, David Richardson, and Herbert Klein, www.slavevoyages.org. A good introductory overview for undergraduates is Lisa Lindsay, *Captives as Commodities: The Transatlantic Slave Trade* (Upper Saddle River, NJ, 2008). Also see Stephanie Smallwood, *Saltwater Slavery: A Middle Passage from Africa to American Diaspora* (Cambridge, MA, 2007), and essays in the special issue, "New Perspectives on the Transatlantic Slave Trade," *William and Mary Quarterly* 58 (January 2001). The most famous account of the Middle Passage is by Olaudah Equiano. See *The Interesting Narrative and Other Writings,* ed. Vincent Carretta (New York, 2003).

On the centrality of labor to the lives of slaves, see Ira Berlin and Philip Morgan, "Labor and the Shaping of Slave Life in the Americas," in Berlin and Morgan, eds., *Cultivation and Culture: Labor and the Shaping of Slave Life in the Americas* (Charlottesville, VA, 1993), 1–45. On various labor systems, see Philip Morgan, "Task and Gang Systems: The Organization of Labor on New World Plantations," in Stephen Innes, ed., *Work and Labor in Early America* (Chapel Hill, NC, 1988), 189–220. For a good overview of issues related to food and provisions, see Judith Carney and Richard Rosomoff, *In the Shadow of Slavery: Africa's Botanical Legacy in the Atlantic World* (Berkeley, 2009), and Ira Berlin and Philip Morgan, eds., *The Slaves' Economy: Independent Production by Slaves in the Americas* (London, 1991).

The general experience of slaves is often best documented in studies of individual plantations. See, for example: B. W. Higman, *Montpelier, Jamaica: A Plantation Community in Slavery and Freedom, 1739–1912* (Kingston, 1998); Burnard, *Mastery, Tyranny, and Desire;* Jerome Handler and Frederick Lange, *Plantation Slavery in Barbados: An Archaeological and Historical Investigation* (Cambridge, MA, 1978); Michael Craton and James Walvin, *A Jamaican Plantation: The History of Worthy Park, 1670–1970* (London, 1970); Veront Satchell, *Hope Transformed: A Historical Sketch of the Hope Landscape, St. Andrew, Jamaica, 1660–1960* (Kingston, 2011). For broader analysis, see J. R. Ward, *British West Indian Slavery, 1750–1834: The Process of Amelioration* (New York, 1988), and Justin Roberts, *Slavery and the Enlightenment in the British Atlantic, 1750–1807* (Cambridge, UK, 2013). Philip Morgan's masterful and monumental *Slave Counterpoint* is required reading for understanding slave life and culture in the Lowcountry. For North Carolina, see Wood, *This Remote Part of the World,* and Marvin Michael Kay and Lorin Lee Cary, *Slavery in North Carolina, 1748–1775* (Chapel Hill, NC, 1999). On the experiences of female slaves in particular, see Hilary Beckles, *Natural Rebels: A Social History of Enslaved Women in Barbados* (New Brunswick, NJ, 1989), and Jennifer Morgan, *Laboring Women: Reproduction and Gender in New World Slavery* (Philadelphia, 2004).

Debates about the survival of African cultures in the Americas stretches back to the pioneering work of Melville Herskovits, but current debates often start with reference to Kamau Brathwaite, *The Development of Creole Society in Jamaica, 1770–1820* (Oxford, 1971), and Sidney Mintz and Richard Price in *The Birth of African American Culture: An Anthropological Perspective* (1976; reprint, Boston, 1992). Mintz and Price emphasized that individual slaves arrived in the Americas as part of "heterogeneous crowds" and that resulting slave cultures represented a mixture of various West African practices, along with European influences. More recent scholars who support the basic idea of hybrid cultures include Philip Morgan, "The Cultural Implications of the Atlantic Slave Trade: African Regional Origins, American Destinations, and New World Developments," in David Eltis and David Richardson, eds., *Routes to Slavery: Direction, Ethnicity, and Mortality in the Transatlantic Slave Trade* (London, 1997), 124–45; Trevor Burnard, "The Atlantic Slave Trade and African Ethnicities in Seventeenth-Century Jamaica," in David Richardson, Suzanne Schwarz, and Anthony Tibbles, eds., *Liverpool and Transatlantic Slavery* (Liverpool, 2007); Alexander Byrd, *Captives and Voyagers: Black Migrants across the Eighteenth-Century British Atlantic World* (Baton Rouge, LA, 2008); and Gregory O'Malley, "Diversity in the Slave Trade to the Colonial Carolinas," in LeMaster and Wood, eds., *Creating and Contesting Carolina.* Scholars who emphasize more the maintenance and influences of specific African cultures in specific parts of the Americas include Michael Gomez, *Exchanging Our Country Marks: The Transformation of African Identities in the Colonial and Antebellum South* (Chapel Hill, NC, 1998); Gwendolyn Midlo Hall, *Slavery and African Ethnicities in the Americas: Restoring the Links* (Chapel Hill, NC, 2005); and John K. Thornton, *Africa and Africans in the Making of the Atlantic World,* 2nd ed. (Cambridge, MA, 1998).

On the issue of creolization generally, see Verene Shepherd and Glen L. Richards, *Questioning Creole: Creolisation Discourses in Caribbean Culture* (Kingston, 2002). The creolization of musical traditions in Jamaica is discussed in Richard Rath, "African Music in Seventeenth Century Jamaica: Cultural Transit and Transition," *William and Mary Quarterly* 50 (October 1993): 700–726. For slave religion, see Sylvia Frey and Betty Wood, *Come Shouting to Zion: African American Protestantism in the American South and British Caribbean to 1830* (Chapel Hill, NC, 1998). On burial practices, see Brown,

The Reaper's Garden, as well as Erik Seeman, *Death in the New World: Cross-Cultural Encounters, 1492–1800* (Philadelphia, 2010).

Information on the variety of forms of slave resistance appears in many of the sources cited above, but for specific studies, see Craton, *Testing the Chains,* and Michael Mullin, *Africa in America: Slave Acculturation and Resistance in the American South and British Caribbean, 1736–1831* (Urbana, IL, 1992). For the Lowcountry, see Peter Charles Hoffer, *Cry Liberty: The Great Stono River Slave Rebellion of 1739* (Oxford, 2012).

six. Creole Societies

The debate over absenteeism is addressed in Trevor Burnard, "Passengers Only: The Extent and Significance of Absenteeism in Eighteenth-Century Jamaica," *Atlantic Studies* 1 (2004): 178–95. See also Maurie McInnis, *In Pursuit of Refinement: Charlestonians Abroad, 1740–1860* (Columbia, SC, 1999), and Julie Flavell, *When London Was Capital of America* (New Haven, CT, 2010). An excellent biography of the powerful absentee planter-politician William Beckford is Perry Gucci, *William Beckford: First Prime Minister of the London Empire* (New Haven, 2013). Also see Richard Pares, *A West India Fortune* (New York, 1950). For other social groups in Barbados, see Karl Watson, *The Civilised Island, Barbados: A Social History, 1750–1830* (Barbados, 1979), and Jill Sheppard, *The Redlegs of Barbados: Their Origins and History* (New York, 1977). For Jamaica, see Brathwaite, *The Development of Creole Society,* and for the Leewards, see Zacek, *Settler Society.*

For discussion of Scottish migration and Scots' experiences in the Caribbean, see Douglas Hamilton, *Scotland, the Caribbean, and the Atlantic World, 1750–1820* (Manchester, 2005), and Alan Karras, *Sojourners in the Sun: Scottish Migrants in Jamaica and the Chesapeake, 1740–1800* (Ithaca, NY, 1993). On the Irish, see Kristen Block and Jenny Shaw, "Subjects without an Empire: The Irish in the Early Modern Caribbean," *Past and Present* 210 (February 2011): 33–60. Although focused on Nevis, Michelle Terrell's *The Jewish Community of Early Colonial Nevis: A Historical Archaeological Study* (Gainesville, FL, 2005) also provides useful background on Jewish colonists in other British island colonies. Two new books explore the life of Thomas Jeremiah while offering good overviews of Charleston society during the Revolutionary era. See William Ryan, *The World of Thomas Jeremiah: Charles Town on the Eve of the American Revolution* (New York, 2010), and J. William Harris, *The Hanging of Thomas Jeremiah: A Free Black Man's Encounter with Liberty* (New Haven, 2009).

On disease and mortality in the region, see Brown, *The Reaper's Garden,* and Peter McCandless, *Slavery, Disease, and Suffering in the Southern Lowcountry* (Cambridge, UK, 2011).

Several new studies of women and family life in the Greater Caribbean have appeared in recent years, but the authors also note that a great deal of work remains to be done. Good starting places for the islands are: Natalie Zacek, "Searching for the Invisible Woman: The Evolution of White Women's Experiences in Britain's West Indian Colonies," *History Compass* 7 (January 2009): 329–41; Zacek, "Between Lady and Slave: White Working Women in the Eighteenth-Century Leeward Islands," in Douglas Catterall and Jodi Campbell, *Women in Port: Gendering Communities, Economies, and Social Networks in Atlantic Port Cities, 1500–1800* (Leiden, 2012), 127–50; Trevor Burnard, "A Failed Settler Society: Marriage and Demographic Failure in Early Jamaica," *Journal of Social History* (Autumn 1994): 63–83; and Sarah Pearsall, " 'The Late Flagrant Instance of Depravity in My Family': The Story of an Anglo-Jamaican Cuckold," *William and Mary Quarterly* 60 (July 2003): 549–82. For the situation of women in the Lowcountry, see Lorri Glover, *All Our Relations: Blood Ties and Emotional Bonds among the Early South Carolina Gentry* (Baltimore, 2000); Cara Anzilotti, *In the Affairs of the World: Women, Patriarchy, and Power in Colonial South Carolina* (Westport, CT, 2002).

Many of the general studies noted above contain excellent analysis of social and cultural life in the region, but also see Michael Craton, "Reluctant Creoles: The Planter's World in the British West Indies," in Bernard Bailyn and Philip Morgan, eds., *Strangers within the Realm: Cultural Margins of the First British Empire* (Chapel Hill, NC, 1991). A good study of religion that incorporates a Greater Caribbean framework is Nicholas Beasley, *Christian Ritual and the Creation of British Slave Societies, 1650–1780* (Athens, GA, 2010). On the Great Awakening in South Carolina, see Harvey H. Jackson, "Hugh Bryan and the Evangelical Movement in Colonial South Carolina," *William and Mary Quarterly* (October 1986): 594–614. On clubs and societies, see George Rogers, *Charleston in the Age of the Pinckneys,* 2nd ed. (Columbia, SC, 1984). On the influence of Africans on foodways and medicine, see essays in David Buisseret and Steven Reinhardt, eds., *Creolization in the Americas* (College Station, TX, 2000), along with Kathleen S. Murphy, "Translating the Vernacular: Indigenous and African Knowledge in the Eighteenth-Century British Atlantic," *Atlantic Studies* 8 (2011): 29–48.

Louis Nelson offers an excellent overview of church architecture in Jamaica and South Carolina while highlighting distinct adaptations to local conditions in "The Diversity of Countries: Anglican Architecture in Virginia, South Carolina, and Jamaica," in David Shields, ed., *Material Culture in Anglo-America: Regional Identity and Urbanity in the Tidewater, Lowcountry, and Caribbean* (Columbia, SC, 2009). See also Roger Leech's essay on architecture in the Leeward Islands in the same volume.

Several studies explore the history of urban areas in the region, although as several authors note, cities and towns have not received enough scholarly attention. One essay that compares and contrasts urban centers in the Greater Caribbean is Trevor Burnard and Emma Hart, "Kingston, Jamaica, and Charleston, South Carolina: A New Look at Comparative Urbanization in Plantation Colonial British America," *Journal of Urban*

History 39 (March 2013): 213–34. Other studies of specific towns include: James Robertson, *Gone Is the Ancient Glory: Spanish Town, Jamaica, 1534–2000* (Kingston, 2005); Pedro Welch, *Slave Society in the City: Bridgetown Barbados, 1650–1834* (Kingston, 2003); Emma Hart, *Building Charleston: Town and Society in the Eighteenth-Century British Atlantic World* (Charlottesville, VA, 2009).

SEVEN. Trade, Politics, and War in the Eighteenth Century

The career of Gedney Clarke is outlined by S. D. Smith in "Gedney Clarke of Salem and Barbados: Transatlantic Super-Merchant," *New England Quarterly* 76 (December 2003): 499–549. An excellent study of London's role in trade to and from the Greater Caribbean is Nuala Zahedieh, *The Capital and the Colonies: London and the Atlantic Economy, 1660–1700* (Cambridge, MA, 2012). On trade between the islands and the mainland, see Richard Pares, *Yankees and Creoles: The Trade between North America and the West Indies before the American Revolution* (Cambridge, MA, 1956). On interimperial trade in the region, see Christian Koot, *Empire at the Periphery: British Colonists, Anglo-Dutch Trade, and the Development of the British Atlantic, 1621–1713* (Athens, GA, 2011). Abraham Redwood's story is outlined in Matthew Parker, *The Sugar Barons: Family, Corruption, Empire, and War in the West Indies* (New York, 2011). Parker's book provides a very readable overview of the islands during the seventeenth and eighteenth centuries.

Studies of individual commodities are also useful entries into the trade of certain colonies and often contain a good deal of information on economic issues more generally. A good example is John McCusker's influential work, *Rum and the American Revolution: The Rum Trade and the Balance of Payments of the Thirteen Continental Colonies* (New York, 1989), which contains a wealth of information on sugar plantations. For other examples, see Chris Evans, "The Plantation Hoe: The Rise and Fall of an Atlantic Commodity, 1650–1850," *William and Mary Quarterly* 69 (January 2012): 71–100.

The impact of the West Indies on Britain's economy, industrialization, and abolitionism is the subject of the so-called Williams Debate, although many of the particular issues fall outside the time frame of this book. Eric Williams outlined his argument in his classic work, *Capitalism and Slavery* (1944; reprint, Chapel Hill, NC, 1994). A recent entry into the debate that outlines key issues, and that contains a wealth of information on Jamaica in the later part of the eighteenth century, is David Beck Ryden, *West Indian Slavery and British Abolition, 1783–1807* (Cambridge, UK, 2010).

Politics and political institutions in the Greater Caribbean have received far less attention than in the mainland colonies, particularly those north of the Mason-Dixon Line. Nevertheless, several studies have been done, most focusing on the eighteenth century, and covering local issues as well as the colonies' political relationship to Britain. The best starting point for the islands is the relevant chapters in Andrew O'Shaughnessy, *An Empire Divided: The American Revolution and the British Caribbean* (Philadelphia, 2000). More specific studies include George Metcalf, *Royal Government and Political Conflict in Jamaica, 1729–1783* (London, 1965); Elsa Goveia, *Slave Society in the Leeward Islands at the End of the Eighteenth Century;* and Watson, *The Civilised Island.*

The literature on politics in the Lowcountry is richer. An excellent short overview of political culture is Robert Weir, "'The Harmony We Were Famous For': An Interpretation of Pre-Revolutionary South Carolina Politics," *William and Mary Quarterly* 26 (October1969): 473–501. The rising power of the assembly, and much more, is addressed in Jack P. Greene, *The Quest for Power: The Lower Houses of Assembly in the Southern Royal Colonies, 1689–1776* (Chapel Hill, NC, 1969). In addition, see Rebecca Starr, *A School for Politics: Commercial Lobbying and Political Culture in Early South Carolina* (Baltimore, 1998); Richard Waterhouse, *A New World Gentry;* and, more recently, Jonathan Mercantini, *Who Shall Rule at Home?: The Evolution of South Carolina Political Culture, 1748–1776* (Columbia, SC, 2007). For Georgia, see Kenneth Coleman, *Colonial Georgia,* as well as works cited in chapter 4 above.

Not surprisingly, given that the Greater Caribbean was the source of almost constant warfare, military concerns feature prominently in the region's scholarship. Seventeenth-century conflicts are explored in Dunn, *Sugar and Slaves,* and the Bridenbaughs, *No Peace Beyond the Line.* The classic, and still most important, work on the topic for the eighteenth century is Richard Pares, *War and Trade in the West Indies, 1739–1763* (Oxford, 1936). In addition, see Duncan Crewe, *Yellow Jack and the Worm: British Naval Administration in the West Indies, 1739–1748* (Liverpool. 1993). On the role of disease in shaping military campaigns, see McNeill, *Mosquito Empires.* For the use of enslaved Africans in the Revolution and earlier, see Philip Morgan and Andrew O'Shaughnessy, "Arming Slaves in the American Revolution," in Christopher Brown and Philip Morgan, *Arming Slaves: From Classical Times to the Modern Age* (New Haven, CT, 2006), 180–208. Fred Anderson's magisterial *The Crucible of War: The Seven Years' War and the Fate of Empire in British North America, 1754–1766* (New York, 2001) places events in the Greater Caribbean in a broad context, as well as outlining debates over keeping Canada or Guadeloupe at the Treaty of Paris. On the latter point, see also the opening chapter in Theodore Draper, *The Struggle for Power: The American Revolution* (New York, 1995). On the war with the Black Caribs in St. Vincent, see Bernard Marshall, "The Black Caribs—Native Resistance to British Penetration into the Windward Side of St. Vincent, 1763–1773," *Caribbean Quarterly* 19 (December 1973): 4–19.

EPILOGUE. The Political Crisis of the 1760s

The best overview of the political situation in the islands during the 1760s and 1770s is O'Shaughnessy, *An Empire Divided*. In addition, see Selwyn Carrington, *The British West Indies during the American Revolution* (Holland, 1988). For a specific analysis of Jamaica, see T. R. Clayton, "Sophistry, Security, and Socio-Political Structures in the American Revolution, or Why Jamaica Did Not Rebel," *Historical Journal* 19 (1986). For the political situation in South Carolina and Georgia, see the works cited above, particularly Weir, *Colonial South Carolina*, Greene, *The Quest for Power*, and Pressly, *On the Rim of the Caribbean*.

Index

proprietors of, 85–90, 95–96; slaves and slavery in, 56, 88, 101–2, 105, 112, 123–24, 126, 128, 129, 130, 134, 140, 172, 210; slave trade to, 101, 117–18, 143; and trade with Native Americans, 92–95; wealth of, 104, 149. *See also* Charleston; naval stores; rice; Stono Rebellion; Yamasee Indians: and war

Lowcountry, Georgia, 4, 25–26, 96, 106–11, 188; and crisis with Britain, 206, 212–13; exports from, 110, 181; and migrants from Caribbean, 110; and migrants from Lowcountry, 109–10; Parliamentary funding for, 108, 212; population of, 107, 110–11; and restrictions on slavery, 107, 108; slavery in, 110–11, 210; trustees' plan for, 106–7, 108. *See also* Savannah

Lucas, John, 89

lumber. *See* timber

Lynch, Thomas, 92

Lyttleton, William Henry, 200

Madeira, 46, 71, 171

mahogany, 13, 80

malaria, 5, 16, 96, 126, 157, 194. *See also* disease

Manigault, Peter, 104, 151, 167

Manning, Edward and Elizabeth, 160–61

Marie Bonadventure (ship), 50–51

Maroons, 64, 78–79, 140–41, 143–44

marriage, 128–30, 158–61

Martinique, 185, 193, 197, 200

Massachusetts, 45, 65, 102, 176–77, 183, 184, 208

Mathews, Maurice, 89

Maynard, Satus, 146–47

medicine, 170–71

Methodists, 138, 163, 164

militias, 143, 154, 187, 197, 210; use of slaves in, 194–95

mixed-race individuals, 13, 155, 160–61

Modyford, Thomas, 67–68, 69, 71–72, 73, 75

molasses, 46, 49, 51, 180, 183, 185

Molasses Act, 185–86, 204

Montserrat, 2, 11, 58, 197; exports from, 60; geography of, 11, 58; Irish in, 34, 154, 193, 196; landholdings on, 61. *See also* Leeward Islands

Moore, Roger, 105

Moravians, 138, 163, 164

Morgan, Henry, 71–72, 75, 132

Mosquito Coast, 13

mosquitoes, 16, 52–53, 122, 157

Muslims. *See* Islam

Myngs, Christopher, 70

Nanny (Maroon leader), 141. *See also* Maroons

Native Americans, 1, 7, 9, 18–26, 210; and agriculture, 19, 23–24; and population size and disease, 20, 25–26; and slaves and slave trade, 36, 44–45, 54, 55, 93–95, 184–85. *See also* Caribs; Cusabo Indians; Kiawah Indians; Westo Indians

naval stores, 85, 96–97, 105–6, 108, 110, 123

Navigation Acts, 100–101, 179–80, 208–9

navy and army, British, 195–96, 209

Nevis, 2, 7, 59, 67, 126, 154, 197, 206; colonization of, 34; early wealth of, 58; exports from, 60–61, 178; geography of, 11, 14, 58; slaves in, 58, 61. *See also* Leeward Islands

New England, 2, 32, 65, 67, 90, 166; life expectancy in, 157; rum distilleries in, 183; and trade with islands; 44–45, 51, 71, 183–86; and trade with Lowcountry, 94; and trade with the French, 186, 204; wealth of, 149, 182. *See also* Massachusetts; Rhode Island

Newport, Christopher, 31
Newport, Rhode Island, 150, 184
newspapers, 169–70
New York, 13, 90, 101, 169, 183,
184; exchanged for Surinam,
197
Noell, Martin, 50, 65
North Carolina, 3, 29, 86, 94, 105

Obeah, 136–37, 141, 144
Oglethorpe, James, 106–7, 141,
199

Parke, Daniel, 190–91
Parliament, 38, 150, 160, 185,
186, 198, 202; and funding for
Georgia, 108, 212; and policies
after Seven Years War, 205,
207, 209–10. *See also* Navigation
Acts
Pembroke, Earl of, 36
Penn, William, 65
Pennsylvania, 90, 101, 183, 184
Phibbah, 160
Pinckney, Charles, 103, 167
Pinckney, Eliza Lucas, 89, 103,
162, 167
pineapples, 15, 146, 170, 171, 184
Pinheiro, Esther, 162
Pitt, William, 200, 202
Port Royal, Jamaica, 13, 71, 72,
73–75, 154, 169, 170, 172; British
navy in, 195, 196; earthquake in,
17, 75–77, 184; fire in, 76
Port Royal, South Carolina, 2, 22,
88, 90, 92
Powell, Henry, 35–36, 44, 50
Powell, John, 35
Poyning's Law, 189–90
Price, Charles, 151
privateering, 9, 64, 70–72, 73, 92,
177, 199; and conflict with
planters, 70–72, 95; early English
ventures, 27–32; as source of
capital for plantation development, 74–75
Providence Island, 12, 64–65, 66

Queen Anne's War, 59, 76, 78, 195,
197, 198
Quincy, Josiah, 150–51, 160, 170, 189

Ralegh, Walter, 29–30
Ravenel, Henry and Mary, 159
Redwood, Abraham, 184
regions, 1–3, 213–14
Regulators, 211
Reid, James, 161
religion, 4, 74, 76, 163–66; among
enslaved Africans, 134–38, 143.
See also Church of England
Rhode Island, 150, 183, 184, 185
rice, 6, 84–85; in Cape Fear area,
106; capital requirements for,
97–98; debate about origins of,
99–100; exports of, 100–102, 110,
180–81, 208–9; in Georgia,
109–11; production of, 97–99;
size of plantations for, 102; and
task system, 6, 120–22
Roaring River plantation, Jamaica,
120
Royal African Company, 72, 132
rum, 46, 49, 51, 136, 180; consumption of, 46, 171, 183; and
triangular trade, 184–85

Saint Domingue, 75, 199, 209.
See also French colonies
Saladoid, 18, 20–21
Salzburgers, 107
Santo Domingo, 29, 47, 65. *See also*
Spanish colonies
Savannah, Georgia, 4, 107–8, 110,
123, 169
Schaw, Janet, 169
schools, 152, 166–67
Scots, 90, 107, 152–53
seasoning, 15, 126
Senegambia, 117, 118, 132, 134–35
Seven Years War, 110, 178, 199–201,
209, 212–13. *See also* Treaty of
Paris
Sewee, 23
Shaftesbury, Earl of, 85, 87, 91